Divine Feminine Energy

5 Steps to Become Dangerously Confident, Get What You Want, and Thrive as a High Value Woman

Taylor Harper

© Copyright 2025 – Taylor Harper – All rights reserved

The content within this book may not be reproduced, duplicated, or transmitted without direct written permission from the author or the publisher.

Under no circumstances will any blame or legal responsibility be held against the publisher, or author, for any damages, reparation, or monetary loss due to the information contained within this book, either directly or indirectly.

Legal Notice

This book is copyright protected. This book is only for personal use. You cannot amend, distribute, sell, use, quote, or paraphrase any part, or the content within this book, without the consent of the author-publisher.

Disclaimer Notice

Please note that the information contained within this document is for educational and entertainment purposes only. All effort has been executed to present accurate, up-to-date, and reliable, complete information. No warranties of any kind are declared or implied. Readers acknowledge that the author is not engaging in the rendering of legal, financial, medical, or professional advice.

Table of Content

About Me and Why I Wrote This Book 7
Introduction 9
Step 1: AWAKENING - Seeing the Truth You've Been Avoiding 12
Chapter 1: The Woman You've Been Pretending to Be 13
    The Exhaustion of Wearing a Mask 13
    Why You're Not Broken, Just Buried 15
    The High Value Woman Nobody Told You About 17
    Permission to Want Everything You Desire 19
    Key Takeaways 21
Chapter 2: The Invisible Cage You Built for Safety 23
    How Trauma Made You Forget Who You Are 23
    The Armor You Wear That's Crushing Your Soul 26
    When Being Strong Became Your Prison 28
    Recognizing the Patterns That Keep You Stuck 30
    Key Takeaways 32
Chapter 3: Your Feminine Essence Was Never Lost 33
    Divine Feminine Energy Already Lives Inside You 33
    Why You Learned to Suppress Your Softness 35
    The Difference Between Being and Doing 37
    Reclaiming What Society Tried to Steal 39
    Key Takeaways 42
Step 2: HEALING - Making Peace With Your Past 44
Chapter 4: The Root of Your Self-Sabotage 45
    There Is No Such Thing as Self-Sabotage 45
    The Parts of You That Are Trying to Protect You 47
    Negative Loyalty Patterns Blocking Your Abundance 49
    Breaking Free From Inherited Limitations 51
    Key Takeaways 54
Chapter 5: Healing the Wounded Feminine Within 55

Understanding Your Enmeshment or Abandonment Trauma 55

The Completion Process for Deep Trauma Resolution 58

Integrating Your Rejected and Shadow Selves 60

Releasing Shame Without Bypassing the Pain 62

Key Takeaways 64

Chapter 6: You Can Have Yourself AND Have Love 66

The False Choice Between Autonomy and Connection 66

Why You Swing Between Compliance and Rebellion 68

Creating Safety Within So You Can Soften Outside 70

Building the Foundation of Secure Attachment 72

Key Takeaways 75

Chapter 7: Boundaries Are Love Not Walls 76

What Boundaries Really Mean and Why They Matter 76

How Violating Your Own Boundaries Destroys Self-Worth 79

Setting Limits Without Guilt or Apology 81

The Feminine Art of Holding Your Ground 83

Key Takeaways 86

Step 3: EMBODIMENT - Becoming Who You Truly Are 87

Chapter 8: Dangerous Confidence From the Inside Out 88

Confidence Is Not What the World Told You 88

Building Unshakeable Worth Independent of Others 90

The Prize Mentality That Changes Everything 93

Ending the Addiction to External Validation 95

Key Takeaways 98

Chapter 9: Embodying Your Magnetic Feminine Power 100

Accessing Feminine Qualities That Don't Require Safety 100

Water, Flexibility and Strength in Softness 102

Sensuality as Sacred Self-Connection 104

Movement, Ritual and Honoring Your Cycles 106

Key Takeaways 109

Help Her Find Her Way 110

Chapter 10: The Language of High Value Communication 111

Speaking Your Truth Without Armor or Attack 111

Vulnerability as Power Not Weakness 113

Expressing Needs Without Neediness 115

Listening With Intuition and Holding Space 117

Key Takeaways 120

Chapter 11: Your Body Is Your Temple Not Your Enemy 121

Healing Your Relationship With Your Physical Form 122

Understanding Your Menstrual Cycle as Wisdom 124

Nourishment Over Punishment 127

Beauty Rituals That Connect You to Divinity 130

Key Takeaways 132

Step 4: RELATING - Creating Love and Connection on Your Terms 133

Chapter 12: Recognizing Love From Trauma Bonds 134

Why You Keep Attracting the Same Toxic Patterns 135

Red Flags You've Been Trained to Ignore 137

The Difference Between Chemistry and Compatibility 139

When to Stay and When to Walk Away 141

Key Takeaways 144

Chapter 13: Dating as a High Value Woman 145

The Energy That Attracts Quality Not Quantity 146

Why Chasing Destroys Polarity and Attraction 148

Letting Him Lead Without Losing Yourself 151

Standards That Filter Out Men Who Waste Your Time 154

Key Takeaways 158

Chapter 14: Creating Relationships Where You Feel Safe 159

What Emotional Safety Actually Looks and Feels Like 160

The Foundation of True Intimacy 162

Communicating Needs in Ways That Bring You Closer 165

Building Partnerships Based on Growth Not Codependency 168

Key Takeaways 171

Chapter 15: The Sacred Feminine in Sisterhood 172

Healing Competition Wounds With Other Women 173

- Why Sisterhood Is Your Secret Weapon ... 175
- Building Your Soul Tribe of Empowered Women ... 178
- Rising Together in Collaboration Not Isolation ... 181
- Key Takeaways ... 184

Step 5: THRIVING - Manifesting and Creating Your Reality ... 186

Chapter 16: Abundance Is Your Natural State ... 187
- Why You Block Your Own Blessings ... 188
- Releasing Scarcity and Embracing Overflow ... 191
- The Art of Receiving Without Guilt ... 194
- Money, Love and Success as Reflections of Worth ... 197
- Key Takeaways ... 200

Chapter 17: Manifestation Without Spiritual Bypassing ... 201
- What Manifestation Really Is Beyond the Hype ... 202
- Aligning Subconscious Beliefs With Conscious Desires ... 205
- Taking Aligned Action Not Just Visualizing ... 209
- Trusting Divine Timing While Taking Responsibility ... 212
- Key Takeaways ... 215

Chapter 18: Thriving as the Most Powerful Version of You ... 216
- Integrating Shadow and Light Into Wholeness ... 217
- Daily Rituals of a Woman Who Knows Her Worth ... 219
- Your Personalized Roadmap to Sustainable Success ... 222
- Living Your Legacy Starting Today ... 225
- Key Takeaways ... 228

Help Another Woman Find This Book ... 229
Bibliography ... 230

About Me and Why I Wrote This Book

I was twenty-three, sitting on the edge of my bed at two in the morning, scrolling through my ex's Instagram again. He had already moved on. I was still wearing his old T-shirt, still in the same apartment, still pretending I was fine.

The truth was, I wasn't fine at all. I had a degree I wasn't using, a job that paid my rent but drained my spirit, and a growing suspicion that I'd spent years performing a version of myself that other people preferred. The girl who didn't need much. The woman who made herself smaller so others could feel bigger.

That night, something inside me snapped. I realized I had been waiting for someone to give me permission to want more. To be more. To stop apologizing for taking up space. No one was coming to give me that permission.

Change didn't happen in one dramatic moment. It came slowly, through small choices that felt terrifying at first. Saying no instead of yes. Skipping a family dinner when I was exhausted. Letting myself rest without guilt. Buying flowers for myself just because I wanted them. Each small act reminded me that my needs mattered.

I also started listening to the parts of myself I had silenced for years: the anger, the desire, the voice that whispered "enough." I learned to sit with discomfort instead of fixing it. I cried in the shower and didn't rush to make it meaningful. I started taking myself on quiet dates to coffee shops, galleries, long walks. I began to feel like someone worth spending time with.

Setting boundaries changed everything. It was messy and awkward. Some people drifted away, and it hurt. But the ones who stayed became real. I stopped attracting men who needed fixing and started connecting with people who wanted partnership, not rescue. I stopped performing for friends and started having conversations that mattered.

What surprised me most was how many women noticed the change. They would ask, "How did you do that? How did you stop caring so much about what people think?" I told them the truth. I hadn't stopped caring. I had simply learned to care about myself too.

That's when I realized this wasn't just my story. It was a pattern I saw everywhere. Brilliant, capable women taught to shrink, to smile, to make others comfortable. Women who confused self-sacrifice with love. Women who believed being "good" meant being small.

I didn't write this book as an expert. I'm still learning, still catching myself in old habits, still figuring out what it means to live from self-respect instead of approval. But I wrote it because I kept having the same conversation with women who felt the same ache I had felt—the quiet exhaustion of being everything for everyone.

Most of the advice out there made it sound simple: "Just love yourself." "Set boundaries." But no one talked about how lonely it can feel at first, how scary it is to disappoint people, how heavy it is to stop performing. I wanted to write something real. Something that tells the truth about what it takes to come home to yourself.

This book isn't a manual. I'm not here to fix you. You don't need fixing. You just need permission to stop betraying yourself. You need words for what you've been feeling and a reminder that you are not alone.

I wish someone had told me that when I was sitting on that bed at two in the morning, convinced something was wrong with me for wanting to be chosen the way I'd been choosing everyone else. Nothing was wrong with me. And nothing is wrong with you.

We've been taught that intuition is paranoia, that anger is unattractive, that standards are arrogance. We've been told that love means sacrifice and that sacrifice means disappearing.

This book is about unlearning all of that. It's about the moment you stop lying to yourself, the healing that begins when you stop performing, and the peace that comes from finally standing in your own truth.

If you've ever felt too much and not enough at the same time, this is for you. I don't have all the answers, but I've been where you are. And I know what it feels like to finally choose yourself.

And I believe you're ready to do the same.

Introduction

You're exhausted from trying to figure out what you're doing wrong. You've read the articles. You've listened to the podcasts. You've analyzed every text message, dissected every interaction, replayed every conversation looking for the moment where you said too much or asked for too little or somehow failed to be the version of yourself that would finally make someone stay.

And despite all of that effort, all that emotional labor, all that bending yourself into shapes you thought would make you more lovable, you're still here. Still confused about why you keep ending up in the same situations. Still wondering if maybe you're just too sensitive, too demanding, too much, or somehow not enough.

Here's what I need you to know: the problem isn't you. It's everything you've been taught about what it means to be a woman worthy of love, respect, and partnership.

You're smart. Probably accomplished in at least some area of your life. You have friends who think you have it together. Maybe you do at work, with your family, in the parts of your life where there are clear rules.

But when it comes to relationships? To knowing what you want and actually asking for it? To setting boundaries without drowning in guilt? That's where everything gets muddy.

You've probably been the "cool girl" at some point. The one who doesn't make things complicated, who goes with the flow, who's understanding when plans change or promises get broken. You've probably spent more time analyzing his behavior than checking in with your own feelings.

And when it didn't work, you turned that magnifying glass on yourself. What did I do wrong? What could I have done differently?

You've worked on yourself. You've gone to therapy. You've identified your attachment style, your childhood wounds. You can articulate exactly where your patterns come from.

But knowing all of that hasn't stopped you from doing it again.

You still say yes when you mean no. You still tolerate behavior that makes you feel small. You still give chances to people who've already shown you they're not capable of meeting you where you are.

Here's what's actually happening.

You've been operating from a framework that was never designed to serve you. A framework that told you your value lies in how accommodating you are, how little you demand. A framework that taught you to prioritize other people's comfort over your own truth.

You've been taught that feminine energy means being passive. That being high value means making yourself as palatable as possible. That love is about sacrificing yourself while getting nothing in return.

None of this is your fault. You were conditioned into it by a culture that rewards women for being accommodating, by relationship advice that tells you to be patient and understanding while men are allowed to be confused and unavailable.

You've been trying to win a game where the rules were rigged against you from the start.

This book is about seeing clearly what's actually been happening. It's about understanding why you've been making the choices you've been making, and why those choices have been leaving you feeling empty.

What you'll find here are concrete tools and a framework for understanding your patterns and what to do about them.

We're going to move through five steps together.

Step 1: Awakening is about seeing the truth you've been avoiding. The masks you've been wearing, the lies you've been telling yourself, the parts of you that got buried.

Step 2: Healing is about making peace with your past by looking at the wounds that have been dictating your choices and learning how to stop letting them run the show.

Step 3: Embodiment is about becoming who you truly are. Not the version you think you're supposed to be, but the woman you actually are when you stop abandoning yourself.

Step 4: Relating is about love, connection, and standards. What healthy relationships actually look like, how to stop settling, and how to recognize when someone isn't capable of what you need.

Step 5: Thriving is about creating your reality in the very real sense of building a life where you're not constantly betraying yourself.

You don't have to read this book linearly. Start where you need to. Take what serves you and leave what doesn't.

This book will probably make you uncomfortable at times. It's going to ask you to look at things you've been avoiding: the ways you've abandoned yourself, the people you've been protecting at your own expense, the standards you've been negotiating away.

That discomfort isn't a sign you're doing something wrong. It's a sign you're waking up.

You already know the truth. You've known it for a while now.

You know when someone isn't treating you right. You know when you're making excuses for behavior that shouldn't require excuses. You know when you're betraying yourself to keep the peace.

You've just been taught not to trust that knowing.

This book is permission to stop doing that.

So if you're tired of pretending, tired of performing, tired of making yourself small, keep reading.

If you're ready to stop abandoning yourself for people who were never going to choose you anyway, keep reading.

This is your invitation to finally choose yourself. Not in some abstract way, but in the real, daily practice of living in alignment with who you actually are and what you actually need.

You don't have to have it all figured out. You just have to be willing to start telling yourself the truth.

That's where everything changes.

Step 1:
AWAKENING - Seeing the Truth You've Been Avoiding

There's a moment that comes for every woman. The one where she realizes everyone can see something about her that she's been desperately trying to hide. That sick drop in the stomach, the sudden awareness that the mask she's been wearing is cracking right down the middle.

That's where we start.

The woman you present to the world is exhausted. She's polished and capable and always fine, even when she's not. She's learned to laugh at jokes that aren't funny, to say yes when she means no, and to make herself smaller so others can feel bigger.

But here's what nobody tells you: that version of yourself was never the problem. The cage you've been living in was built by hands that weren't your own, constructed from fears that don't belong to you, and locked with keys you were told to throw away the moment you learned to be a "good girl."

Your feminine essence didn't disappear. It's not broken or damaged or lost somewhere you can't reach. It's buried, yes, but it's still there. Still alive. Still waiting for you to remember that softness isn't weakness, that wanting more doesn't make you selfish, and that the wild, untamed parts of you were never meant to be tamed at all.

These first three chapters will ask you to look at things you've probably been avoiding. The patterns that keep showing up. The voice in your head that sounds suspiciously like someone who hurt you. The armour you wear that's become so heavy you forget you're wearing it until your body starts breaking under the weight.

This part isn't about fixing you. You were never broken. It's about seeing clearly, maybe for the first time, what's been keeping you from the woman you actually are underneath all the performance and pretending.

Chapter 1:
The Woman You've Been Pretending to Be

"Owning our story and loving ourselves through that process is the bravest thing that we'll ever do." — Brené Brown

You know the feeling. That split second before you walk into a room when you adjust your face, straighten your posture, and become *her*. The version of yourself that's always fine, always capable, always has it together. She's the one who responds to "How are you?" with a bright smile and "Great!" even when your chest feels tight and your mind is screaming.

She's the woman you've been perfecting for years. Maybe decades.

And she's exhausting.

This chapter isn't about fixing you. You don't need fixing. It's about recognizing the mask you've been wearing so long that you've forgotten it's not your actual face. We're going to look at why you built this persona in the first place, what it's costing you to maintain it, and what becomes possible when you finally understand that being "high value" has nothing to do with the performance you've been giving.

You're about to discover that the woman you've been trying so hard to be is standing in the way of the woman you actually are.

The Exhaustion of Wearing a Mask

Your body knows you're lying.

It knows when you laugh at jokes that aren't funny. When you agree with opinions that make your stomach turn. When you say "I'm not upset" while your jaw clenches and your shoulders climb toward your ears. Your body is keeping score of every time you betray yourself for approval, and it's sending you the bill in the form of tension, fatigue, and a vague sense that something is deeply wrong even when everything looks perfectly fine.

The mask isn't always obvious. It doesn't announce itself. You didn't wake up one morning and decide to become someone else. It happened gradually, in small moments of correction and adjustment. The first time someone told you that you were "too much," you dialed yourself down. When your enthusiasm was met with eye rolls, you learned to contain it. When your anger was labeled as "crazy" or "dramatic," you swallowed it and smiled instead.

You learned that certain parts of you were acceptable and others were not. So you emphasized what worked and buried what didn't.

The problem is that maintaining this edited version of yourself requires constant vigilance. You're monitoring every word before it leaves your mouth. Calculating how much emotion is appropriate to show. Wondering if you're being too assertive or not assertive enough. Trying to strike that impossible balance between confident and humble, sexy but not slutty, successful but not threatening, independent but not intimidating.

You're playing a character, and the role is killing you.

Women come to me all the time talking about burnout, and they think it's about their job or their schedule. But when we dig deeper, the real exhaustion isn't from what they're doing. It's from who they're pretending to be while they do it.

You're tired because authenticity is your natural state, and pretending is hard work.

Think about the last time you spent an entire day with someone who truly sees you. Someone you don't have to perform for. Notice how different your body feels in those spaces. Your breath deepens. Your shoulders drop. The background noise in your head quiets down. That's not because you're finally relaxing. It's because you're finally being yourself, and being yourself doesn't require effort.

The mask requires effort. Constant, relentless effort.

And here's what nobody tells you: the mask doesn't just hide you from other people. It hides you from yourself. When you spend years performing a role, you start to lose track of where the performance ends and the real you begins. You forget what you actually think about things because you're so used to calibrating your opinions based on who's in the room. You forget what you actually want because you've trained yourself to want what's acceptable.

You've become so good at being what others need that you've forgotten who you are when nobody's watching.

The worst part? The mask doesn't even accomplish what you hoped it would. You put it on thinking it would make you more lovable, more acceptable, more safe. But the opposite happened. The people who love the mask don't actually love you. They love the performance. And somewhere deep down, you know that. Which means you can never fully relax into their love because you're terrified of what happens when they see behind the costume.

You're lonely inside a crowd of people who think they know you.

Your body is trying to tell you something. The exhaustion, the anxiety, the sense that you're constantly holding your breath—these aren't signs that something is wrong with you. They're signs that something is wrong with the life you're living. They're evidence that you're spending your days being someone you're not, and your authentic self is suffocating under the weight of the pretense.

You can't heal burnout by sleeping more or taking a vacation. You heal it by coming home to yourself.

Why You're Not Broken, Just Buried

There's a story you've been telling yourself. It goes something like this: if you just work hard enough, achieve enough, fix enough of your flaws, become disciplined enough, positive enough, healed enough—then you'll finally be worthy. Then you'll finally be enough.

But what if the entire premise is wrong?

What if you're not a project that needs completion? What if there's nothing fundamentally defective about you that requires fixing?

I need you to sit with this for a moment because it contradicts everything you've been taught. Our culture is built on the idea that you're not okay as you are. Every advertisement, every self-help book, every Instagram post of someone's "transformation" is designed to convince you that your current state is unacceptable and that worthiness is something you earn through effort and achievement.

You've internalized this so deeply that you can't even imagine an alternative.

The voice in your head that catalogs your flaws, compares you to other women, and finds you lacking—you think that's your voice. You think that's reality. You think that critical narrator is telling you the truth about who you are.

It's not.

That voice is the accumulation of every message you've received about who you should be. It's your mother's anxiety about what the neighbors think. Your father's discomfort with your emotions. The boys who made fun of your body in middle school. The teacher who told you to stop asking so many questions. The boyfriend who said you were "too needy." The culture that taught you that your value is tied to your appearance, your achievement, and your ability to make others comfortable.

None of that is you. That's just the soil you grew up in.

Underneath all that conditioning, underneath the shame and the fear and the desperate need to be acceptable, you're still there. The essence of who you were before the world told you who to be. She's not gone. She's just buried.

Think about yourself as a child, before you learned to edit yourself. You had preferences. Strong ones. You knew what you liked and what you didn't, and you weren't afraid to say so. You felt your emotions fully and expressed them without calculation. You were creative and curious and alive. You didn't spend hours worrying about whether you were enough. You just were.

That version of you didn't disappear. She got covered up.

Every time you were punished for being too loud, too sensitive, too much—you added another layer. Every time your needs were dismissed as inconvenient, you learned to stop having needs. Every time your boundaries were violated and you were told it was your fault, you decided that boundaries weren't safe. Layer by layer, year by year, you built walls around the core of who you are.

Not because you're weak. Because you're smart.

You adapted. You survived. You figured out what you needed to do to stay safe and loved and accepted in an environment that wasn't built to honor your full humanity. The mask wasn't a mistake. It was brilliant strategy.

But here's what happens when you spend your life in survival mode: you forget that you're not just trying to survive anymore. The threats that required the mask may no longer exist, but you keep wearing it because it's all you know. You keep performing because you've forgotten there's another option.

You're not broken. You're just operating from old programming that no longer serves you.

The work ahead isn't about becoming someone new. It's about remembering who you were before the world taught you to be small. It's about excavating the parts of yourself that you buried because they weren't safe to show. It's about removing the layers that don't belong to you and reconnecting with the essence that's been there all along.

This is what makes you different from a project. Projects get built from scratch. You don't need to be built. You need to be uncovered.

The High Value Woman Nobody Told You About

When you hear "high value woman," what comes to mind?

If you're like most women, you probably picture someone who looks a certain way. She's put together. Successful. Confident. She has her life figured out. She never seems stressed or overwhelmed. She's the woman you see on Instagram with the perfect aesthetic, the impressive career, the enviable relationship, and the caption about gratitude and morning routines.

That's not what I'm talking about.

The version of "high value" that's been sold to you is just another mask. Another performance. Another set of standards you're supposed to meet to prove your worthiness. It's the same old game dressed up in new language.

Real value has nothing to do with how you look, what you've achieved, or how well you've curated your life for public consumption.

A high value woman is someone who knows her worth is inherent. Not earned. Not conditional. Not up for debate.

She's not high value because she's mastered the art of looking like she has her shit together. She's high value because she's stopped pretending. She's learned that authenticity is more powerful than perfection, and that showing up as she truly is will always attract better things than performing for approval ever could.

This woman doesn't wake up every morning feeling confident and powerful. She has days when she doubts herself. Moments when she feels scared or inadequate or completely lost. But she's learned that those feelings don't diminish her value. They're just part of being human.

She doesn't have impeccable boundaries because she read the right book or followed the right formula. She has boundaries because she got tired of betraying herself to keep other people comfortable. She decided that her peace was more important than being liked, and she built her life around that truth.

She's not always soft and feminine and graceful. Sometimes she's angry. Sometimes she's exhausted. Sometimes she's a mess. And she's learned that she's still worthy in those moments. That her value doesn't fluctuate based on her mood or her ability to be pleasant.

The high value woman you've been chasing doesn't exist. She's a fantasy. A composite of everyone else's ideas about what makes a woman valuable. You could spend your whole life trying to become her and still feel empty because you're pursuing an image instead of substance.

What if instead of trying to meet someone else's standards, you started living from your own?

What if "high value" meant you value yourself enough to stop performing, stop shrinking, stop dimming your light to make others comfortable? What if it meant you trust yourself enough to make decisions based on what feels right to you instead of what looks right to everyone else?

That kind of value can't be measured by external markers. You can't put it on a resume or show it off in a photo. But you can feel it. It's the difference between walking into a room and scanning for approval versus walking in and knowing you belong there just by existing. It's the difference between needing validation and welcoming it when it comes but not collapsing when it doesn't.

True value is quiet. It doesn't announce itself or defend itself or perform for an audience. It just is.

And the wild thing is, this kind of value is magnetic. Not because you're trying to attract anyone, but because authenticity is rare and powerful. When you stop performing, you stop attracting people who only want the performance. You start drawing in people who can handle your full humanity. People who aren't threatened by your complexity. People who don't need you to be smaller to feel bigger.

You become dangerous to everything that required your smallness to survive.

Being a high value woman isn't about becoming someone impressive. It's about becoming yourself. Fully. Unapologetically. Without the need to justify or explain or soften your existence to make it palatable for others.

That's the woman nobody told you about. That's the woman who's been waiting underneath all the pretending.

Permission to Want Everything You Desire

You've been taught to want small.

Not explicitly. Nobody sat you down and said, "Make sure you don't want too much." But you learned it anyway. You learned it when you expressed excitement about something and someone rolled their eyes. When you shared a dream and were met with skepticism or concern instead of encouragement. When you asked for what you wanted and were called greedy or ungrateful or unrealistic.

So you adjusted. You learned to minimize your desires. To ask for less. To settle for good enough. To tell yourself that wanting more was selfish or immature or evidence that you hadn't done enough work on yourself.

You convinced yourself that wanting was the problem.

But desire isn't your enemy. Desire is your compass. It's how your soul communicates what would make you come alive. And you've been taught to ignore it, override it, explain it away, or feel ashamed of it.

You want more money? You're told that's shallow and materialistic. You should focus on gratitude for what you have. You want a better relationship? You're told you're being picky or unrealistic, that relationships require compromise and you need to adjust your expectations. You want recognition for your work? You're told that real satisfaction comes from internal validation, not external approval.

All of these messages contain partial truths, which is what makes them so insidious. Yes, gratitude matters. Yes, relationships require compromise. Yes, internal validation is important. But none of those truths mean you should stop wanting what you want.

You've been sold a spiritualized version of settling. Told that desire is attachment and attachment is suffering, so the path to peace is to want less. To need less. To be content with whatever shows up.

That's not enlightenment. That's resignation dressed up in spiritual language.

Wanting isn't the same as being entitled to having. You can desire something without demanding that the universe deliver it on your timeline. You can want what you want and still be grateful for what you have. These aren't contradictory states.

But you've been so conditioned to feel guilty about your desires that you can barely admit them to yourself, let alone speak them out loud. You've learned to hide them, minimize them, rationalize them away. You say "I want" and then immediately follow it with "but" and a list of reasons why it's not reasonable or possible or appropriate for you to actually pursue it.

Here's what I need you to understand: your desires are not random. They're not character flaws. They're not evidence that you haven't done enough healing or that you're spiritually immature.

Your desires are information.

They tell you what direction your life wants to grow. They show you where you're not in alignment. They reveal the gap between who you're being and who you're capable of becoming.

When you ignore them, dismiss them, or shame them, you cut yourself off from the guidance system that could lead you toward your most authentic life.

You don't have to know how your desires will manifest. You don't have to have a plan or a strategy or proof that they're achievable. You just have to stop pretending they don't exist.

What if you gave yourself permission to want what you actually want, not what you think you should want or what's safe to want or what other people think is appropriate for someone like you to want?

What if you let yourself want the big house, the successful business, the passionate relationship, the financial freedom, the recognition, the adventure, the creative expression, the ease, the pleasure, the support, the love?

What if wanting those things didn't make you selfish or shallow or spiritually bankrupt? What if it just made you human?

Your desires aren't the problem. Your relationship with your desires is the problem. You've been taught to distrust them, police them, suppress them. And in doing so, you've disconnected from the very thing that could guide you toward the life you're meant to live.

This is your permission slip. Not to have everything you want handed to you without effort or challenge. But to stop apologizing for wanting it. To stop shrinking your dreams to fit other people's limited vision of what's possible for you. To stop pretending that you're fine with less when your soul is screaming for more.

You're allowed to want everything you desire. You're allowed to pursue it. You're allowed to believe it's possible even when you don't know how it will happen.

The woman you've been pretending to be doesn't want much. She's learned to be small and grateful and satisfied with crumbs. The woman you actually are has appetites. Big ones. And they're not going away just because you've spent years trying to starve them.

Stop feeding the mask. Start feeding your soul.

Key Takeaways

- The exhaustion you call burnout often comes from constantly managing other people's perceptions instead of living your own truth.
- The persona you've built didn't appear overnight; it's the sum of every moment you toned yourself down to stay acceptable.
- Your body keeps an honest record of every compromise—each forced smile and each emotion swallowed for the sake of peace.
- The constant self-monitoring to seem balanced, capable, or likable is a quiet form of self-erasure.
- Approval once felt like safety, but it slowly became a cage that keeps you repeating an outdated survival script.

- The curated version of "high value" is another costume; real worth begins where the performance stops.
- Authentic power shows up when you no longer trade comfort for belonging or silence for acceptance.
- The calm you feel with people who truly see you isn't relaxation—it's recognition.
- Your desires aren't excessive; they're data about what your life is trying to become next.
- Growth starts the moment you stop negotiating with your own aliveness to make others comfortable.

Chapter 2:
The Invisible Cage You Built for Safety

"Why do you stay in prison when the door is so wide open?" — Rumi

You think you're free because nobody's physically holding you back. You can go where you want, say what you think, make your own choices. On paper, you have all the freedom in the world.

So why does it feel like you're living inside invisible walls?

The cage you're in wasn't built by someone else. You constructed it yourself, brick by brick, as a response to a world that didn't feel safe. Every rule you follow that doesn't make sense to you, every limit you accept without questioning, every time you stop yourself before anyone else has to: that's a bar in your cage.

You built it to protect yourself. And it worked. But now the thing that kept you safe is keeping you small, and you can't figure out how to get out because you've forgotten it's even there.

This chapter is about recognizing the cage. Understanding why you built it, how it's shaped your life, and what it's costing you to stay inside. Because until you can see the walls, you can't dismantle them. And until you dismantle them, you'll keep wondering why you feel trapped in a life that looks perfectly fine from the outside.

How Trauma Made You Forget Who You Are

Trauma doesn't always look like what you think it does.

You're waiting for the big event. The obvious wound. The thing you can point to and say, "That's what broke me." But most of the trauma that shapes you is quiet. It's not the dramatic moment that everyone rallies around. It's the thousand small moments when you learned that parts of you weren't acceptable.

Your dad walked out of the room every time you cried. Your mom gave that nervous laugh when you asked questions that made her uncomfortable. The teacher humiliated you in front of the class. The friend group went silent when you walked up. The boyfriend made you feel insane for having needs.

Each moment was survivable. You got through it. You moved on. But somewhere in your nervous system, a decision got encoded: this part of me isn't safe to show. This need isn't okay to have. This emotion is too big. This desire makes people uncomfortable.

You didn't consciously decide to change. You just noticed what got you rejected and what got you accepted, then adjusted accordingly.

The point isn't only the event. It's the adaptations that stayed active long after the threat passed.

You started entering rooms already listening, scanning for tone and temperature, calibrating your presence before you spoke. The adaptation worked so well it became invisible. Automatic. You stopped noticing you were doing it.

This is what makes early conditioning so effective. It doesn't announce itself. It just runs in the background, shaping every interaction without your conscious input.

The rules got installed young. Don't be too loud. Don't take up space. Don't ask for too much. Don't show that you're hurt. The rules were implicit, absorbed through repetition and consequence rather than explanation. And because they were never stated explicitly, you never thought to question them.

You just followed them. Still do.

Your body signals safety or alarm before your thoughts catch up. When your stomach tightens and your breath gets shallow as you're about to speak up in a meeting, that's not drama or overthinking. That's procedural memory. Your nervous system remembers what happened the last fifty times you made yourself visible, and it's trying to protect you from a repeat.

The problem is that your body doesn't distinguish between past and present very well. It doesn't care that you're not in your childhood home anymore, that your boss isn't your critical parent, that the people in this room aren't the ones who punished you for existing fully.

Your body just knows: visibility once meant danger. So visibility still triggers the alarm.

This is why you can understand intellectually that you're allowed to have boundaries, express opinions, take up space, but still feel paralyzed when the moment comes to actually do it. Your thinking brain says one thing. Your nervous system says another. And when those two systems are in conflict, the nervous system wins every time.

You're not walking around with a wound. You're walking around carrying rules that once kept you safe but now keep you contained.

And here's the part that makes this so hard to see: you've been following these rules for so long that they feel like truth. Like reality. Like just how things are.

You think everyone monitors their words this carefully. Everyone second-guesses their instincts this much. Everyone feels this level of anxiety about being seen.

They don't. Most people carry conditioning too, but you've made self-regulation into an Olympic sport.

Your body remembers what your mind has explained away. It remembers every time authenticity got punished. Every time vulnerability led to abandonment. Every time you showed up fully and it wasn't safe.

So now, even when you're in objectively safe situations, your physiology doesn't believe it. Heart rate climbs. Breath gets tight. Muscles brace. All the signals that say: be careful, monitor yourself, don't let too much through.

You're not in that environment anymore. The people who couldn't handle your full presence don't have to define everyone else. The conditions that required constant vigilance aren't the only conditions available to you.

But your nervous system doesn't know that yet. It's still running the old protocol, watching for punishment that isn't coming, bracing for rejection that may never arrive.

The cage is made of rules. Old rules. Rules that made sense once. Rules that no longer serve you but still govern your behavior because you've never examined them closely enough to see them for what they are: outdated strategies that once protected you but now keep you trapped in a version of reality that no longer exists.

The Armor You Wear That's Crushing Your Soul

You know what your armor looks like. Maybe it's perfectionism. The email you rewrite four times before sending. The presentation you stay up until 2 AM perfecting even though the first version was fine. The constant mental loop checking for mistakes, vulnerabilities, anything someone could criticize.

Maybe it's hyper-independence. The automatic "I've got it" when someone offers help. The pride in never needing anyone. The belief that asking for support is weakness, so you carry everything yourself and resent people for not noticing you're drowning.

Maybe it's agreeableness. The reflexive "I'm fine with whatever" when someone asks your preference. The way you absorb other people's moods and adjust yours to match. The chronic inability to locate your own opinion when someone asks what you think.

Maybe it's control. The detailed plans, the backup plans for the backup plans, the inability to relax until every variable is accounted for. The anxiety that spikes when something unexpected happens because you didn't see it coming.

Whatever form your armor takes, it started as protection. You needed it. It worked. It kept you safe when being undefended would have been dangerous.

But you're still wearing it, even though the threat is gone. And armor you can't take off becomes a cage.

Perfectionism shifts the focus from your actual work to your anxiety about error. Walk into a room carrying that energy and people register the stress, not the competence. They feel your fear of falling short before they see what you've accomplished.

Hyper-independence creates distance. When you refuse help automatically, people stop offering. When you signal that you don't need anyone, they believe you. Then you wonder why nobody shows up for you, not realizing you've been actively pushing them away while telling yourself it's strength.

Agreeableness makes you a blank space. People know you're nice. They don't know who you are. There's no friction, no edge, nothing to grab onto. They like you fine. They don't feel close to you because there's no actual person there to be close to, just a pleasant mirror reflecting their preferences back at them.

Control creates rigidity. Life requires flexibility, adaptation, the ability to work with what shows up instead of only what you planned for. When you can't tolerate deviation from the plan, you can't tolerate life. And trying to force reality into your predetermined structure is exhausting for everyone involved.

Your armor isn't the problem. The problem is that you've worn it so long you think it's your skin.

With the armor on, relational proximity stops before contact. People respect you, trust your competence, appreciate what you bring. They struggle to feel you. There's a surface they can't get past, and eventually they stop trying.

The armor tells you that without it, you'll be destroyed. That your perfectionism is what makes you valuable. That your independence is what makes you strong. That your agreeableness is what makes you likable. That your control is what keeps your life from falling apart.

None of that holds up under examination.

Your value doesn't fluctuate with your performance. Your strength doesn't require isolation. Your likability doesn't depend on your lack of preferences. Your life doesn't need your constant management to function.

But you won't believe that until you test it. Until you send the email at draft two instead of draft five and watch nothing bad happen. Until you accept help with something small and notice that people feel closer to you, not less respectful. Until you state a clear preference and discover that having boundaries makes you more interesting, not less likable. Until you let one variable unfold without your intervention and see that you can handle whatever comes.

The armor isn't keeping you safe anymore. It's keeping you separate.

Here's a test for each type:

Perfectionism: Send your next email at version two. Notice the urge to keep refining. Send it anyway. Track what actually happens versus what your anxiety predicted would happen.

Hyper-independence: Accept help with something minor. Let someone make the appointment, carry the box, handle the logistics. Watch what happens in your body when you're not carrying it all yourself.

Agreeableness: Give a clear, brief no to a small request. No explanation, no apology, just "That doesn't work for me." Notice the impulse to soften it, justify it, make the other person feel better about your boundary. Don't.

Control: Leave one small variable unplanned. Show up without knowing exactly how it will go. Monitor your physiological response. Breath, heart rate, muscle tension. Notice that you can tolerate more uncertainty than your control habit led you to believe.

You built the armor to survive. Survival isn't the same as living. If you want to actually live, you're going to have to remove it piece by piece and discover what it feels like to move through the world without all that weight.

The armor was lying to you. It told you that without it, you'd be destroyed. The truth is, without it, you'll finally be available for real connection.

When Being Strong Became Your Prison

Nobody questions strength. When you're the strong one, people admire you. They rely on you. They come to you when they need someone who can handle hard things without falling apart.

And you've been playing that role for so long that you don't know how to stop.

Being strong wasn't always a burden. At first, it felt empowering. When everyone else was falling apart, you held it together. When chaos erupted, you stayed calm. When problems needed solving, you solved them. Your capacity to carry heavy things got you through situations that would have broken other people.

People noticed. They appreciated your steadiness. They felt safe around your reliability. They learned they could count on you.

But somewhere along the way, strength stopped being something you could choose and became something you had to maintain. You couldn't show vulnerability because people were depending on your stability. You couldn't ask for help because you were the person other people came to for help. You couldn't fall apart because you were the one who held everything together.

Strength became a fixed assignment. No rotations. No breaks. No one to hand the load to when you needed rest.

The strong one carries things. That's the job description. And you've been doing that job so long that you've forgotten it's optional.

You started believing that your value was tied to your capacity to handle weight. That if you showed strain, people would lose respect for you. That if you admitted struggle, you'd be letting everyone down. That if you stopped being the steady one for even a moment, everything would collapse.

So you kept going. Kept carrying loads that were too heavy. Kept absorbing other people's stress on top of your own. Kept saying "I'm fine" when fine was nowhere near accurate.

And people believed you. If you always deliver stable outcomes, they calibrate their expectations to that data. They assume you have capacity. They don't see the cost because you don't show it.

They have no idea that behind the competence is someone who fantasizes about disappearing. Not because she wants to die, but because she's so tired of carrying weight that was never hers to carry in the first place.

You became a prisoner of your own capability.

The prison is invisible. Your suffering doesn't register because you've gotten so good at maintaining the exterior. You keep showing up functional, so people keep treating you as if you're unbreakable. They keep bringing you their problems, leaning on you, expecting you to have answers.

And you keep delivering because you don't know how to tell them that you're at capacity. That you need someone to hold weight for you. That you're exhausted from being everyone's solid ground when what you need is somewhere soft to land.

You think asking for support would make you weak. What's actually happening is that refusing to ask for support is making you resentful, isolated, and one bad day away from collapse.

Strength without the ability to be vulnerable isn't strength. It's a fixed role that doesn't bend. And when a role doesn't bend, it eventually breaks.

Real capacity includes knowing your limits. Admitting when you're at threshold. Asking for what you need before you hit depletion. Letting people see you when you're not operating at full capacity and trusting that they won't abandon you for being human.

But you won't believe that's safe until you test it. Until you tell someone "I'm not okay" and watch them stay. Until you ask for help and discover that people feel honored to support you, not burdened by it. Until you let yourself be held instead of always doing the holding.

The version of strength you've been performing isn't sustainable. You're trying to be superhuman. You're human. You have limits. You have needs. You have moments when you can't carry everything, and that's not a flaw in your design. That's just how bodies and nervous systems work.

This week, identify three things that are not your responsibility. Things you've been carrying that belong to someone else. Hand them back. Not with resentment or drama, just with clarity: this is yours to handle.

Watch what happens when you stop being the one who carries everything. Watch how much energy returns when you're only responsible for your actual load.

Your prison doesn't have locks. It's held together by your belief that you don't have permission to put things down. That belief is what's trapping you.

Recognizing the Patterns That Keep You Stuck

You tell yourself you want to change. You read the books, listen to the podcasts, set the intentions. You understand intellectually that the way you're living isn't working. That the patterns you're repeating are making you miserable.

And yet, you keep repeating them.

You date the same type of emotionally unavailable person in different packaging. You take on more than you can handle and then resent everyone when you're overwhelmed. You say yes when you mean no and then feel bitter about being taken advantage of. You push away the people who try to get close and then feel lonely when they stop trying.

You know you're doing it. You can see the pattern. But somehow, you can't stop yourself from running it again.

Patterns aren't conscious choices. They're automatic sequences that your nervous system executes before your thinking brain gets involved. By the time you realize what you're doing, you're already deep into the pattern, wondering how you ended up here again.

Your patterns aren't random. They're solutions to problems you had in the past. The issue is that you're still executing those solutions even though the original problem no longer exists.

The pattern made sense once. It kept you safe, connected, functional in an environment where those things weren't guaranteed. But you're not in that environment anymore. The strategy that protected you then is limiting you now.

Here's where patterns show up: in the gap between trigger and response.

Someone offers help. Before you can consider whether you actually want the help, "No thanks, I've got it" is already out of your mouth.

Someone criticizes your work. Before you can assess whether the feedback is useful, you're already defensive or shut down.

Someone expresses interest in getting closer. Before you can evaluate whether you're interested back, you're already listing reasons why it won't work.

The pattern fires in that gap. Trigger, impulse, automatic action, predicted outcome, actual cost.

Your nervous system is running old code. The software is from a version that assumed you had zero margin, no options, that safety required constant vigilance and any deviation would result in disaster.

That operating system is outdated. You have margin now. You have options. You have resources you didn't have when that code got written.

But until you update the system, it keeps running the old protocol. The first step isn't changing the pattern. It's seeing the pattern clearly. Not judging it, not trying to immediately fix it, just observing how it operates.

Modification comes after measurement. First you track the sequence, then you can intervene in it.

For the next seven days, track three moments: when someone offers you help, when someone criticizes you, when someone invites you closer. Note your first physical response. Stomach tightens, breath shortens, shoulders rise, whatever happens in your body before thought kicks in. Then note the thought that follows. Then note the automatic action you take.

Just observe. Don't try to change it yet.

Once you have data on how the sequence runs, you can experiment with altering one element. Not the whole pattern, just one piece. Breathe twice before responding. Delay your response by ten minutes. Say "Let me think about that" instead of your automatic answer.

Small interventions in the automatic sequence. That's how patterns shift. Not through willpower or discipline, but through conscious interruption of the automatic loop. Your patterns will keep you stuck until you recognize them for what they are: outdated strategies that once served you but are now operating on assumptions that no longer match your reality.

The cage is made of rules you follow without questioning. The armor is equipment you wear without noticing. The patterns are code that runs without your input. All of it can be examined. All of it can be updated. But first, you have to see it clearly enough to know what needs changing.

Key Takeaways

- The limits that keep you contained were learned as safety rules and now run so quietly that they feel like reality.
- What shaped you was often a series of small corrections that taught you which parts of you were welcome and which were costly.
- Your nervous system reacts to visibility before thought can intervene because it remembers outcomes from older rooms with stricter rules.
- The body flags alarms through tight breath and braced muscles even when the present moment is not dangerous.
- Perfectionism, hyper independence, excessive agreeableness and rigid control began as protection and now function as barriers to contact.
- Respect and competence cannot replace felt closeness when armor blocks people from reaching the person underneath.
- Strength turned into a fixed assignment becomes a cell where asking for help feels forbidden and resentment grows in silence.
- Patterns repeat because they are old solutions that still execute between trigger and response before choice is available.
- Measurement precedes change when you track the sequence in your body and language and insert one small pause to break the loop.
- Dismantling the cage starts with testing new permissions in low stakes moments so the nervous system can learn that safety exists outside the old rules.

Chapter 3:
Your Feminine Essence Was Never Lost

"The most common way people give up their power is by thinking they don't have any."
— Alice Walker

You've spent years trying to become something. More confident, more successful, more attractive, more lovable. You've been working on yourself like you're a project that needs completion, a problem that needs solving.

But what if the entire framework is backwards?

What if nothing essential is missing? What if what's essential has simply been quieted? What if everything you've been searching for is already inside you, just covered by layers of conditioning that taught you to hide it?

Your feminine essence isn't something you need to cultivate or create. It's not a skill you learn or a state you achieve through enough meditation and self-help books. It's the core of who you are. It's been there since before you learned to edit yourself for acceptance.

The work isn't about becoming her. It's about removing everything that's covering her up.

This chapter is about recognizing that your feminine energy was never lost. It's about understanding why you went quiet, what that quieting has cost you, and what becomes possible when you finally let yourself be what you've always been underneath all the performance and protection.

Divine Feminine Energy Already Lives Inside You

You arrived in this life with a distinctly feminine imprint. A way of sensing and shaping the world that's been part of you since the beginning. It wasn't random or mistaken. That was your nature, and it came with a specific energy signature that's been woven into you from the start.

Feminine energy isn't something you acquire. It's something you are.

But you've spent so much time being told what femininity should look like that you've disconnected from what it actually feels like. You've been handed a script about what makes a woman valuable, desirable, acceptable, and you've been trying to perform that script instead of embodying your actual nature.

The script says femininity is soft, quiet, accommodating, decorative. It says real women are nurturing, selfless, intuitive in ways that serve others but never disruptive. It says you should be sexy but not sexual, confident but not threatening, strong but still need rescuing.

That script is garbage. It has nothing to do with actual feminine essence.

Real feminine energy moves, responds, adapts. It holds power without aggression. It's the force that creates life, literally and metaphorically. It's the capacity to receive, to transform, to birth new realities. It's the ability to hold complexity, to feel deeply, to know things that can't be explained through logic alone.

Your feminine essence is already complete. It doesn't need improvement. It doesn't need to be earned or proven or perfected. It exists whether you acknowledge it or not, whether you express it or not, whether you've done the inner work or not.

The only question is whether you're allowing it to move through you or whether you're blocking it.

And right now, you're blocking it. Not because you're doing something wrong, but because you learned that expressing your full feminine nature wasn't safe. That it made you vulnerable to judgment, objectification, dismissal. That it was better to hide it than to risk what happened when you showed it.

So you covered it up. You developed strategies to protect it. You trained yourself to lead with logic instead of instinct, with planning instead of flow, with doing instead of being. You learned to operate from your head because moving from your body felt too exposed.

And it worked. You survived. You succeeded. You proved you could function in a world that wasn't built to honor the feminine.

But functioning isn't fulfillment. And you can't thrive while denying half of who you are.

This energy is trying to come through. You feel it in moments when you're alone and don't have to perform. When you're in nature and something in your body relaxes. When you're with someone who feels safe and suddenly you're softer, more open, more yourself.

Those moments aren't exceptions. That's your baseline. That's who you are when you're not defending against a world that taught you that feminine power is weakness.

The feminine essence doesn't need to be created within you. It just needs to be allowed. It needs permission to exist without apology, without justification, without the constant monitoring that's been draining your energy for years.

Nothing is missing. Nothing is lacking. You're just obscured. And obscured is fixable.

All you have to do is stop suppressing what wants to emerge. Notice when your shoulders tense before you speak and release them instead. Stop editing your natural responses. Stop second-guessing your instincts. Stop performing a version of femininity that was designed by people who were threatened by the real thing.

Your feminine essence is already here. It responds the moment you stop resisting it.

Why You Learned to Suppress Your Softness

Softness got you hurt.

Not the first time you expressed it. Maybe not even the tenth time. But eventually, you learned that showing softness in a hard world is dangerous.

You were vulnerable with someone and they used it against you. You expressed emotion and got called dramatic. You asked for what you needed and were labeled needy. You showed tenderness and someone mistook it for weakness.

Each time, you made a note. Softness equals risk. Vulnerability equals exposure. Openness equals giving people ammunition they can use to hurt you later.

So you stopped being soft. Not completely, not all at once, but gradually. Hardness became the safer entry point. You learned to show strength before vulnerability. To make sure people knew you could handle yourself before you let them see that you had needs.

The world didn't make this easy. You grew up watching women get punished for softness. Your mother, your teachers, the women in movies and magazines. The ones who stayed soft got walked on, taken advantage of, dismissed. The ones who succeeded learned to be hard, strategic, untouchable.

You absorbed that lesson. Softness is a liability in a world that rewards toughness.

But here's what nobody told you: suppressing softness doesn't make you strong. It makes you rigid. And rigidity breaks under pressure in ways that flexibility never does.

You built walls because you needed protection. The walls worked. They kept you safe from people who would have exploited your openness. But walls don't just keep danger out. They keep everything out. Including the connection, intimacy, and joy that can only enter through openness.

You're safe now, but you're also alone. Not physically alone. You might have plenty of people around you. But you're alone in the way that matters because nobody can reach the real you through all that protection.

Softness isn't weakness. Softness is strength that doesn't need to prove itself. It's the capacity to stay open even when you've been hurt. To keep feeling even when feeling is painful. To remain tender in a world that's constantly trying to harden you.

It went quiet while you were busy surviving. And you learned to function so well without it that you forgot it was there.

You can feel the absence, though. You feel it in the tightness in your chest that never quite releases. In the way you can't fully relax even when you're supposedly relaxing. In the hardness you wear that's become so habitual you don't notice it anymore.

Your body wants to soften. Your nervous system is tired of being on high alert. Your heart wants to open. But you've trained yourself so thoroughly to stay defended that softening feels like surrendering, and surrendering feels like giving someone else the power to destroy you.

So you stay hard. And you tell yourself it's strength. And you wonder why nothing feels satisfying even when you're achieving everything you set out to achieve.

Softness isn't something you can think your way into. You can't logic yourself into letting your guard down. Your mind is the part that's convinced you need the walls. Your body is the part that knows the walls are crushing you.

The path back to softness isn't through more striving. It's through less. It's through learning to recognize when you're bracing and choosing to release instead. It's through finding people and spaces where softness is safe and practicing being undefended there until your nervous system learns that openness doesn't always lead to pain.

You learned to suppress your softness because the world made it clear that softness was dangerous. You're allowed to unlearn that now. You're allowed to reclaim what went quiet and discover that you can be soft without being weak, open without being defenseless, tender without being destroyed.

Your softness is ready to re-emerge the instant safety returns.

The Difference Between Being and Doing

You know how to do. You're exceptional at it. You set goals, make plans, take action, produce results. You measure your value by your output, your worth by your accomplishments, your legitimacy by your productivity.

Doing is how you prove you deserve to exist. If you're not producing, achieving, improving, then what's the point of you?

That's masculine energy. And there's nothing wrong with masculine energy. You need it. It gets things done. It builds, creates, moves things forward. But it's not the only energy available to you, and living exclusively in doing mode is exhausting you in ways you don't even recognize anymore.

Feminine energy is about being. Not doing nothing. Not passive waiting. But existing fully in the present moment without needing to accomplish anything to justify your presence.

You don't know how to do that. You don't even know what it means.

Being is sitting with your coffee in the morning without checking your phone. It's taking a bath without using the time to plan tomorrow's tasks. It's having a conversation without trying to fix the person or steer the outcome. It's feeling your feelings without immediately strategizing how to get rid of the uncomfortable ones.

Being is presence. Pure presence. With no agenda, no goal, no purpose beyond experiencing what's happening right now.

And you're terrible at it because you've been conditioned to believe that value comes from productivity. That if you're not actively working towards something, you're wasting time. That rest is only acceptable after you've earned it through sufficient doing.

You're running yourself into the ground trying to do enough to finally feel like you're enough. And it's not working because enough isn't a place you arrive at through achievement. Enough is a state you inhabit through being.

Masculine energy moves towards. It takes action, solves problems, pushes forward. Feminine energy receives. It allows, attracts, opens.

You've been taught that receiving is passive, weak, unambitious. So you've cut yourself off from one of your most powerful capacities. You give constantly. You do constantly. You produce constantly. And you can't figure out why you feel so depleted.

You're depleted because you're only running on one energy. You're all output, no input. All action, no rest. All doing, no being.

Your body needs both. Your nervous system needs both. Your core self needs both. But you've been operating in masculine override for so long that you've forgotten how to access the feminine.

Being doesn't mean doing nothing. It means being present with what is instead of constantly trying to change it, fix it, improve it. It means trusting that you're allowed to exist without justifying your existence through productivity.

This terrifies you because you've tied your entire identity to what you accomplish. If you're not the woman who handles everything, achieves everything, stays on top of everything, then who are you?

You're the woman underneath all that doing. The one who's been buried under tasks and goals and endless self-improvement projects. The one who's allowed to just be here, taking up space, breathing, existing, without needing to earn that right through constant achievement.

Feminine energy isn't about sitting still and doing nothing. It's about moving from a different center. Instead of forcing and pushing and making things happen, you're allowing and attracting and letting things unfold.

That requires trust. Trust that you don't have to control everything. Trust that life can happen without your constant management. Trust that you're valuable even when you're not producing.

You don't trust that. You've been proving your value through doing for so long that stopping feels like disappearing.

But here's what happens when you learn to be instead of only do: you stop burning out. You stop feeling like you're running on a treadmill that never ends. You stop resenting everything and everyone because you've finally given yourself permission to rest.

Being replenishes what doing depletes. You can't keep extracting without replenishing. Eventually, there's nothing left to extract.

You're at that point now. You've been running on fumes, trying to do more with less, pushing through exhaustion because stopping feels impossible.

It's not impossible. It's just unfamiliar. And unfamiliar feels unsafe when you've spent your entire life measuring your worth by what you produce.

Start small. Five minutes a day where you're not doing anything productive. Not meditating with a goal of becoming more mindful. Not resting so you can work harder tomorrow. Just being. Sitting. Breathing. Existing without purpose.

Watch what happens in your body when you give yourself permission to exist without an agenda. When you shift from doing to being, your breath deepens. Your pulse slows. The body registers safety. Notice the resistance, the guilt, the voice that says this is a waste of time. Notice that voice, and then notice that you're still breathing, still here, still valuable even while doing absolutely nothing.

That's feminine energy. That's being. And once you taste it, you finally remember what nourishment feels like.

Reclaiming What Society Tried to Steal

As you start to live from presence instead of constant performance, it becomes easier to see how the culture around you shaped that performance in the first place.

Society has been lying to you about what it means to be a woman.

They told you to be feminine but punished you when you were. They said be confident but not threatening. Be sexy but not sexual. Be ambitious but not aggressive. Be nurturing but not a doormat. Be independent but still need a man.

The expectations were designed to be impossible to follow. Because the point wasn't to help you succeed. The point was to keep you off balance, constantly adjusting, never quite right, always trying to fit into a box that was deliberately made too small.

You internalized those contradictions. You tried to be all the things you were supposed to be, even though they directly opposed each other. And when you failed, which you always did because the rules were rigged, you blamed yourself instead of questioning the expectations.

You decided you were the problem. Too much of this, not enough of that. If you could just get the balance right, if you could just figure out the correct way to be a woman, then you'd finally be acceptable.

But there is no correct way. There's just your way. And your way has been buried under decades of messaging about who you should be instead of who you are.

Society tried to steal your feminine power by convincing you it was something to be ashamed of. They sexualized your body and then shamed you for having sexuality. They demanded emotional labor and then dismissed you as overly emotional. They benefited from your intuition and then told you to stop being so sensitive.

They took everything powerful about feminine essence and reframed it as weakness, liability, something that needed to be controlled and contained.

And you believed them. Not because you're naive, but because the message was everywhere. In every movie, every magazine, every comment from family members, every interaction with men who were uncomfortable with your power.

You learned to dim it. To make it smaller. To apologize for taking up space. To second-guess your instincts. To explain away your knowing. To rationalize your desires until they were small enough to be acceptable.

That ends now.

Your feminine essence doesn't need society's approval. It doesn't need to fit into anyone's definition of acceptable womanhood. It doesn't need to make itself palatable for people who are threatened by it.

Your intuition isn't too sensitive. It's incredibly accurate, and people who don't want to be seen clearly are uncomfortable when you see them.

Your emotions aren't too much. They're appropriate responses to situations that others have numbed themselves to avoid feeling.

Your sexuality isn't shameful. It's a powerful life force that you're allowed to own and express on your terms.

Your standards aren't too high. They're exactly what you need to create a life that honors you instead of using you.

Your needs aren't inconvenient. They're valid information about what your system requires to function well.

Reclaiming what society tried to steal means looking at every message you received about what makes a woman valuable and asking: does this serve me, or does it serve a system that benefits from my smallness?

Most of what you've been taught falls into the second category.

You've been taught to prioritize everyone else's comfort over your own truth. To make yourself smaller so others can feel bigger. To suppress your power so you don't threaten fragile egos. To edit your desires so they fit into someone else's idea of appropriate.

None of that is feminine energy. That's just oppression dressed up as virtue.

Real feminine power doesn't apologize. It doesn't shrink. It doesn't perform for approval. It just is. Fully. Unapologetically. Without needing anyone's permission to exist in its full magnitude.

You're allowed to want what you want. Feel what you feel. Know what you know. Be as much as you are. And anyone who can't handle that isn't your person.

Society will keep trying to convince you that you're too much. That you need to tone it down, be more reasonable, stop being so intense. Every time you hear that message, recognize it for what it is: an attempt to keep you manageable.

You're not here to be manageable. You're here to be fully yourself. And fully yourself includes all the power, passion, intensity, and presence that you've been taught to suppress.

The theft happened gradually. Small compromises, tiny adjustments, little moments of shrinking that seemed insignificant at the time. But they added up. And now you're a fraction of what you could be.

Reclamation happens the same way. Small moments of choosing your truth over their comfort. Tiny acts of taking up space. Little decisions to honor your knowing instead of deferring to someone else's opinion.

Each time you choose yourself, you get a piece back. Each time you refuse to shrink, you expand. Each time you express what you've been suppressing, you reclaim territory that was always yours.

Your feminine essence was never lost. It was just stolen, piece by piece, by a world that benefited from your diminishment.

Take it back.

Not in defiance, but in alignment. You're simply returning what was always yours.

Key Takeaways

- Your feminine essence never disappeared; it simply went quiet beneath layers of adaptation.
- You were taught to perform femininity instead of feeling it, to act graceful instead of moving naturally.
- Real feminine energy is not decoration or compliance but a living intelligence that responds, senses, and creates.

- Logic became your armor when intuition started to feel dangerous, yet your intuition never stopped speaking.
- Softness was misread as weakness, so you learned to harden and now mistake tension for safety.
- The walls you built to avoid being hurt also block tenderness, connection, and genuine pleasure.
- Doing became your proof of value, but being is where your nervous system finally exhales.
- Restoring balance means allowing as much as acting, listening as much as directing.
- Society profits from your self-doubt and trains you to equate compliance with worth.
- Every time you choose honesty over performance, you recover a fragment of power that was always yours.

Step 2:
HEALING - Making Peace With Your Past

The mask is off. The cage is visible. The armour has been named. And maybe right now there's a voice in your head asking, "Great. Now what? I'm aware that I'm a mess. How does that help?"

Here's the truth: awareness without action just turns into another cage. Spending years knowing exactly why things are the way they are while still repeating the same patterns, still attracting the same type of person, still ending up in the same place wondering why nothing ever changes.

Healing isn't about understanding trauma. It's about resolving it.

This is the part where most books fail. They tell women to love themselves more, set better boundaries, and think positive thoughts, as if years of conditioning and pain can be erased with a bubble bath and some affirmations.

But the real issue isn't effort. It's fighting invisible battles with parts of yourself you don't even know exist. Parts that are terrified of change because change means risk, and risk means potential pain.

Self-sabotage isn't sabotage at all. It's a protection mechanism that made perfect sense at one point in your life, probably when you were too young to have any other options. Now it's outdated software running on autopilot, making decisions based on threats that don't exist anymore.

These next four chapters are about making peace with the parts that have been running the show from behind the scenes. The wounded feminine that's been in hiding. The loyalty to family patterns that keep you broke or alone or playing small. The boundaries you've been violating in yourself long before anyone else got the chance.

This work isn't pretty. There's no bypassing the pain here, no shortcut around the grief. But on the other side of that feeling? Freedom.

Chapter 4:
The Root of Your Self-Sabotage

"Until you make the unconscious conscious, it will direct your life and you will call it fate." – Carl Jung

You've been calling it self-sabotage. The pattern where you get close to what you want and then do something that derails it. The relationship that was going well until you picked a fight over nothing. The job opportunity you didn't apply for even though you were qualified. The goal you set and then abandoned halfway through.

You think there's something wrong with you. Some glitch in your wiring that makes you undo what you've built. Some unconscious desire to fail that keeps pulling you back every time you try to move forward.

But what if you're not sabotaging yourself at all?

What if every behavior you've labeled as self-destructive is actually a protection mechanism that once kept you safe? What if the part of you that seems to be working against you is actually working for you, just based on outdated information about what safety requires?

This chapter is about understanding that there's no such thing as self-sabotage. There are only parts of you operating from different priorities, with different information, trying to keep you alive and connected in the ways they learned were necessary. Once you stop fighting these parts and begin understanding them, real change starts to happen.

There Is No Such Thing as Self-Sabotage

The term self-sabotage implies intent. It suggests that some part of you is deliberately trying to ruin your life, destroy your chances, keep you small.

That's not what's happening.

What you're calling sabotage is actually a part of you trying to protect you from a perceived threat. The behavior that looks self-destructive from the outside makes perfect sense from the inside once you understand what that part is trying to prevent.

You get close to success and suddenly you can't focus, you procrastinate, you make mistakes that seem careless. That's not sabotage. Its goal isn't to ruin anything; it's to keep you safe from what it still perceives as danger. Maybe you grew up watching a parent get torn down for their achievements. Maybe you learned that standing out meant becoming a target. Maybe success in your family meant losing connection because they couldn't celebrate what they envied.

So now, when you get close to achieving something, that protective part activates. It creates friction, generates doubt, manufactures obstacles. You might notice it as sudden fatigue before an important step, or the urge to "just check one more thing" instead of acting.

You meet someone who's emotionally available and genuinely interested, and you start finding problems that don't exist. You pick fights, create distance, test their commitment until they leave. That's protection in disguise. It's a part of you that learned love doesn't last, that people who claim to care will eventually leave, that letting someone in means giving them the power to destroy you.

So when someone gets close, that part creates problems to prove its point. It pushes them away before they can leave on their own. It maintains control over the inevitable abandonment instead of being blindsided by it later.

You set a boundary and then immediately apologize for it, walk it back, make exceptions. That's self-protection following old instructions. It's a part of you that learned boundaries led to rejection. That saying no meant being labeled difficult, selfish, unlovable. That your needs were less important than keeping peace and maintaining connection.

So when you try to set a limit, that part panics. It tries to soften the boundary, qualify it, make it more palatable. Not because you don't deserve boundaries, but because it's trying to protect you from the isolation it believes boundaries will cause.

Every pattern you've labeled as self-sabotage is a part of you doing its job. The problem isn't the part. The problem is that the part is operating on old information. It's trying to protect you from threats that existed in your past but may not exist in your present.

That protective part doesn't know that you're not a child anymore. It doesn't know that you have resources now that you didn't have then. It doesn't know that the people in your current life aren't the people who hurt you before.

It just knows what it learned: this situation is dangerous, and here's what we do to stay safe.

When you understand this, everything shifts. You stop fighting yourself. You stop judging the part that seems to be sabotaging you. Instead, you start getting curious about what it's trying to protect you from.

What does this part believe will happen if I succeed? What's it trying to prevent? What threat does it think it's defending me against?

Once you identify the belief underneath the behavior, you can update it. You can show that part evidence that the old threat no longer exists. You can demonstrate that you have new tools, new resources, new options that weren't available when that protective strategy got installed.

The behavior that looks like sabotage is actually loyalty. Loyalty to old survival strategies. Loyalty to beliefs that once kept you safe. Loyalty to the version of you that needed protection and figured out how to get it.

You're adaptive, just still operating on outdated software. And outdated software can be updated once you stop pathologizing it and start understanding the purpose it was designed to serve.

The Parts of You That Are Trying to Protect You

You don't operate as a single, seamless self. You're a system of parts, each with its own job, its own perspective, its own priority.

There's the part that wants to take risks and grow. The part that wants to stay safe and avoid pain. The part that craves connection. The part that needs independence. The part that's ambitious. The part that's exhausted. The part that wants to be seen. The part that wants to hide.

These parts don't always agree. In fact, they often have completely opposing goals. And when they conflict, you experience it as internal warfare. As confusion about what you actually want. As the feeling of being at war with yourself.

But none of these parts are your enemy. They're all trying to help you, just in different ways, based on different experiences and different information about what you need.

The part that makes you procrastinate isn't lazy. It's protecting you from the vulnerability of being judged on your work. It learned that if you don't finish, you can't fail. That potential is safer than performance because no one can criticize what you haven't done yet.

The part that makes you defensive when criticized isn't immature. It's protecting you from shame, from the old fear that any mistake will expose you as not enough.

The part that makes you stay busy constantly isn't just ambitious. It's protecting you from having to feel what comes up when you're still. It learned that rest means facing things you'd rather avoid, that stopping means remembering things you've worked hard to forget.

The part that makes you withdraw when someone gets close isn't afraid of intimacy. It's protecting you from abandonment. It learned that people leave, that caring about someone gives them power to hurt you, that distance is safer than disappointment.

These parts developed for good reasons. They're not random. They're not defects. They're intelligent responses to experiences that required adaptation.

The problem is that parts don't update themselves automatically. They keep running the same strategy that worked once, even when the situation has changed, even when that strategy is now creating more problems than it solves.

Your anxious part is still protecting you from dangers that existed in childhood. Your perfectionist part is still trying to earn love from people who withheld it. Your avoidant part is still guarding against betrayals that happened years ago.

They're doing their jobs. They're just doing their jobs in circumstances that no longer require those particular defenses.

This is why willpower doesn't work. You can't force a protective part to stand down through discipline or determination. It's not going to stop protecting you just because your conscious mind says it should.

The only way to update a part is to acknowledge what it's trying to do and then provide evidence that its strategy is no longer necessary.

You have to talk to it. Not metaphorically. Actually engage with it. When you notice yourself procrastinating, instead of pushing through or beating yourself up, pause. Ask the part that's making you procrastinate what it's protecting you from. Notice where that question lands in your body. Maybe your chest tightens or your stomach pulls in. That's the part answering. Listen to what comes. It might be a feeling, an image, a memory, a belief.

Then you can address that concern directly. If the part is afraid of judgment, you can acknowledge that fear is real and valid, and also show it that you can handle judgment now in ways you couldn't when that fear got installed. That criticism doesn't destroy you the way it once did. That your worth isn't contingent on everyone's approval.

When a part feels heard and sees that you have new resources available, it relaxes. It doesn't need to protect you as intensely because you've demonstrated that you can handle what it was trying to prevent.

This is the work. Not fighting the parts that seem to sabotage you, but understanding them. Not forcing them into submission, but updating the information they're working with.

Your parts aren't the enemy. They're doing their best with the information they have. Update the information they're using, and the strategy updates itself.

Negative Loyalty Patterns Blocking Your Abundance

You have invisible contracts with the people who shaped you. Agreements you never consciously made but follow anyway because breaking them feels like betrayal.

These contracts govern what you're allowed to have. How much success is acceptable. What kind of happiness is permitted. What you can access without somehow abandoning the people you came from.

Your mother struggled financially, so you have a contract that says having more money than she did means you're disloyal. That being comfortable when she never was means you think you're better than her. That enjoying what she couldn't have is a form of judgment.

So you sabotage your earning potential. Not consciously. But you make decisions that keep you at her level. You spend what you make. You undercharge for your work. You don't pursue opportunities that would take you too far beyond what she achieved.

You're not trying to stay poor. You're trying to stay connected. Because on some level, you believe that having what she couldn't have means losing her. That success would create a distance you can't tolerate.

Your father was critical of people he saw as show-offs, so you have a contract that says visibility is dangerous. That claiming your accomplishments means becoming the kind of person he despised. That confidence equals arrogance in his eyes.

So you downplay your achievements. You don't promote your work. You stay small in rooms where you could take up space. You do believe in yourself, yet that belief collides with the old rule that visibility means rejection.

And maybe your family struggled, so you absorbed another rule: that ease is suspicious, that effort equals worth. So you make everything harder than it needs to be. You reject help. You choose the difficult path even when an easier one exists.

These loyalty patterns are invisible because they feel like truth. They feel like reality, like just how things are, like the natural order you're supposed to follow.

But they're not truth. They're contracts you agreed to without realizing you were signing anything. And they're keeping you limited in ways you don't recognize because you can't see the contract that's governing your choices.

You think you're just being realistic about money. That you're just not good at earning. That financial struggle is your normal. You don't see that you're following a rule that says having more means abandonment.

You think you're just humble about your achievements. That confidence isn't your personality. That staying quiet is just who you are. You don't see that you're following a rule that says visibility means rejection.

You think you just have a strong work ethic. That you value effort and discipline. That ease feels wrong because you haven't developed the skills for it. You don't see that you're following a rule that says suffering is the price of worth.

These patterns are particularly insidious because they trigger most intensely when you start to exceed what the people you came from had. The guilt shows up. The fear of separation. You might feel it as a drop in your stomach, a heaviness that makes expanding uncomfortable. The unconscious need to sabotage what you've built so you can return to familiar ground.

Breaking these contracts doesn't mean rejecting the people who installed them. It means recognizing that you can love them without living by their limitations. That you can honor where you came from without staying there forever.

Your success doesn't diminish them. Your abundance doesn't prove they were wrong. Your happiness doesn't mean you've forgotten their struggles.

You can have more and still belong. You can succeed beyond their level and still love them. You can create what they couldn't and still honor where you came from.

But first, you have to see the contract. You have to identify the invisible rule that's governing your relationship with money, success, visibility, ease, joy.

What did you learn about people who have what you want? What judgments did your family hold about wealth, confidence, happiness? What would it mean about you if you exceeded their level? What are you afraid you'd lose?

Once you see the contract, you can renegotiate it. You can decide that loyalty doesn't require limitation. That love doesn't require sacrifice. That honoring your family doesn't mean inheriting their restrictions.

You can write a new contract. One that allows you to have abundance and connection. Success and belonging. Happiness and love.

The old contract was written by fear; your signature can be replaced with freedom.

Breaking Free From Inherited Limitations

You inherited more than eye color or laughter. You inherited beliefs, patterns, ways of seeing the world that got passed down like DNA.

Your grandmother believed women should be small and quiet, so your mother learned to shrink, and you learned to shrink, and now you're passing that same contraction to your daughter without anyone ever saying it explicitly.

It's in the way your mother apologized for taking up space. The way she made herself smaller when your father was in a mood. The way she sacrificed her needs and called it love. You watched. You absorbed. You replicated.

Your father believed emotions were weakness, so he shut his down, and your brother learned to shut his down, and you learned that caring too much makes you vulnerable in ways men respect and women endure.

You saw it each time your father handled stress by going silent, praised stoicism, dismissed tears. You listened. You adapted. You applied those same rules to yourself.

These inherited limitations don't announce themselves. They don't come with disclaimers that say "this belief is optional" or "this pattern is just one family's interpretation."

They arrive disguised as truth, as the unquestioned way things have always been.

You don't question them because you don't even see them. They're the water you swim in. The air you breathe. The foundation you build your life on without ever examining whether that foundation is solid.

You think you're making free choices. That you're deciding based on your own values, your own assessment of what's possible. You don't realize how many of your decisions are actually just replications of patterns you witnessed and internalized before you were old enough to question them.

You stay in a mediocre job not because you can't find better, but because you inherited the belief that work is supposed to be hard and unfulfilling. That you're lucky to have anything. That asking for more is entitled.

You settle in relationships not because you don't know you deserve better, but because you inherited the model that love requires tolerating mistreatment. That partnership means sacrifice. That loneliness together is better than risk alone.

You struggle with money not because you can't earn it, but because you inherited the belief that there's never enough. That financial security is for other people. That wanting comfort makes you greedy.

These aren't your beliefs. They're hand-me-downs. But you're living by them as if they're natural law.

Breaking free from inherited limitations starts with seeing them. With recognizing which beliefs are actually yours and which ones you're just carrying because no one in your lineage questioned them before you.

Ask yourself: where did I learn this? Who taught me this was true? Is this actually my experience, or is this what I was told to expect?

Pause before answering. The body often knows before the mind admits it.

Most of what you believe about what's possible for you comes from watching what was possible for the people who raised you. Their ceiling became your ceiling. Their fears became your fears. Their limitations became your inheritance.

But inheritance is optional. You can accept it, or you can decline it.

You can look at the belief that financial struggle is inevitable and say: that was true for them, and it doesn't have to be true for me.

You can look at the pattern of tolerating bad relationships and say: that's how they loved, and I'm learning a different way.

You can look at the limitation around success and say: their fear of visibility doesn't have to be my fear.

This isn't about rejecting your family or pretending their experiences don't matter. It's about recognizing that their experiences were shaped by their circumstances, their traumas, their era, their resources.

You have different circumstances. Different resources. Different options.

You're allowed to exceed their limitations without disrespecting their struggles. You're allowed to have what they couldn't have without implying they should have had it too. You're allowed to break patterns without blaming them for installing those patterns in the first place.

But you can't break what you can't see. And right now, most of what's limiting you is invisible because it's been there so long you think it's just how you are.

It's not how you are. It's what you learned. And what was learned can be unlearned once you bring it into consciousness and decide whether it still serves you.

The limitations you inherited aren't destiny; they're coordinates you can step beyond once you remember you're free to move.

Key Takeaways

- What you've labeled self-sabotage is actually a part of you protecting you from repeating old pain.
- Behaviors that seem destructive are rooted in survival strategies that made sense when they first formed.
- The closer you get to what you deeply desire, the louder the protective mechanisms become, trying to keep you safe.
- Every internal conflict reflects parts of you operating with different priorities, not a lack of self-control.
- Understanding the hidden purpose behind your patterns creates space to choose differently rather than repeating old cycles.
- Inherited family beliefs silently dictate how much success, money, and joy you allow yourself.
- Unspoken loyalty can limit your potential as you unconsciously try not to surpass those who raised you.
- The discomfort you feel around abundance or visibility is often linked to fears of betraying family expectations.
- True freedom comes when you rewrite the rules you never consciously agreed to.
- Your family's limits were shaped by their history, not yours, and you're allowed to redefine what's possible.

Chapter 5:
Healing the Wounded Feminine Within

"I am not what happened to me, I am what I choose to become." — Carl Jung

You can read every book on feminine energy, practice every ritual, speak every affirmation, and still feel like something fundamental is missing. As if you've learned the language of wholeness but still speak in fragments.

That's because surface-level practices can't touch wounds that live in your body, your nervous system, the parts of you that split off when staying whole felt too exposed.

The wounded feminine isn't an idea to analyze—it's a lived reality in the body. It's the part of you that learned femininity itself was unsafe. That being soft meant being hurt. That opening meant being violated. That trusting meant being betrayed.

And it's still operating from that place, still protecting you from dangers that may no longer exist, still running strategies that once kept you alive but now keep you isolated, defended, half-present in your own life.

This chapter is about going deeper than theory. It's about understanding the specific wounds that shape how you move through the world, and learning the process that actually resolves trauma at its root instead of just managing symptoms. You reach it by allowing yourself to feel what the body has been holding.

Understanding Your Enmeshment or Abandonment Trauma

Most of your relationship patterns come down to one of two core wounds: enmeshment or abandonment. Sometimes both, in different relationships or different contexts.

These wounds shape everything. How close you let people get. How much of yourself you reveal. Whether you chase connection or run from it. Whether you lose yourself in relationships or refuse to fully enter them.

Enmeshment trauma happens when you learn that having boundaries means losing love. When the people who were supposed to care for you couldn't tolerate your separateness. When your needs, feelings, thoughts, desires had to match theirs or you faced consequences.

Maybe your mother needed you to be an extension of her. Your accomplishments were hers. Your failures reflected on her. Your emotions had to align with hers because she couldn't handle the discomfort of your different experience.

Maybe your father required you to think like him, value what he valued, want what he wanted. Disagreeing meant rejection. Having your own perspective meant you were disloyal, ungrateful, didn't appreciate everything he'd done for you.

You learned that love requires giving yourself up. That connection means erasing your edges. That to be close to someone, you have to become them.

So now, when relationships deepen, you start disappearing. You lose track of your preferences because you're so focused on matching theirs. You can't locate your feelings because you've trained yourself to absorb their emotional state instead. You don't know what you think because you've been reading the room and adjusting your position before you even check in with yourself. Your shoulders tighten, breath shortens, and your body subtly mirrors the other person's posture before you even notice.

You might label this flexibility or kindness. What it actually is: enmeshment trauma still running the show.

Intimacy begins to feel like disappearing. Like you can't have yourself and have connection. Like closeness requires choosing them over you, every time.

Abandonment trauma is the opposite wound, but it creates equally painful patterns. This happens when you learn that needing people leads to pain. That depending on someone means giving them power to hurt you. That love is temporary and loss is inevitable.

Maybe your parents were physically there but emotionally absent. You learned that expressing needs didn't get them met, it just exposed your vulnerability. So you stopped expressing them.

Maybe someone you loved left. Died, divorced, disappeared. And the message you took from that was: don't get attached because attachment leads to devastation.

Maybe you were neglected, forgotten, consistently deprioritized. You learned that you're not important enough to stay for, that people will always choose something or someone else over you.

So now, you don't let people close enough to hurt you. You maintain distance even in relationships that are supposed to be intimate. You test people, push them away, convince yourself you don't need anyone so you can't be disappointed when they leave. Your chest constricts, eyes avert, or you distract yourself with busyness when someone gets too close.

You tell yourself it's self-reliance. What it actually is: abandonment trauma keeping you protected by keeping you alone.

Closeness starts to feel risky and unstable. Like vulnerability equals giving someone ammunition. Like opening means setting yourself up for inevitable loss.

Both wounds create the same problem: you can't access real intimacy. Either you lose yourself trying to maintain connection, or you maintain yourself by avoiding real connection.

Neither strategy works. Enmeshment leaves you empty, constantly giving from a depleted place, resentful that no one sees you because you've made yourself invisible. Abandonment leaves you isolated, craving connection while simultaneously ensuring you never get close enough to actually receive it.

Healing begins the moment you recognize which wound is active. Or if you have both, recognizing which one activates in which context.

Do you lose yourself in relationships? Struggle to say no? Feel responsible for other people's emotions? Have trouble accessing your own needs and desires when someone else is in the room? That's enmeshment.

Do you keep people at arm's length? Struggle to ask for help? Feel uncomfortable when someone tries to take care of you? Sabotage relationships when they get too close? That's abandonment.

Once you see the wound clearly, you can start addressing it. Not by thinking about it differently, but by giving your nervous system new experiences that contradict what the wound taught you to expect.

For enmeshment: practice staying connected to yourself while staying connected to someone else. Small things. Notice your preference when someone asks where to eat. State a boundary without apologizing. During a conversation, silently repeat, "I'm still here," before answering. Say no and see that the relationship survives.

For abandonment: practice letting people in without immediately pushing them away. Small risks. Accept help with something minor. When someone offers care, pause for ten seconds and allow yourself to receive before you deflect. Share something vulnerable. Ask for what you need and see that asking doesn't guarantee rejection.

The wound won't heal through understanding alone. It heals through experience. Through your nervous system learning that the old threat doesn't exist anymore. That you can have boundaries and still be loved. That you can need people and still be secure.

The Completion Process for Deep Trauma Resolution

Understanding your wounds is necessary. But understanding doesn't heal them. You can know exactly why you do what you do and still keep doing it because the wound lives deeper than your thinking mind can reach.

Trauma isn't stored in your thoughts. It's stored in your body, your nervous system, the parts of you that fragmented when the original experience was too much to handle as a unified self.

This is why talking about trauma can help you make sense of it but doesn't resolve it. Why insight feels powerful in the moment but doesn't change your automatic responses. Why you can spend years in therapy understanding your patterns and still repeat them.

You need a process that works with the body, the nervous system, the fragmented parts. That goes to where the wound actually lives instead of just discussing it from a distance.

A deep completion practice is designed for exactly this. This process works directly with the body and the parts that split. It's not just mental insight—it requires embodied experience that actually completes what was left incomplete.

Here's how it works.

You start with a trigger. Something in your present life that creates a disproportionate emotional response. Maybe someone criticizes you and you feel shame so intense it's paralyzing. Maybe someone gets close and you feel panic so strong you have to create distance immediately. Maybe you achieve something and instead of celebrating, you feel terror.

That emotional charge is your body telling you: this situation is activating an old wound. The intensity of your reaction isn't about the present moment. It's about an unresolved past experience that this moment is reminding your system of.

You follow that emotional charge back. Not through memory, but through sensation. You ask your body: when did I first feel this? And you let your system take you there. To the original moment when this emotional pattern got created.

You might get a specific memory. You might get an age, a feeling, an image, a sense of what was happening even if you don't have clear details. Notice your breath shorten, your shoulders tense, or your stomach tighten as the memory surfaces. Trust what comes. Your system knows where the wound is.

Once you've identified that moment, you invite your adult self into that scene and stay present with what unfolds. Not to change what happened, but to be with your younger self in a way that no one was with her then.

You ask her what she needed. What she was feeling. What she wanted that she didn't get. And you give it to her. Not just conceptually. You feel it in your body. You let her feel what it would have been like to be seen, protected, validated, held, whatever she needed that was absent.

This is where the healing happens. Not in understanding that you were hurt, but in your nervous system experiencing what it would have felt like to receive what you needed. That somatic experience creates new neural pathways. It gives your system evidence that the wound can be complete. That you don't have to keep running protection strategies designed for a situation that's now resolved.

Then you bring that younger part back into your present self. You integrate her. She doesn't have to stay frozen in that traumatic moment anymore, trying to get needs met that never got met, running patterns that made sense then but create problems now.

She can come home. She can relax into your adult self who has resources, options, power she didn't have then. And when she integrates, the pattern she was running stops. Because the wound that created it is complete.

This isn't a one-time process. You have multiple wounds, multiple moments that created fragmentation. Each one needs its own completion. But every wound you complete gives you access to more of yourself. More capacity. More presence. More ability to respond to your current life instead of reacting from past pain.

The process is simple. It's not easy. It requires you to feel what you've been avoiding. To go toward the pain instead of running from it. To stay present with young parts of you that are still holding experiences you wanted to forget.

But it works because it completes what remained unfinished and restores a sense of security in the body.

Integrating Your Rejected and Shadow Selves

You're not just carrying wounds from what happened to you. You're carrying wounds from what you had to reject about yourself in order to survive what happened.

The parts of you that were too much, too intense, too messy for the people around you to handle. The anger that wasn't allowed. The neediness that was punished. The sexuality that was shamed. The ambition that threatened fragile egos. The sensitivity that was dismissed as weakness.

Those parts never disappeared—they've been running beneath awareness, shaping behavior from the shadows.

Your rejected anger shows up as passive aggression, resentment that builds until you explode over something minor, or complete emotional shutdown that looks like not caring when you actually care too much.

Your rejected neediness shows up as independence so extreme it's isolation, doing everything yourself even when you're drowning, or attracting people who need you so you can meet your need for connection without having to admit you have needs.

Your rejected sexuality shows up as shutting down entirely, performing sexuality without actually feeling it, or sexualizing situations that aren't sexual because you don't know how to access intimacy any other way.

These shadow parts don't disappear just because you reject them. They go underground and run covert operations that sabotage what you're trying to build on the surface.

Healing happens through integration, not elimination. By bringing those rejected parts back into consciousness and finding ways to express them that don't recreate the original trauma.

This starts with acknowledging what you rejected. What parts of yourself did you decide were unacceptable? What did you learn you had to hide in order to be loved?

Were you too loud, too emotional, too demanding, too sexual, too angry, too sensitive, too ambitious, too much in some way that got you punished or rejected?

That part didn't go away. It's just been operating without your conscious guidance, trying to get its needs met through indirect strategies that usually backfire.

Integration means making room for that part again. Not in the unregulated way it showed up when you were young, but in a mature form that serves you now.

Your anger can transform from reactivity to assertive boundary-setting, clear communication, the ability to say no without guilt.

Your neediness can shift from hidden dependence to open requests for support, the capacity to ask for help, to receive, to acknowledge that interdependence is strength.

Your sexuality can move from shutdown or performance to embodied desire, pleasure in your body, the ability to connect through physical intimacy without shame or dissociation.

But first, you have to stop treating these parts like enemies. Stop trying to eliminate them. Stop being ashamed that they exist.

They're not the problem. The problem is that they had to go underground because expressing them wasn't secure. Now they're running programs from the shadows, creating patterns you can't control because you can't see them.

Bring them into the light. Acknowledge them. Thank them for trying to get your needs met even when you were pretending you didn't have those needs.

Then find new ways to express what they represent. Ways that work in your current life instead of recreating past trauma.

This isn't about becoming unfiltered or unleashing every impulse. It's about integrating what you split off so you can access your full range of human experience without the parts you rejected sabotaging you from the shadows.

You're not whole without your shadow. You're just performing wholeness while half of you operates underground, trying to be seen, trying to be heard, trying to be included in the life you're living.

Let it come home. When you acknowledge these parts, take a deep breath and feel your spine lengthen—as if your system finally has room for all of you.

Releasing Shame Without Bypassing the Pain

Shame is the feeling that you are fundamentally defective. Not that you did something wrong, but that you are something wrong. That your existence is the problem.

And shame is the glue that holds your wounds in place. As long as you're ashamed of what happened to you, ashamed of how you responded, ashamed of the parts of you that developed from trauma, you can't heal those wounds. Because shame keeps them hidden, and you can't heal what you won't look at.

Shame softens only when you face it directly instead of avoiding it. And that means feeling what you've been avoiding.

You've been trying to heal by thinking your way past the pain. By understanding it, reframing it, finding the lesson in it. By jumping straight to forgiveness or acceptance or the place where you're okay with what happened.

That's skipping over the pain. Using spiritual concepts to avoid feeling what needs to be felt.

Real healing requires you to stop rushing to insight without feeling and start actually feeling. To sit with the pain you've been running from. To let yourself acknowledge how much it hurt, how wrong it was, how much you needed something you didn't get.

This feels risky because you're afraid that if you let yourself feel it fully, you'll get stuck there. That the pain will swallow you. That you won't be able to come back from it.

But the opposite is true. You're stuck because you won't feel it. The pain you're avoiding is taking up space in your system, creating symptoms, running patterns, keeping you defended. Once you actually feel it, complete it, let it move through you, it can release. But not before.

Shame keeps you from feeling the pain because shame tells you the pain is your fault. That you deserved it. That something about you caused it or attracted it or made you vulnerable to it.

None of that is true. What happened to you wasn't your fault. How you responded to what happened was the best you could do with the resources you had at the time. The parts of you that developed from trauma are adaptations, not defects.

But you can't believe that intellectually. You have to feel your way to it. You have to let yourself grieve what was lost, rage at what was wrong, ache for what you needed but didn't receive.

Before revisiting painful memories, ground yourself—feel your feet on the floor, place a hand on your chest, remind your body that you're secure now.

You have to stop protecting everyone else's feelings about what happened and start honoring your own. Stop minimizing it because others had it worse. Stop explaining it away because you understand why they did what they did. Stop forgiving before you've fully felt.

Your anger is valid. Your grief is valid. Your sense of betrayal, abandonment, violation is valid. Even if the people who hurt you didn't mean to. Even if they were doing their best. Even if they had their own trauma. Your pain is still real, still yours, still deserving of space.

Let yourself have it. The full weight of it. Not forever, but fully. Let yourself feel how much it hurt to not be protected. To not be seen. To not be loved in the way you needed. To have to become someone else in order to survive.

This isn't about staying in victim consciousness. It's about giving yourself permission to acknowledge the reality of what happened before you try to transcend it.

You can't transcend what you won't admit was wrong in the first place.

Once you've felt it, once you've let the pain move through instead of keeping it locked inside, something shifts. Shame starts to loosen. Because shame thrives in hiding, and you just brought everything into the light.

You realize the pain wasn't proof of your defectiveness. It was proof of your humanity. It was a natural response to an unnatural situation. And responding to pain with pain doesn't make you broken. It makes you human.

The shame dissolves when you stop trying to be okay with what wasn't okay. When you stop performing forgiveness you don't feel. When you stop pretending you're healed when you're actually just numb.

Real healing isn't pretty. It's not a straight line from wound to wholeness. It's messy and nonlinear and sometimes you feel worse before you feel better because you're finally feeling what you've been avoiding.

But on the other side of that feeling is freedom. You no longer carry the past as shame but as integrated knowledge, a memory that informs healthier choices instead of defining who you are.

You don't have to be ashamed of what happened to you. You don't have to be ashamed of how it shaped you. You don't have to perform being over it before you're actually through it.

You just have to be willing to feel it. All of it. Until it's complete. And then you can release it, not because you've bypassed the pain, but because you finally let yourself have it.

Key Takeaways

- Surface-level healing can't resolve wounds embedded deeply within your nervous system.
- Enmeshment wounds make relationships feel suffocating, forcing you to erase your boundaries to maintain connection.

- Abandonment wounds lead you to keep people distant to prevent the loss you anticipate.

- Healing trauma requires providing your nervous system with new experiences, proving old threats no longer apply.

- You release trauma by revisiting the original wound and experiencing the emotional support you previously lacked.

- The behaviors you judge harshly in yourself are often adaptive responses from rejected parts operating beneath awareness.

- Embracing your shadow aspects dissolves the patterns of resentment and passive aggression caused by suppression.

- Shame dissolves when you fully acknowledge your pain without minimizing it or protecting others from discomfort.

- Genuine forgiveness emerges naturally once you've allowed yourself to fully grieve the impact of your wounds.

- Integration of your wounded parts restores emotional availability, helping you move from defensiveness into authentic connection.

Chapter 6:
You Can Have Yourself AND Have Love

"Love rests on two pillars: surrender and autonomy. Our need for togetherness exists alongside our need for separateness." — Esther Perel

It happens in the quiet moments, when someone asks what you need and you don't know what to say. When you shrink a little to keep the peace. When you feel the pull between honesty and belonging.

The lie is this: you have to choose between being yourself and being loved.

That having boundaries means people will leave. That expressing your needs makes you a burden. That showing your full self will result in rejection. That to keep relationships, you have to give yourself up.

So you've been choosing. Sometimes you choose yourself and accept loneliness. Sometimes you choose connection and abandon yourself. But you never imagine there's a third option where you don't have to choose at all.

This chapter is about dismantling that false binary. About understanding that the belief you have to sacrifice yourself for love is a trauma response, not a truth. About learning that real intimacy doesn't require self-abandonment, it requires the opposite. And about discovering that the relationships worth having are the ones where you can be fully yourself and fully connected at the same time.

The False Choice Between Autonomy and Connection

Somewhere early in your life, you learned that being yourself and being close to someone were mutually exclusive. That you could have your own thoughts, feelings, needs, desires, or you could have love. But not both.

Maybe your parents couldn't handle your differentness. Your preferences that didn't match theirs felt like rejection to them. Your boundaries felt like attacks. Your separate identity threatened their sense of control or their need for you to reflect well on them.

So you learned: connection requires conformity. To stay close, you have to mirror. To be loved, you have to match.

Or maybe the opposite happened. Maybe the people who were supposed to love you were so absent, so unreliable, so conditional that you learned depending on anyone was a setup for disappointment. That needing people gave them power to hurt you. That autonomy was the only way to stay intact.

So you learned: connection requires dependence, and dependence is dangerous. To stay whole, you have to stay separate.

Either way, you developed the belief that you can't have both. That intimacy and autonomy are opposing forces. That you're either merged with someone and losing yourself, or you're independent and alone.

This belief creates an impossible situation. Because you need both. You're human. You're wired for connection and you're wired for individuation. You can't thrive without intimate relationships, and you can't thrive without a coherent sense of self.

But you keep defaulting to one side or the other. You feel it in your body, the tension between wanting closeness and needing space. Never finding equilibrium because you don't believe equilibrium is possible.

You get into a relationship and slowly start disappearing. You stop voicing preferences. You absorb their moods. You adjust your life around theirs. You tell yourself this is what partnership requires, but really, you're just running the old program that says love means erasing your edges.

Eventually, you can't take it anymore. You feel suffocated. Resentful. Invisible. So you pull back. You create distance. You reclaim your space. And in doing so, you lose the connection you were trying to maintain.

Or you stay fiercely independent. You don't let anyone close enough to influence you. You maintain complete control over your life, your choices, your space. You tell yourself this is freedom, but really, you're just running the old program that says needing people means losing yourself.

Eventually, you can't take the loneliness. You crave intimacy. You want someone to know you. So you try to let someone in. And in doing so, you panic and push them away before they can get too close.

You're caught in a pendulum swing. Merge and lose yourself, or separate and lose connection. Back and forth. Never landing in the middle because you don't believe the middle exists.

But it does exist. The middle is called secure attachment. It's the place where you can be deeply connected to someone and deeply connected to yourself at the same time. Where intimacy doesn't require self-abandonment. Where autonomy doesn't require isolation.

You can have your own thoughts and share them. Your own feelings and express them. Your own needs and ask for them to be met. And the relationship doesn't end. In fact, it deepens. Because real intimacy isn't built on sameness. It's built on two whole people choosing to be close without either one disappearing.

The false choice between autonomy and connection is a trauma response. It's based on experiences where that choice was real. Where being yourself did lead to disapproval. Where needing people did lead to pain.

But that was then. You're not in that situation anymore. The people in your current life don't have to be the people from your past. The patterns that were true in your family don't have to be true in your relationships now.

You can have yourself and have love. The work is remembering that the choice was never real.

Why You Swing Between Compliance and Rebellion

It feels like you're choosing how to show up, but most of the time you're simply reacting from old code.

Compliance says: I'll give you what you want so you don't leave me. I'll be agreeable, flexible, easy. I'll anticipate your needs and meet them before you have to ask. I'll shape myself around you so you never have reason to reject me.

Rebellion says: I won't give you anything so you can't control me. I'll do the opposite of what you want. I'll resist your influence, reject your input, prove that you don't get to tell me who to be.

Both strategies are trying to solve the same problem: how do I stay connected without losing myself? But neither one works because neither one is actually about the present relationship. They're both reactions to past relationships where connection and autonomy really were in conflict.

Compliance comes from enmeshment. From learning that differentiation was dangerous. That having your own opinions, preferences, needs meant losing love. So you learned to give yourself up preemptively. To erase your edges before they could create friction.

You became the person other people needed you to be. And it worked. You stayed connected. But you lost yourself in the process, and now you don't know how to be in a relationship without disappearing.

Rebellion comes from the same wound, just a different response. At some point, you couldn't take the self-erasure anymore. You hit a breaking point where compliance felt like death, so you swung to the opposite extreme.

You began saying no to everything, sometimes just to prove you still could. Resisting influence. Doing things your way even when another way might work better. Not because you actually wanted to do it differently, but because agreeing felt like giving in. Like losing the battle for your autonomy.

So now you're in relationships where you're constantly pushing back, creating unnecessary conflict, turning everything into a power struggle. You think you're protecting your independence. What you're actually doing is staying controlled by the thing you're rebelling against.

Both compliance and rebellion keep you trapped. Compliance keeps you trapped in other people's expectations. Rebellion keeps you trapped in opposition to those expectations. Neither one lets you be free because neither one is about what you actually want. They're both just reactions to the fear of being controlled.

Real autonomy isn't compliance or rebellion. It's the ability to make choices based on what serves you, regardless of what anyone else wants or expects.

Sometimes that looks like agreeing. Not because you're afraid to disagree, but because you genuinely align with what's being proposed.

Sometimes that looks like saying no. Not because you're automatically opposing, but because what's being asked doesn't work for you.

Sometimes that looks like compromise. Not because you're giving yourself up, but because you care about the other person and you're willing to meet in the middle when it matters.

The difference is conscious choice. Compliance and rebellion are both automatic. They happen before you even check in with yourself. You comply because that's your default programming. You rebel because that's your default programming.

Freedom is checking in with yourself first. Asking: what do I actually want here? Not what will keep the peace. Not what will prove I'm independent. What do I genuinely want?

Then acting from that place. Even if it sometimes looks like compliance. Even if it sometimes looks like rebellion. Because when it's coming from conscious choice instead of automatic reaction, it's neither. It's just you, responding authentically to what's in front of you.

You can't have yourself and have love while you're swinging between compliance and rebellion. Because both strategies are forms of self-abandonment. Compliance abandons your authentic response. Rebellion abandons your actual preference in service of opposing someone else's.

You only get to have both when you stop reacting and start choosing. When you break the pendulum and find your center. When you learn that you can consider someone else's needs without erasing your own, and that you can honor your own needs without making everything a battle.

That's where real connection begins, between two people centered enough to stay open even when it's uncomfortable.

Creating Safety Within So You Can Soften Outside

You can't relax into intimacy without inner stability. And you can't feel stable with another person until you feel stable with yourself.

This is what most relationship advice gets wrong. It tells you to trust people, to open up, to be vulnerable, to let your guard down. As if the problem is that you're choosing to stay defended and you just need to choose differently.

But you're not choosing to stay defended. Your nervous system is keeping you defended because it doesn't believe it's protected. And it won't believe it's protected until you demonstrate that you can take care of yourself even when someone else disappoints you, hurts you, or leaves you.

The work isn't convincing yourself to trust other people. The work is building such a strong foundation with yourself that other people's behavior can't destabilize you.

When you know you can handle rejection and survive disappointment, those experiences stop controlling you. When you know you can recover from betrayal, betrayal stops making you close off completely.

You soften not because the world is reliable, but because you are. Not because people won't hurt you, but because you trust yourself to handle it if they do. You notice it in your body as your shoulders drop and your breath deepens.

This is what it means to create an internal sense of security. You're not waiting for external conditions to be perfect before you allow yourself to be open. You're building the capacity to stay open even when conditions aren't perfect.

That capacity comes from self-trust. From knowing that you'll honor your boundaries even when it's uncomfortable. That you'll leave situations that aren't good for you even when staying feels easier. That you'll choose yourself even when choosing yourself means disappointing someone else.

Every time you keep a promise to yourself, you build self-trust. Every time you set a boundary and maintain it, you build self-trust. Every time you walk away from something that's wrong for you, you build self-trust.

And as self-trust builds, the need for external security decreases. You stop needing guarantees before you open. You stop needing people to prove themselves before you let them in. You stop requiring perfect behavior before you're willing to stay present.

Because you know that if it goes wrong, you'll handle it. That you're not at the mercy of other people's choices. That you can take care of yourself no matter what happens.

This doesn't mean you stop having needs or stop wanting support. It means you stop collapsing when those needs aren't met or that support isn't available. You feel the disappointment, the hurt, the frustration, and you stay intact.

Your worthiness doesn't depend on someone else seeing it. Your capacity for love doesn't depend on someone else returning it. Your stability doesn't depend on someone else providing it.

You become your own secure base. The place you return to when external circumstances are chaotic. The ground you stand on when everything else is shifting.

And from that place, you can actually be intimate with people. Not because they've earned your trust through perfect behavior, but because you trust yourself enough to risk being seen, being disappointed, being human.

You can express needs without making the other person responsible for your entire emotional state. You can ask for what you want without needing them to say yes for you to be okay. You can show vulnerability without needing them to handle it perfectly.

You can let people be imperfect, make mistakes, have limitations. Because their imperfection doesn't threaten your foundation. You're not relying on them to be your entire source of security.

The relationships that last aren't the ones where nobody ever gets hurt. They're the ones where both people are anchored enough in themselves that they can handle the inevitable moments of hurt without the relationship dissolving.

You don't need someone who will never let you down. You need to build the capacity to stay present when they do. To communicate about it. To repair it. To decide whether the pattern is workable or whether you need to walk away.

But you can't do any of that from a place of internal instability. You can't show up authentically when you're terrified that one wrong move will destroy everything. You can't be intimate when you're constantly monitoring whether the other person is going to abandon you.

You have to build your own security first. Then you can bring that security into connection with someone else. And from there, you can build something real. Something that can hold complexity, conflict, imperfection, humanness.

Something where you get to be both fully yourself and fully connected. You carry your foundation with you, and that's what makes intimacy sustainable.

Building the Foundation of Secure Attachment

Secure attachment isn't something you either have or don't have. It's something you build. And you build it through repeated experiences that teach your nervous system a new pattern.

The old pattern says: opening leads to pain. Needing people makes you vulnerable. Showing your real self results in rejection. Stay defended, stay in control, stay prepared for the worst.

The emerging pattern says: opening can lead to connection. Needing people can result in support. Showing your real self attracts people who can actually love you. You can be vulnerable and survive. You can take risks and recover if they don't work out.

But your nervous system won't believe the new pattern just because you tell it to. It needs consistent, repeated evidence. Experiences that contradict what it learned to expect.

This is why one good relationship can't undo years of insecure attachment. Your system needs more data than that. It needs consistent experiences over time that demonstrate the new pattern is actually reliable.

You build secure attachment by practicing vulnerability in small doses with people who've shown they can handle it. Not by opening completely to anyone who seems interested, but by taking calculated risks with people who've demonstrated some level of trustworthiness.

You share something small and see how they respond. Do they listen? Do they respect what you've shared? Do they use it against you later? Do they dismiss it? Do they try to fix it when you just needed them to hear it?

Their response gives you information. Information you use to decide whether to take another small risk or whether to maintain your current level of distance.

Over time, if they consistently respond well, you take slightly bigger risks. You share more. You ask for more. You let them see more of who you actually are.

And if they keep showing up, keep responding with care, keep demonstrating that your vulnerability is honored, your system starts to update its expectations. Your body begins to register calm where it once braced for loss. It starts to believe that maybe opening doesn't always lead to pain. Maybe needing someone doesn't always result in disappointment.

This is earned security. Not the fantasy that someone will never hurt you, but the reality that someone can hurt you and still work to repair it. That conflicts can happen and the relationship can survive. That you can express needs and they can say no sometimes and the connection doesn't dissolve.

Secure attachment also means you're not making the other person responsible for regulating your entire emotional system. You're managing your own state. You're not requiring them to constantly reassure you. You're able to self-soothe when they're not available.

You're bringing your emotional stability to the relationship instead of expecting the relationship to provide it.

That doesn't mean you don't lean on them. It means you're not collapsing into them. You're not outsourcing your sense of security to their presence or their validation.

You know you're building secure attachment when you can be close without losing yourself. When you can have conflict without fearing the relationship will end. When you can express needs without anxiety about whether expressing them will push the person away.

When you can receive love without immediately questioning it or testing it or sabotaging it. When you can give love without depleting yourself. When you can be separate from your partner for periods of time and know the connection remains intact.

Secure attachment feels like being able to breathe fully with another person. Like you can show all of yourself and the relationship has room for it. Like the other person's needs matter and your needs matter and you can work together to honor both.

It's not perfect. Securely attached people still have conflicts, disappointments, moments of disconnection. The difference is they have the tools to navigate those moments without the relationship fracturing.

They can name what's wrong. They can listen to feedback without getting defensive. They can repair when they've caused harm. They can forgive when they've been harmed. They can stay present through discomfort instead of running or shutting down.

You build this foundation one interaction at a time. By showing up honestly. By honoring your needs and respecting theirs. By staying when it's hard instead of leaving at the first sign of difficulty. By leaving when the pattern becomes harmful instead of staying out of fear of being alone.

By learning that you can have yourself and have love. That connection doesn't require self-abandonment. That autonomy doesn't require isolation.

That there's a third option where you're whole and they're whole and you choose to share that wholeness with each other. Not to complete each other, but to enhance each other. Not to fix each other's wounds, but to provide a secure space where healing can happen.

That's what becomes possible when you stop choosing between yourself and connection. When you build a foundation strong enough to hold both. When you finally live from the truth that the choice was never real at all.

Key Takeaways

- You learned early that expressing your true self could threaten connection, leaving you trapped in cycles of hiding or isolation.

- • Believing intimacy requires sacrificing boundaries leads you to repeatedly abandon your own needs.

- • Compliance arises as a survival strategy, where anticipating others' needs feels safer than risking rejection.

- • Rebellion against closeness is another strategy of control, intended to protect you from being consumed by others' expectations.

- • True autonomy emerges when your decisions come from genuine desire rather than fear of rejection or control.

- • A secure relationship is one where intimacy does not cost you your individuality or independence.

- • Building internal safety allows you to remain open even when external circumstances become unstable or disappointing.

- • Real intimacy requires trusting yourself enough to handle disappointment rather than expecting flawless behavior from your partner.

- • Secure attachment develops through consistent experiences of vulnerability being met with respect and care.

- • You don't have to sacrifice yourself to experience deep connection; true partnership thrives when both people remain fully themselves.

Chapter 7:
Boundaries Are Love Not Walls

"Daring to set boundaries is about having the courage to love ourselves even when we risk disappointing others." — Brené Brown

Boundaries are not distance. They are design. You've been taught that they're selfish. That saying no makes you difficult. That having limits means you're not generous enough, flexible enough, loving enough.

So you say yes when you mean no. You tolerate behavior that feels wrong. You give more than you have to give. And you tell yourself this is what it means to be a good person, a good partner, a good woman.

But here's what nobody told you: boundaries aren't barriers to love. They're the framework that makes love possible.

Without them, there's no container for intimacy. There's just enmeshment, resentment, and the slow erosion of yourself until there's nothing left to give and nobody left to give it.

This chapter is about understanding what boundaries actually are, why you struggle to set them, and how to establish limits that honor both yourself and your relationships. Because the truth is, people who love you want you to have boundaries. They want to know where you end and they begin. They want clarity more than compliance. And they definitely don't want you sacrificing yourself to keep them at ease.

What Boundaries Really Mean and Why They Matter

A boundary is simply the line that defines where you end and another person begins. It's the acknowledgment that you're a separate being with your own thoughts, feelings, needs, desires, and limits. That your experience is valid even when it differs from someone else's.

A boundary is a decision about your own behavior, not a mandate for someone else's.

Boundaries aren't about controlling other people's behavior. They're about defining what you will and won't accept in your own life. What you will and won't participate in. What treatment you'll tolerate and what treatment is non-negotiable.

They are not walls. Walls block everything. Boundaries let in what is healthy and filter out what is harmful. They are about discernment, not isolation.

But you've been conditioned to see boundaries as rejection. As proof that you're not loving enough. As evidence that you're selfish, high-maintenance, demanding.

You learned this early. When you said no as a child and got punished for it. When you expressed what you needed and were told you were asking for too much. When you set a limit and the people around you acted wounded, accused you of not caring, made you feel guilty for having needs.

So you learned to sacrifice your limits to maintain connection. To prioritize other people's ease over your own capacity. To give until you were empty because giving was how you proved your worth.

And now you're an adult who doesn't know how to say no without feeling like a terrible person. Who takes on more than you can handle because declining feels impossible. Who stays in situations that drain you because leaving feels cruel.

You think you're being kind. What you're actually being is depleted. And depletion doesn't serve anyone.

When you have no boundaries, you become resentful. You give and give and give, and eventually you start keeping score. You notice what you're not getting in return. You feel used, taken advantage of, invisible. And you blame other people for taking what you kept offering.

But they didn't take anything. You gave it. You didn't set a limit, so they had no way of knowing they were crossing one.

This is what happens when you expect people to read your mind. When you think boundaries mean making other people guess what you need and respecting it without you having to say it out loud.

That's not how it works. People cannot honor limits you never name.

Clear boundaries create clarity. They eliminate guessing. They let people know what works for you and what doesn't. What you can offer and what you can't. What you're available for and what's outside your bandwidth.

Use the three C's: clear, concise, consistent.

When you have clear limits, people know where they stand with you. They know what to expect. They know that when you say yes, you mean it. That when you say no, you mean that too. That you're not going to agree to something and then resent them for it later.

This creates trust. Real trust. Not the false trust of someone who never disagrees or never has needs. But the trust that comes from knowing someone will tell you the truth about what works for them instead of pretending everything is fine until they explode or disappear.

Boundaries also protect your capacity. You only have so much to give. If you're giving it to everyone and everything without discernment, you'll have nothing left for the people and things that actually matter to you.

Every yes to something that doesn't serve you is a no to something that does. Every hour you spend doing something you don't want to do is an hour you can't spend on what actually lights you up.

Notice your breath shorten right before a reluctant yes. That is your cue to pause.

Your time, your energy, your emotional capacity are finite resources. Boundaries are how you allocate them intentionally instead of letting other people's needs and expectations dictate where they go.

This isn't selfish. This is self-preservation. And self-preservation is what allows you to show up fully in the places where you actually want to be present.

You can't love others well when you're running on empty. You can't be generous when you're depleted. You can't give from overflow when you're giving from deficit.

Boundaries ensure you have something to give. They create the container that makes sustainable generosity possible. They protect the resource that is you so you don't burn out trying to be everything to everyone.

The people who matter will respect your limits. The people who don't respect them are showing you exactly why you need them.

How Violating Your Own Boundaries Destroys Self-Worth

Every time you say yes when you mean no, you betray yourself. Every time you tolerate behavior that feels wrong, you send yourself the message that your feelings don't matter. Every time you give more than you want to give, you teach yourself that other people's needs are more important than yours.

This isn't abstract. This is how self-worth gets destroyed. It seems minor in the moment. It compounds over time.

You think it's not a big deal. It's just one favor. One instance of tolerating something that bothered you because addressing it felt too hard.

But your nervous system doesn't see it that way. Your body registers every instance of self-abandonment. Every moment when you chose someone else's comfort over your own truth. Every time you betrayed what you knew was right for you.

And it adds up. Not consciously. You're not keeping a running tally of every boundary violation. But your system is. And with each one, you trust yourself a little less.

Because if you can't count on yourself to protect you, who can you count on? If you won't honor your own limits, why would anyone else? If you don't treat your needs as valid, how can you expect others to?

You start to feel shaky inside. Ungrounded. Like you can't trust your own judgment. Because you can't. You've trained yourself to override your internal guidance system in favor of external approval.

You ignore the tightness in your chest that says this doesn't feel right. You dismiss the voice that says you don't want to do this. You talk yourself out of the boundary before anyone else has to because you've already decided your needs aren't legitimate.

This is what happens when you make other people's ease more important than your own integrity. You lose your center. You lose the internal compass that tells you what's okay and what's not. And without that compass, you drift. You end up in situations and relationships that don't serve you because you stopped listening to the signals that would have steered you away.

Your body is giving you information all the time. Treat these signals like data, not drama. Tension in your jaw when someone asks for something. Heaviness in your stomach when you're about to agree to something you don't want to do. Fatigue that comes from giving beyond your bandwidth.

But you've learned to ignore those signals. To push past them. To tell yourself they're not important. That you're just being difficult or sensitive or selfish.

So the body gets louder. The tension becomes chronic. The drain becomes burnout. The signals escalate because you're not listening to the quiet ones.

And still, you keep violating your boundaries. Because at this point, you don't even know where your boundaries are. You've overridden them so many times that you can't locate the line between what's okay and what's not.

You think everyone else's needs are clearer, more urgent, more valid than yours. You've lost the ability to differentiate between what you want and what you think you should want. Between what feels right and what feels like it would make others happy.

This is the cost of chronic boundary violation. Not just resentment toward others, but a fundamental disconnection from yourself. You can't be grounded in your own experience when you're constantly dismissing it. You can't build self-worth when you're repeatedly demonstrating to yourself that you're not worth protecting.

The path back starts with small promises. Not to other people. To yourself.

Keep one small promise today. Let it be measurable and easy to keep.

Notice when something feels off. Don't immediately talk yourself out of it. Just notice. Let the feeling be there without needing to fix it or explain it away.

Then take one small action that honors what you noticed. Decline the invitation. End the conversation. Leave the situation. Not dramatically. Just clearly.

Each honored limit restores self-trust one inch at a time. You show your system that you're paying attention. That you'll protect yourself when something doesn't feel right. That your internal signals matter.

And slowly, the ground beneath you stabilizes. You start to feel solid again. Not because anyone else changed, but because you stopped betraying yourself. You stopped giving away your integrity for the sake of keeping others convenient.

Self-worth doesn't come from other people validating you. It comes from you validating yourself. From treating your needs as legitimate. From protecting your limits even when it disappoints someone. From proving to yourself, through your actions, that you matter.

You matter. And boundaries are how you demonstrate that to yourself every single day.

Setting Limits Without Guilt or Apology

You've been apologizing for your boundaries your entire life. "I'm sorry, but I can't." "I'm sorry, I need to leave." "I'm sorry, that doesn't work for me."

Stop apologizing.

A boundary is information. It does not require an apology.

When you apologize for your boundary, you're sending two messages. To the other person, you're saying: I know this is an inconvenience and I feel bad about it. To yourself, you're saying: having limits is wrong and I should feel guilty about it.

Neither message is true. And both undermine the boundary you're trying to set.

Requests do not need apologies. They need clear responses. Yes or no. Available or not. Willing or unwilling. Clear information lets them make decisions based on reality instead of hoping you'll cave if they push.

And you don't need to feel guilty for having limits. Guilt is appropriate when you've done something wrong. Having boundaries isn't wrong. It's human.

But you've been conditioned to feel guilty any time you prioritize your needs. Any time you're not immediately available. Any time you say no to someone who wants a yes.

That guilt is old programming. It's the internalized voice of everyone who taught you that your needs were an inconvenience. That being accommodating was virtuous and having requirements was selfish.

You're not selfish for having boundaries. You're self-aware. You know your limits. You know what you can give sustainably versus what will deplete you. And you're choosing to operate within those limits so you don't burn out.

That's not selfishness. That's wisdom.

When you set a boundary without apologizing, it sounds like this:

"That does not work for me." "I am not available for that." "I cannot take that on." "That is outside my capacity right now." "I am ending this conversation." "I am not comfortable with that."

Notice what's missing: explanations. Justifications. Long stories about why you can't do it. Apologies for the inconvenience.

Just the boundary. Clear and simple.

You don't owe anyone a detailed explanation of why something doesn't work for you. The fact that it doesn't work is enough. You don't need to prove that your boundary is legitimate. You don't need to make it sound reasonable enough that they'll approve of it.

Your boundary is legitimate because you said so. That's the only justification required.

Explanations invite debate. Clarity closes the loop.

When you start adding explanations, you open the door for negotiation. You give people information they can use to talk you out of your boundary. "But if the reason you can't do it is X, what if we adjust Y? Then would you be able to?"

No. The boundary stands. Not because the logistics make it impossible, but because you don't want to.

That's hard for you to say. "I don't want to" feels too simple. Too honest. Too vulnerable. Like it's not a good enough reason.

But it's the best reason. It's the truth. And when you can say "I don't want to" without needing to justify it, you've reclaimed your power.

Sometimes boundaries require action from you, not compliance from them. Use this format:

"When X happens, I will do Y."

Examples: "When calls come after 9 pm, I will answer tomorrow." "When the conversation becomes insulting, I will leave the room."

Most people won't push back on a clear boundary. They might be disappointed. They might have preferred a different answer. But if you deliver your no with confidence, they'll accept it and move on.

The people who do push back are showing you exactly why you need boundaries with them. People who respect you accept your no the first time. People who don't respect you will keep pushing, testing, trying to find the angle that gets you to change your answer.

Those people aren't safe. Your boundary is working. It's filtering out the people who don't honor your limits.

Let it filter. That's the point.

You'll feel guilty at first. If guilt spikes, inhale for four, exhale for six, then restate your boundary once. Every time you set a boundary without apologizing, the old programming will kick in. The voice that says you're being mean, difficult, too much. That you should have said yes. That you're letting people down.

Notice the guilt. Don't act on it. Feel it, and set the boundary anyway.

Over time, the guilt will quiet. Your nervous system will learn that setting boundaries doesn't result in disaster. That people don't abandon you for having limits. That the relationships that matter survive your honesty.

And the ones that don't survive weren't relationships built on genuine care. Relationships that require your compliance are not relationships. They are arrangements.

You're building something different now. Relationships where you can be honest. Where your limits are respected. Where you don't have to shrink or hide or apologize for taking up space.

And that starts with setting boundaries clearly, confidently, without apology. Because you have nothing to apologize for.

The Feminine Art of Holding Your Ground

There's a misconception that feminine energy is soft, yielding, accommodating. That being feminine means saying yes, going with the flow, making things easy for everyone.

That is not feminine power. That is conditioning disguised as virtue.

Real feminine power knows how to hold ground. It can be soft and immovable at the same time. It doesn't need to harden or fight or defend. It just stands in its truth and doesn't budge.

Think of water. Water is soft. It flows around obstacles. It adapts to whatever container it's in. But water also carves canyons through stone. It shapes coastlines. It can't be compressed or controlled. It finds its level and stays there.

Water adapts, and it shapes stone. Soft does not mean weak.

That's feminine boundary-setting. Not rigid. Not aggressive. Just clear and consistent.

You don't have to raise your voice to hold a boundary. You don't have to get angry or harsh or cold. You can stay warm, stay open, and still be completely unmovable on what doesn't work for you.

"I hear that you'd like me to reconsider. My answer is still no."

"I understand you're disappointed. This is still my decision."

"I can see this is frustrating for you. I am not changing my mind."

Keep your tone warm, your sentence short, your volume steady.

This is what makes people uncomfortable. They're used to women who either collapse under pressure or harden into defensiveness. They're not used to women who can stay soft and still hold their ground.

That combination is disorienting. It removes the tactics that usually work to get you to back down.

If you get defensive, they can accuse you of being difficult. If you get aggressive, they can play victim. But if you stay calm and simply restate your limit without engaging in the argument they're trying to start, there's nothing to push against.

You're not fighting. You're just standing in your truth. And you can stand there all day.

Holding a boundary is a tolerance skill. Practice increases your window. This requires you to tolerate discomfort. Theirs and yours.

They're uncomfortable because they wanted a different answer and they're not getting it. You're uncomfortable because you've been conditioned to believe that disappointing people means you've done something wrong.

But disappointing someone isn't the same as harming them. They'll survive your no. They'll adjust. They'll find another solution. And if they can't, that's information about how dependent they were on your compliance, which is exactly why the boundary was necessary.

Your discomfort is the old programming trying to get you to cave. It's the part of you that learned keeping others at ease was your job. That their upset was your responsibility. That boundaries were cruel.

Feel the discomfort. Breathe through it. Hold your ground anyway.

The more you practice this, the easier it gets. Your nervous system learns that saying no doesn't result in catastrophe. That holding your boundary doesn't mean losing love. That you can disappoint people and the relationship continues.

And something else happens. The people in your life start to trust you more.

Because when your yes means yes and your no means no, people know where they stand with you. They know they're not getting a fake yes that will turn into resentment later. They know that when you show up, you're actually available, not giving from obligation or guilt.

This creates real intimacy. Not the false intimacy of someone who always agrees with you, but the real intimacy of someone who shows you who they actually are and trusts you to handle it.

The feminine art of holding ground isn't about being unmovable on everything. It's about knowing what matters to you and being unmovable on that. It's about flexibility in the things that don't affect your core needs and absolute clarity on the things that do.

You can flow and you can stand firm. You can adapt and you can hold your line. You can be soft and you can be unshakeable.

That's not contradiction. That's integration. That's what it looks like when you stop performing femininity and start embodying feminine power.

And feminine power always knows where its boundaries are. Always honors them. Always holds them with a softness that's more powerful than any wall could ever be.

Softness with limits does not break. It bends, and still holds.

And you're learning to be exactly that.

Key Takeaways

- Boundaries define clearly where your energy ends and another person's begins.
- Saying no isn't an act of rejection; it's an affirmation of what you're genuinely available for.
- You can care deeply about someone and still refuse their requests without feeling guilty.
- A clear boundary reduces confusion and resentment, creating relationships built on honesty rather than obligation.
- When you consistently override your limits, your self-respect erodes because you're training yourself not to trust your own instincts.
- Real generosity is sustainable only when you respect your own capacity and stop giving more than you have.
- Stop apologizing for your boundaries; a simple and direct no is enough without explanations or justifications.
- Boundaries protect you from burnout, allowing you to remain fully present in relationships without resentment.
- Setting limits calmly, firmly, and consistently teaches others how to treat you.
- Genuine intimacy occurs when both people clearly communicate their limits instead of silently hoping others will guess them.

Step 3:
EMBODIMENT - Becoming Who You Truly Are

The hardest part is done. Looking at what was keeping you stuck. Starting to make peace with the parts that were running on fear instead of choice.

Now comes the part where apologizing for taking up space stops.

Most women get stuck here. Not because they haven't healed enough, but because somewhere along the line, they learned that confidence is arrogance, that softness is weakness, and that being magnetic means being manipulative.

So they keep playing small. Keep second-guessing themselves. Keep waiting for someone to give them permission to be powerful, to take what they want, to walk into a room and own it without making themselves smaller to keep everyone else comfortable.

Embodiment isn't a performance. It's not about acting confident until you feel it or faking it until you make it. It's about dropping into your body and remembering that everything you've been trying to become, you already are.

Feminine energy doesn't need cultivation or creation. It's already there, woven into the fabric of who you are, waiting for you to stop suppressing it and let it move through you the way water moves through a river.

Masculine energy became the default because that's what kept you safe. That's what got things done. But safety and aliveness are not the same thing. And the version running on control and independence and constant doing is tired.

These four chapters are about coming home to your body. Learning to speak in a way that opens doors instead of putting up walls. Moving through the world with the kind of confidence that doesn't need to announce itself because it's just that deeply rooted in knowing who you are.

Chapter 8:
Dangerous Confidence From the Inside Out

*"Confidence is not 'they will like me.' Confidence is 'I'll be fine if they don't.'" —
Christina Grimmie*

Readiness is a reward, not a requirement. You've been waiting to feel confident before you act. Waiting until you're sure, until you're ready, until you've proven to yourself that you're capable enough, worthy enough, good enough to take up space.

Confidence is the byproduct of action.

You don't build confidence by convincing yourself you're confident. You build it by doing things that scare you and surviving them. By taking action before you feel ready. By proving to yourself, through evidence, that you're more capable than your fear wants you to believe.

The strongest form of confidence is quiet and steady. It doesn't scan the room for approval. It doesn't need constant validation. It doesn't need permission or approval to exist. You notice it in your body when it's real: steadier breath, slower pulse, fewer mental rehearsals.

This chapter is about building that kind of self-trust. The kind that doesn't need permission or approval to exist. The kind that makes you ungovernable because praise or rejection no longer control you.

Confidence Is Not What the World Told You

The world taught you that confidence is loud. That it's walking into a room and commanding attention. That it's being the most attractive, the most successful, the most impressive person there.

That is performance, not confidence. And performance requires an audience. It needs validation, attention, proof that the act is working. It collapses the moment someone isn't impressed.

Real confidence is quiet. It doesn't need to announce itself. It doesn't need to prove anything. It just exists, solid and unshakeable, regardless of who's watching or what they think.

Confidence isn't believing you're better than everyone else. It's knowing you're exactly who you need to be. It's trusting that you can handle whatever comes without needing to be perfect, without needing to have all the answers, without needing everyone to agree that you're doing it right.

You've been confusing confidence with certainty. Thinking that confident people never doubt themselves, never feel fear, never wonder if they're making the right choice.

Confident people act with fear in the room. They move forward while uncertain. They take risks while afraid. They make decisions without knowing if they'll work out. In the body it looks like exhaling and moving before the mind demands another guarantee.

You've also been taught that confidence comes from external achievements. That once you get the degree, the job, the relationship, the body, then you'll finally feel confident.

But external validation doesn't create internal conviction. It creates dependence. You feel good when you're getting praise and crumble when you're not. Your sense of worth becomes hostage to circumstances you can't always control.

Real confidence does not depend on circumstances. It doesn't come from what you have or what you've achieved. It comes from your relationship with yourself. From trusting that you'll show up for yourself even when things fall apart. That you'll honor your values even when it costs you. That you'll stay true to who you are even when being someone else would be easier.

This kind of inner steadiness can't be taken from you. People can reject you, criticize you, disappoint you, leave you. And you stay intact. Not because their opinions don't matter, but because your opinion of yourself matters more.

The world wants you to believe confidence is something you earn through being impressive enough. That's a lie designed to keep you performing, striving, trying to prove your worth through accomplishments that never feel like enough.

You don't earn confidence. You claim it, then collect evidence through action.

You decide that you're allowed to take up space, have opinions, make choices, exist fully without needing anyone's permission.

That decision doesn't require proof. It doesn't require credentials. It just requires the willingness to stop waiting for external validation before you give yourself internal permission.

You've been taught to look outside yourself for confirmation that you're worthy. To check everyone else's reactions to determine if you're doing it right. To make yourself smaller when your presence makes others uncomfortable.

That's the opposite of confidence. That's self-abandonment with extra steps.

Real confidence comes from an internal locus of evaluation. From measuring yourself against your own standards instead of everyone else's. From knowing what you value and living accordingly, even when other people don't understand or approve.

It's the ability to hear criticism without absorbing it as truth. To receive praise without becoming dependent on it. To make decisions based on what's right for you instead of what will get the best reaction.

This doesn't mean you don't care what anyone thinks. It means you care what you think first. You consider other perspectives. You take in feedback. But you don't let external opinions override your internal knowing.

The world told you confidence was something you'd feel once you fixed everything that's wrong with you. Once you were smarter, prettier, more successful, more lovable.

The truth is, confidence comes from accepting yourself as you are right now. Not in a resigned way, but in a way that says: I'm human, I'm imperfect, I'm learning, and I'm worthy anyway. Not because I've proven it, but because worthiness isn't something you earn. It's something you are.

You've been waiting for confidence to arrive so you can start living. Start living as yourself and let confidence catch up.

Building Unshakeable Worth Independent of Others

Your inherent value is not up for debate. It's not determined by whether someone loves you, hires you, validates you, or sees your value. It's intrinsic. It exists because you exist.

But you don't believe that. You've spent your entire life measuring your worth through other people's responses. Feeling valuable when they approve and worthless when they don't. Using their reactions as a mirror to tell you who you are.

That's not a mirror. That's a funhouse reflection distorted by their limitations, their wounds, their projections. And you've been trying to fix yourself based on a reflection that was never accurate to begin with.

Building unshakeable worth starts with disconnecting your value from external validation. Not because other people's opinions are meaningless, but because they can't tell you something you need to know for yourself.

Other people can see parts of you. They can appreciate your gifts, acknowledge your efforts, recognize your impact. But they can't determine your worth. Only you can do that.

And you do it by deciding it's true. Not by proving it, not by earning it, but by claiming it as a fact that doesn't require evidence.

This feels wrong because you've been taught that confidence without proof is arrogance. That you're supposed to stay humble, stay small, stay uncertain about your value until someone else confirms it for you.

But humility isn't self-doubt. Humility is recognizing that everyone has value, including you. Arrogance is believing your value makes you better than others. Confidence is knowing your value doesn't make you better or worse than anyone. It just makes you worthy of your own respect.

You've been treating your worth like it's conditional. Like it increases when you succeed and decreases when you fail. Like it's something you can lose if you're not careful.

But dignity doesn't fluctuate. Your performance fluctuates. Your circumstances fluctuate. Your mood, your productivity, your ability to meet expectations. Those things go up and down. Your inherent value does not.

You are not more worthy on days when everything goes right. You are not less worthy on days when you fall apart. Your worth is a constant. And treating it like a variable is what keeps you on the emotional rollercoaster of needing constant validation to feel okay.

Building unshakeable worth means anchoring into that constant. Recognizing that your value isn't determined by your achievements, your appearance, your likability, or your productivity. It's determined by the fact that you're a human being, and human beings have inherent worth.

This doesn't mean you don't strive for growth. It means you stop believing that growth is required to earn the right to exist without apology.

You're allowed to want to improve and also know you're fine as you are. You're allowed to have goals and also recognize that reaching them won't make you more valuable than you already are. You're allowed to work on yourself without treating yourself like a problem that needs fixing.

The shift happens when you stop looking outside for confirmation and start generating it from within. When you become your own source of validation instead of constantly seeking it from others.

This doesn't happen overnight. You've spent years outsourcing your sense of worth. Retraining yourself to generate it internally takes practice.

Start small. Notice when you're seeking approval. When you're checking whether someone approved. When you're scanning faces to determine if you said the right thing. When you're replaying conversations to assess whether you performed well enough.

Notice the urge to scan faces; relax your gaze and feel your feet instead.

Just notice. Don't judge it. Just see it.

Then practice giving yourself what you're seeking from them. Tell yourself you handled it well. Acknowledge your own effort. Validate your own experience. Not to replace external validation entirely, but to stop being dependent on it.

External feedback is context, not identity.

Over time, your nervous system learns that you don't need someone else to confirm your worth before you can feel it. That you can approve of yourself without waiting for permission. That your internal validation is just as legitimate as external praise, and far more reliable.

This is when you become unshakeable. Not because nothing bothers you, but because other people's opinions stop determining your internal state. Criticism stings less because you're not using it as proof of your worthlessness. Praise feels good but doesn't become something you need to chase because your worth isn't dependent on getting it.

You stop performing for approval. You stop shrinking to avoid disapproval. You stop making decisions based on what will get the best reaction and start making them based on what actually aligns with who you are.

And that alignment is what creates true confidence. Not the kind that needs constant reinforcement, but the kind that remains steady even when external circumstances shift.

End-of-day check: What did I do well? What aligns with my values? What did I learn?

Say it out loud once: "I approve of how I handled that."

Place a hand on your chest for one breath while you say it.

You know who you are. You know what you value. You know your worth isn't negotiable. When worth comes from within, you stop being steerable by praise or rejection.

The Prize Mentality That Changes Everything

You've been taught to audition for other people's approval. To prove you're worthy of the job, the relationship, the opportunity. To show up with your resume of accomplishments and hope they decide you're good enough.

That framework is backwards. And it's keeping you small.

The prize mentality flips the script. Instead of auditioning for their approval, you're evaluating whether they're worthy of access to you. Instead of proving your value, you're assessing whether they recognize it. Instead of hoping they choose you, you're deciding whether you choose them.

This is discernment, not superiority.

And discernment is what separates women who settle from women who select.

When you see yourself as the prize, you stop chasing. You stop performing. You stop trying to convince people of your value. Because you already know it. And if they don't see it, that's information about them, not evidence against you.

This doesn't mean you think you're better than everyone. It means you know your value, and you're not available for people who don't recognize it or won't honor it.

You've been conditioned to make yourself more palatable, more accessible, more easy to choose. To lower your standards so you're not too demanding. To accept less than you want so you don't risk being alone.

That's fear talking. And fear-based decisions never lead anywhere you actually want to go.

The prize mentality says: I know what I bring. I know what I need. I'm not negotiating on either. If you can meet me there, excellent. If you can't, I'm not diminishing myself to make it easier for you.

I choose where my time goes.

I choose who gets access.

I choose the terms that protect my values.

This applies to romantic relationships, but it applies everywhere. To friendships, work opportunities, collaborations, any situation where you're being evaluated or considered.

Stop auditioning. Start evaluating.

When you're in a job interview, you're not just hoping they hire you. You're assessing whether the role, the culture, the compensation align with what you need. You're asking questions that help you determine if this is a place where you can thrive. You're interviewing them as much as they're interviewing you.

When you're dating, you're not just trying to be chosen. You're determining whether this person can meet your needs, respect your boundaries, match your effort. You're watching how they treat you and using that information to decide if they get continued access.

Do they match my effort, honor my limits, and add to my peace?

When someone offers you an opportunity, you're not just grateful to be considered. You're evaluating whether the terms work for you, whether the relationship is reciprocal, whether the arrangement honors your worth.

This level of discernment requires knowing your value. Because if you don't know what you're worth, you'll accept whatever is offered and call it lucky.

You'll tolerate disrespect because you think that's the best you can get. You'll stay in situations that drain you because you don't believe anything better is available.

But when you know you're the prize, you become selective. You have standards. You're willing to walk away from anything that doesn't meet them because you know your worth isn't contingent on anyone's approval.

This doesn't mean you're inflexible or unreasonable. It means you know what you need and you're not pretending those needs don't exist to make yourself easier to choose.

The prize mentality also shifts how rejection feels. When someone doesn't choose you and you've been auditioning for their approval, rejection feels like evidence that you're not enough. Like they saw the real you and determined you weren't worthy.

But when you see yourself as the prize, rejection becomes direction. It means they weren't the right fit. It means they couldn't meet your standards or didn't recognize your value. And that's fine. Not everyone will. The people who matter will see what you bring and rise to meet it.

You don't need everyone to choose you. You need the right people to choose you. And the right people will only show up when you stop lowering your standards to accommodate the wrong ones.

This mentality changes how you move through the world. You stop seeking permission. You stop waiting to be picked. You stop shrinking to fit into spaces that weren't designed for you.

You show up as yourself, fully. You make your requirements known. You walk away from what doesn't serve you without guilt. You trust that the right opportunities, relationships, and connections will align with who you are instead of requiring you to become someone else.

Stop auditioning. Start selecting. Alignment is attractive.

Ending the Addiction to External Validation

You're addicted to approval. Not in a dramatic way. In a quiet, pervasive way that shapes every decision you make.

You check reactions before you speak. You monitor faces to see if people agree.

You replay conversations to determine if you said the right thing. You feel anxious when someone's upset with you, not because their feelings matter to you, but because their disapproval threatens your sense of worth.

Approval is human. Dependence on approval is captivity.

You've outsourced your sense of okayness to other people's reactions. When they approve, you feel good. When they withdraw approval, you panic. You spend enormous amounts of energy managing other people's perceptions so you can maintain the validation supply that keeps you feeling stable.

But it's never enough. No amount of approval fills the hole because the hole isn't caused by lack of external validation. It's caused by lack of internal validation. And you can't fix an internal problem with external solutions.

Ending the addiction starts with recognizing that seeking validation isn't wrong. It's human. We're wired for connection, and approval signals that we're safe within our group. The problem isn't wanting approval. The problem is needing it to feel okay about yourself.

When approval is a preference, you can enjoy it without depending on it. When it's a requirement, you become controlled by it. Every choice becomes about what will get the reaction you need instead of what actually aligns with your truth.

That is a life organized around other people's reactions.

The first step to breaking the addiction is noticing when you're seeking validation. Not judging it, just seeing it. Watch yourself check someone's reaction. Notice the slight panic when someone doesn't respond the way you hoped. Observe the relief when they approve.

Just witness the pattern. That awareness alone starts to create distance between the impulse and the action.

Notice the seek.

The second step is practicing self-validation. This feels artificial at first because you've trained yourself to believe that self-approval doesn't count. That only external validation is legitimate.

But that belief is keeping you trapped. Your approval of yourself is just as valid as anyone else's approval of you. More valid, actually, because you're the only one who knows your full experience, your intentions, your context.

When you do something well, acknowledge it. Out loud if possible. "I handled that well." "That was a good decision." "I'm proud of how I showed up."

It will feel awkward. Do it anyway. You're retraining your nervous system to generate validation internally instead of seeking it externally.

Name your value out loud once.

The third step is tolerating disapproval without collapsing. Someone's upset with you. They don't like your choice. They think you handled something wrong.

Feel the discomfort. Don't immediately try to fix it, explain it, or change their mind. Just let them be disappointed without making their disappointment your emergency.

You don't have to agree with their assessment. You don't have to defend yourself. You can simply hold your ground and let them have their reaction while you remain stable in your own knowing.

Soften your jaw, lower your shoulders, exhale longer than you inhale.

This is excruciating at first. Your system will scream that you need to repair the rupture, get them to approve again, make it okay. That panic is the addiction talking.

Breathe through it. The discomfort won't kill you. And on the other side of it, you'll discover that you can survive someone's disapproval. That their opinion of you doesn't determine your worth. That you can stay intact even when they're upset.

Tolerate disapproval for 90 seconds before acting.

Each time you do this, the addiction weakens. You're proving to yourself that external validation isn't necessary for your survival. That you can generate your own sense of okayness. That other people's reactions are information, not verdicts.

The final step is making choices based on your values instead of anticipated reactions. Ask yourself: if no one would know, if no one would approve or disapprove, what would I choose?

Then choose that. Even if people won't understand. Even if they'll judge. Even if it means disappointing someone.

Choose by values, not reactions.

This is how you reclaim your life from the tyranny of other people's opinions. By proving to yourself that you can make choices that serve you even when those choices don't get external validation.

Over time, the need for approval diminishes. Not because you stop caring what people think, but because you stop letting what they think override what you know.

You can hear feedback without absorbing it as identity. You can appreciate praise without becoming dependent on it. You can receive criticism without treating it as truth.

Your worth stabilizes. It stops fluctuating based on external circumstances because you're no longer using external circumstances to determine it.

And from that stable place, you become free. Free to speak honestly. Free to make choices that serve you. Free to exist as yourself without constantly checking if that self is acceptable to everyone around you.

The addiction to external validation keeps you small, manageable, controllable. Breaking it makes you noncompliant. Because you're no longer motivated by approval or deterred by rejection.

You're motivated by alignment. With yourself, with your values, with what actually matters to you. You become directional. Clear. Hard to sway.

Not because you don't care what anyone thinks. But because you care what you think first. And that shift changes everything.

Key Takeaways

- Confidence isn't something you wait for; it emerges through taking action before you feel ready.
- Seeking validation from others places your self-worth in their hands, making you vulnerable to their approval or rejection.

- True confidence shows up quietly, without needing to impress, persuade, or justify its existence.
- Building self-trust requires making decisions aligned with your values even when others disagree or misunderstand.
- Your worth doesn't fluctuate with praise or criticism—it remains steady, unaffected by external circumstances.
- Instead of auditioning for others' approval, view yourself as the one evaluating if others align with your standards.
- Approval feels good, but relying on it makes your self-esteem fragile; generating validation internally provides lasting stability.
- Disappointment from others becomes manageable once you realize their reactions don't define your value.
- You become truly confident when external rejection no longer feels like a reflection of your worth.
- Making choices based on your own values rather than anticipated reactions frees you from the control of external judgment.

Chapter 9:
Embodying Your Magnetic Feminine Power

"To be beautiful means to be yourself. You don't need to be accepted by others. You need to accept yourself." — Thich Nhat Hanh

The mind learns first; the body learns last. You've done the hard work of healing. You've set boundaries. You've started to believe in your worth. But something still feels off. You can know all the right things intellectually and still feel disconnected from the woman you're trying to become.

Embodiment is what happens when your body catches up to your mind. It's when you don't just think you're valuable; you feel it in your bones. It's when feminine energy stops being a concept you read about and becomes something you live inside of. This isn't about performing femininity for anyone else. It's about coming home to yourself in a way that's so visceral, so complete, that your presence alone becomes magnetic.

The problem is that most teachings on feminine energy assume you need to feel safe first. They tell you to soften, to be vulnerable, to open up. But what if your life doesn't allow for that right now? What if you're still in survival mode, still dealing with pressure, still navigating situations where letting your guard down feels dangerous? Does that mean you're locked out of your feminine power until circumstances change?

No. You can access your feminine essence right now, exactly where you are. This chapter will show you how to embody qualities that make you feel alive, magnetic, and deeply connected to yourself without requiring perfect conditions. You'll learn to work with your body, your energy, and your natural rhythms in ways that don't ask you to be something you're not.

Accessing Feminine Qualities That Don't Require Safety

Common advice says you must feel secure to soften and receive. While that's true for certain expressions of femininity, it's incomplete. It leaves out all the women who can't afford to let their guard down yet. The single mothers working two jobs. The women rebuilding after trauma. The ones navigating hostile workplaces or unstable relationships. They cannot wait for perfect conditions.

The truth is that feminine essence has many faces. Softness is one. But so is fluidity. So is intuition. So is generative power. Some of these qualities actually help you stay safe. They don't require you to drop your defenses; they give you better tools to work with.

Take water, for example. Water is feminine, but it's not weak. It moves around obstacles instead of fighting them head-on. It finds cracks and seeps through. It can be still on the surface while carrying powerful currents underneath. When you embody the qualities of water, this is not exposure; it is adaptability and strategy. You're choosing flow over force, and that's still feminine even when you're in a situation that requires you to protect yourself.

Flexibility works the same way. A tree that's too rigid breaks in a storm. The one that bends survives. Flexibility doesn't mean giving up your boundaries or your standards. It means you know when to adjust your approach, when to take a different angle, when to pivot instead of pushing. You're still moving toward what you want. You're just not exhausting yourself by trying to control every single variable along the way.

Then there's intuition. This is one of the most powerful feminine qualities, and it has nothing to do with softness. Intuition is your body's early warning system. Signal: a brief belly drop or subtle chest tightness before your mind finds reasons. It's the quiet knowing that guides you toward the right decision even when logic says otherwise. When you tune into your intuition, you're not making yourself more vulnerable. You're making yourself sharper, more aware, more attuned to what's really happening beneath the surface.

Creativity is another one. You don't need to feel safe to create. In fact, some of the most potent creativity comes from women who are navigating chaos. You can write, paint, dance, build, design, cook, garden, problem-solve. Creativity is generative. It's the part of you that makes something out of nothing, that transforms what you have into what you need. That's feminine power, and you can access it even when everything around you feels unstable.

Sensuality begins privately, as presence in your senses. It's the pleasure of feeling warm water on your skin in the shower. The taste of something you actually enjoy eating. The sensation of fabric that feels good against your body. The awareness of your own aliveness. You can cultivate that even when your nervous system is on high alert. In fact, reconnecting with simple sensory pleasure can be one of the fastest ways to remind yourself that you're still here, still whole, still capable of feeling good.

No permission needed. Start where you stand. You don't need the perfect partner, the ideal circumstances, or a life free of stress. You just need to stop waiting for conditions to be right and start working with this current that's available to you now. The energy that doesn't make you weaker but makes you wiser. The energy that doesn't require you to drop your defenses but allows you to move through life with more grace and less grinding effort.

Start paying attention to where you're already doing this without realizing it. Notice when you adjust your approach instead of forcing something. Notice when you follow a hunch that turns out to be right. Notice when you solve a problem in a way that's creative rather than combative. You're already tapping into feminine essence. You just haven't been calling it that.

One-minute flow scan: unclench jaw, lengthen exhale, release shoulders, then choose one softer alternative to today's hardest task.

Water, Flexibility and Strength in Softness

Your body is mostly water. That's not a metaphor; it's biology. And yet, you've probably spent years trying to function like stone. Rigid. Unyielding. Bracing against every impact as if staying hard will keep you safe. But stone cracks under pressure. Water doesn't. Water moves, adapts, flows around what it can't move through. It doesn't lose itself in the process. It just finds another way.

Softness has been sold to you as weakness, but that's only true if you confuse softness with passivity. A supple body is responsive. Responsiveness keeps balance. When you hold tension constantly, you lose that responsiveness. You become slow to react, easy to knock off balance, disconnected from what your body is trying to tell you. Suppleness is what allows you to sense danger before it's obvious, to shift direction before you hit a wall, to move with life instead of constantly colliding with it.

Think about how you hold your body right now. Is your jaw clenched? That's armor, and it makes sense. You've needed it. But armor is exhausting to carry, and it doesn't actually protect you the way you think it does. It just keeps you locked in a state of bracing for impact. You can't be fully alive when you're always braced.

Learning to soften doesn't mean becoming defenseless. It means learning to release the tension that isn't serving you so you can be present, alert, and responsive to what's actually happening. Ease gives you access to your intuition because intuition speaks through your body, not your head. If your body is locked up tight, you can't hear it.

Start small. You don't have to dissolve all your defenses at once. Just notice where you're holding tension that isn't doing anything useful. Maybe it's your jaw. Take a breath and let it go. Not because you're giving up. Because you're choosing to conserve your energy for something that actually matters.

Water doesn't announce its power. It doesn't make a lot of noise. It just moves, consistently, persistently, until it gets where it's going. It chooses the efficient path. You can carve canyons with water if you give it enough time. You can reshape entire landscapes. That's what this current does when you stop trying to force your way through everything. It finds the path of least resistance and flows there. Because it's efficient. Because it knows that pushing harder isn't always the answer.

Flexibility is closely tied to this. Flexibility doesn't mean you bend to everyone else's will. It means you know when to hold firm and when to adjust. Rigid thinking keeps you stuck in patterns that don't work. Flexible thinking lets you see other options. Rigid plans fall apart the moment something unexpected happens. Flexible plans account for the fact that life is unpredictable and build in room to adapt.

This applies to how you move through conflict, too. Rigidity in relationships looks like always needing to be right, always needing the last word, always needing things to go exactly the way you planned. Flexibility looks like being willing to meet someone halfway, to try a different approach, to admit when you were wrong without feeling like your entire sense of self is collapsing. You don't lose anything by being flexible. You gain options. You gain the ability to find solutions instead of just digging deeper into the same argument. Ask once: "What outcome matters most here?" Then adjust tactics, not values.

Strength in softness doesn't mean you tolerate what you shouldn't. It means you respond from a place of groundedness instead of reactivity. When someone crosses a boundary, you don't have to explode to prove you're serious. You can hold your line calmly, clearly, without escalating. That's water energy. That's what happens when you're not operating from a place of constant tension. You have the bandwidth to stay steady even when something would normally set you off.

Your nervous system knows the difference between genuine threat and learned hypervigilance. But if you're always in fight-or-flight mode, it stops being able to tell the two apart. Suppleness is how you signal to your body that it's safe to come down from high alert, at least for a moment. Even if your external circumstances haven't changed, you can create pockets of ease internally. That might look like a warm bath. Anything that reminds your nervous system it's allowed to relax, even briefly.

The more you practice this, the more you'll notice that ease doesn't make you weaker in your dealings with the world. It makes you more present. More aware. More capable of reading situations accurately and responding in ways that actually serve you. What is rigid shatters. What is supple returns.

Sixty-second soften: inhale 4, exhale 6, unclench tongue from palate, soften hands. Then decide.

Sensuality as Sacred Self-Connection

Sensuality has been hijacked. Somewhere along the way, it became something you perform for someone else's consumption instead of something you experience for your own pleasure. It got tied up with sexuality, with desirability, with whether or not you're "attractive enough" by someone else's standards. Sensuality begins privately, as presence in your senses. It's about feeling alive in your own skin.

Your body is constantly sending you information. The temperature of the air on your skin. The texture of the fabric you're wearing. The feeling of your feet on the ground. The taste of your coffee. The sound of rain. Most of the time, you're tuned out of all of it because you're living in your head, thinking about what you need to do next, replaying conversations, worrying about the future. You're physically here, but you're not fully inhabiting your body.

Sensuality is the practice of coming back. It's the practice of noticing what it feels like to be in a body, to have senses, to experience the world through touch and taste and sound and sight. It's not complicated. It's not some advanced spiritual practice. It's just paying attention to what's happening right now in your physical experience.

Start with something simple. When you eat, actually taste your food. Not while scrolling on your phone. Not while standing at the counter rushing through it. Sit down. Put the food in your mouth. Notice the texture, the flavor, the way it feels to chew and swallow. That's sensuality. When you take a shower, feel the water. Notice whether it's too hot or too cold, how it feels on your shoulders, your back, your face. That's sensuality. When you get dressed, choose clothes that feel good on your body, not just clothes that look good in a mirror. That's sensuality.

It is foundational. Your relationship with your body determines your relationship with everything else. If you're disconnected from your body, you're disconnected from your intuition. You're disconnected from your emotions. You're disconnected from the signals that tell you when something is right or wrong for you. You're operating on autopilot, and autopilot keeps you stuck in the same loops.

Sensuality is how you break out of autopilot. It's how you remember that you're not just a brain in a jar. You have a body, and that body is capable of pleasure. Not just sexual pleasure, though that's part of it. Pleasure in the full spectrum. The pleasure of movement. The pleasure of rest. The pleasure of warmth. The pleasure of being touched in ways that feel good, whether that's a massage or a hug or your own hand running through your hair.

Productivity culture trains numbness. Numbness erases signals. Productive people don't stop to notice how things feel. They just push through. But that's how you end up numb. That's how you end up so disconnected from your body that you can't even tell what you want anymore, let alone what you need.

Reconnecting with sensuality isn't selfish. It's self-preservation. It's how you stay connected to the part of you that knows what's good for you. Your body has wisdom that your mind doesn't. It knows when you're safe. It knows when you're not. It knows what nourishes you and what depletes you. But you can't access that wisdom if you're not listening. And you can't listen if you're not present.

This doesn't require a partner. It doesn't require anyone else at all. In fact, it's better if you start by exploring this alone. Because when you learn to give yourself pleasure, to notice what feels good without needing someone else to validate it, you stop outsourcing your sense of aliveness to other people. You stop waiting for someone else to make you feel desired or beautiful or worthy of attention. You source aliveness from within.

Right now, what sensation feels nourishing? What movement would increase ease by two percent?

Move your body in ways that feel good. Not in ways that punish you or force you into a mold. Dance in your living room. Stretch on the floor. Walk outside and feel the sun on your face. Your body wants to move. It wants to feel alive. Give it that.

Touch yourself with kindness. Not just sexually, though that's valid too if it feels right. But also just... touch. Run your hands over your arms, legs, belly, and register where tension holds and where ease returns. You're not doing this to fix anything. You're doing this to be present. To inhabit your body instead of just dragging it around like luggage.

The more you practice this, the more you'll notice that your body starts to trust you again. It stops feeling like something separate from you, something you have to manage or control. It starts feeling like home. And when your body feels like home, everything else shifts. You stop tolerating things that don't feel good just because you think you should. You start making choices based on what actually nourishes you instead of what you think you're supposed to want. You start living from the inside out instead of the outside in.

Two-minute sensory reset: one scent, one texture, one sound. Name them out loud. Return to task.

Movement, Ritual and Honoring Your Cycles

Your body isn't meant to be static. It's meant to move, to shift, to flow through different states. But modern life treats your body like a machine that should perform the same way every day. Wake up at the same time. Produce at the same level. Feel the same energy. Ignore what your body is actually asking for and just keep going.

That's not how bodies work. Especially not female bodies. Your energy moves in cycles. Your mood moves in cycles. Your creativity, your focus, your capacity for different kinds of work all move in cycles. If you're trying to override those cycles and function the same way every single day, you're fighting against your own nature. And you're losing.

Choose movement that circulates energy rather than depletes it. Dance. Yoga. Walking. Swimming. Stretching on your bedroom floor. Anything that gets you out of your head and into your body.

The type of movement you need changes depending on where you are in your cycle. Sometimes you need something intense, something that lets you discharge excess energy and feel powerful. Other times you need something slow and grounding, something that helps you settle. Mismatch equals disconnection, not discipline.

Pay attention to what your body is asking for. That's not the same as being lazy or undisciplined. It's listening. It's honoring the fact that you're not a machine. You're a living system with rhythms that deserve to be respected.

Ritual is how you mark those rhythms. Ritual doesn't have to be complicated or spiritual in the traditional sense. It just has to be intentional. It's the difference between mindlessly going through your routine and creating moments that signal to your body and mind that something is shifting.

Morning: Three minutes. Breathe, stretch, taste.

Evening: Three cues. Dim light, warm water, slower breath.

Rituals around sleep tell your nervous system it's safe to let go, to stop being on high alert, to rest. If you're struggling with sleep, it's not because there's something wrong with you. It's because your body doesn't feel safe enough to fully relax. Ritual helps build that steadiness.

Then there's your menstrual cycle, if you have one. This is the most obvious cycle your body moves through, and it's the one most women have been taught to ignore, suppress, or feel ashamed of. You're supposed to function the same way whether you're menstruating or ovulating, whether you're in your follicular phase or your luteal phase. But that's absurd. Your hormones shift dramatically throughout the month, and those shifts affect everything. Your energy. Your mood. Your focus. Your tolerance for stress. Your desire for socializing versus solitude.

Track three signals only: energy, focus, social appetite. Adjust one commitment accordingly.

In the first half of your cycle, after your period, you might feel more outgoing, more energized, more willing to take on new projects. That's a good time to schedule things that require a lot of social energy or creative output. In the second half, especially the week before your period, you might feel more introspective, more sensitive, more in need of quiet and rest. That's not weakness. That's your body asking you to slow down and turn inward.

If you try to push through that and maintain the same pace all month long, you'll burn out. You'll feel like something's wrong with you because you can't keep up with the version of yourself from two weeks ago. But nothing's wrong. You're just trying to live in a way that ignores your body's natural rhythm.

Honoring your cycle doesn't mean you stop working or cancel all your plans every time you get your period. It just means you give yourself permission to adjust. To say no to things that feel like too much. To rest more. To lower your expectations for how much you can accomplish when your body is asking you to be gentle with it.

The same goes for seasonal cycles. Winter isn't the same as summer. Your body knows this even if your calendar doesn't care. Winter is for slowing down, for turning inward, for conserving energy. Summer is for expansion, for being out in the world, for taking action. If you're trying to live at summer pace in the middle of winter, you're going to feel exhausted and wonder why nothing's working.

Name the season you are in today and pick pace to match.

Rituals mark the shift and train your system to follow it. And when you're living in alignment with your own rhythms, you stop feeling like you're constantly swimming upstream. You start moving with the current. You start trusting that your body knows what it needs, and you stop overriding that knowing with what you think you're supposed to do.

Today's alignment:
- What pace matches my current cycle or season
- What movement circulates energy

- One ritual I will keep

Key Takeaways

- Feminine energy isn't limited to softness—it also includes adaptability, creativity, intuition, and strength under pressure.
- Embodiment happens when knowledge moves beyond concepts and becomes something you physically feel and live.
- You don't have to wait for perfect conditions to access your feminine essence; you can embody it exactly where you are now.
- Softness isn't weakness—it's choosing to respond instead of react, staying grounded in yourself rather than becoming rigid or defensive.
- Intuition is your body's way of guiding you, providing subtle cues that often arrive long before your mind can rationalize them.
- Sensuality is about being fully present in your body, experiencing pleasure through your senses without needing external validation.
- Movement isn't about pushing yourself harder, but about aligning with your body's natural rhythms and cycles.
- Ritual provides structure, signaling to your nervous system when it's safe to shift gears and let down defenses.
- Honoring your natural cycles prevents burnout, teaching you when to rest, when to push forward, and how to trust your internal guidance.
- Your presence becomes magnetic when you truly inhabit your body and live from an internal state of ease rather than external approval.

Help Her Find Her Way

"Helping one person might not change the whole world, but it could change the world for one person." – Unknown

I f you've made it this far, something in this book has resonated with you. Maybe you've recognized yourself in these pages. Maybe you've finally found words for experiences you thought were yours alone.

Here's the truth: there's a woman out there right now searching for exactly what you've found. She's scrolling through reviews, trying to figure out if this book will finally help her make sense of why she keeps choosing the wrong people, why she can't set boundaries, why she's exhausted from being the "understanding one."

You can help her find this book. By taking 60 seconds to leave an honest review on Amazon, you'll show her she's not alone and give her the sign she needs that this book might be exactly what she's looking for.

I appreciate all reviews, whether positive or negative, and I read them personally. Your honest feedback helps one more woman realize she's not the problem and begin choosing herself.

Scan to leave a review

It costs nothing and takes less than a minute. But for her, it could be everything.

Thank you from the bottom of my heart.

Chapter 10:
The Language of High Value Communication

"Speak your mind, even if your voice shakes." — Maggie Kuhn

Words reveal who you are before anything else does. The way you speak to others, the way you ask for what you need, the way you hold a boundary or express a feeling creates the entire container of your relationships. Most women have been taught to communicate in ways that make them smaller. You can hear it in the pause before their real opinion, the smile that hides disagreement, the apology that replaces conviction. Softer in tone but weaker in message. Apologetic when they should be clear. Silent when they should speak.

High value communication isn't about being the loudest voice in the room or proving you're right. It's about saying what you mean without wrapping it in so many qualifiers that the message gets lost. It's about expressing your needs without making yourself small in the process. It's about learning to speak from a place of groundedness instead of reactivity, so that what you say lands with the weight it deserves.

This chapter will teach you how to communicate in ways that build connection instead of defense. You'll learn how to speak your truth without attacking or collapsing. How to use vulnerability as a tool for deeper intimacy instead of a performance for validation. How to express what you need without sounding desperate or demanding. And how to listen in a way that actually hears what's underneath the words, not just what's being said on the surface.

The women who get what they want don't just think differently. They speak differently. It starts with the words you choose and with the power you stop giving away when you speak them.

Speaking Your Truth Without Armor or Attack

You've been taught to protect yourself when you speak. Add disclaimers. Soften the blow. Make sure no one gets upset. The result is that often, people can't understand what you're saying because you've buried it under so many cushions. The other half, you come out swinging because you've held it in so long that when it finally comes out, it explodes.

Neither of these works. Armor makes you hard to reach. Attack makes people shut down or fight back. What you want is clarity. Directness that doesn't require cruelty. Honesty that doesn't need to be wrapped in apology.

Start by noticing how you dilute your own message. Do you say "I'm sorry, but..." before stating a preference? Do you phrase requests as questions when they're actually non-negotiables? Do you laugh nervously after saying something serious to soften the impact? Notice your body when it happens: shoulders lift, throat tightens. That is your cue that you are editing yourself mid-sentence.

High value communication is saying what you mean the first time. Not aggressively. Not rudely. Just clearly. If you don't want to do something, you say no. You don't say "I'm not sure" or "Maybe" or "Let me think about it" when you already know the answer. If something bothers you, you address it directly instead of hinting around it and hoping the other person picks up on your mood.

This doesn't make you difficult. It makes you trustworthy. People know where they stand with you. They're not left guessing what you really meant or trying to decode your emotional temperature. You've given them the gift of clarity, which is one of the most generous things you can do in any relationship.

The flip side is that you have to stop making other people guess what you need. If you want something, ask for it. Not in a roundabout way. Not by dropping hints and then getting upset when no one notices. Ask directly. Use words. Be specific. "I need help with this." "I'd like you to do that." "This matters to me."

You might worry that being this direct makes you sound demanding. It doesn't. What sounds demanding is when you've built up resentment because you never asked for what you needed and now you're bitter that no one gave it to you. Asking clearly, early, without accusation, that's just communication.

When you do need to address something difficult, lead with your experience instead of your judgment. There's a difference between "You always do this" and "When this happens, I feel dismissed." One is an attack. The other is information. One puts the other person on the defensive. The other invites them into understanding.

Your job isn't to control how someone reacts to your truth. Your job is to deliver it with as much integrity as possible. If they get defensive, that's data. If they shut down, that's also data. You're not responsible for managing their emotions. You're responsible for being honest about yours.

This gets easier the more you practice. The first few times you speak directly, it might feel harsh or uncomfortable. You're used to padding everything. But directness becomes natural once you realize it doesn't damage relationships. What damages relationships is dishonesty, passive aggression, and unspoken resentment. Clarity, even when it's uncomfortable, builds trust.

One shift that changes everything: stop explaining yourself to death. When you set a boundary or state a preference, you don't owe anyone a dissertation on why. "No, I can't" is a complete sentence. "That doesn't work for me" doesn't require a list of reasons. The more you over-explain, the more you signal that your decision is up for negotiation. It's not. You've already decided. Now you're just informing the other person.

If they push back, you repeat yourself once. Calmly. Without getting louder or angrier. Just the same message, delivered again. Most people will stop pushing if they realize you're not going to budge. The ones who keep pushing after that are showing you they don't respect your boundaries, and that's information you can use.

Speaking your truth also means owning your mistakes without collapsing into shame. When you've messed up, you say so. You don't defend it, minimize it, or deflect blame. You just acknowledge it. "I was wrong about that." "I handled that poorly." "I should have done this differently." Then you course-correct. You don't drown in guilt or beg for forgiveness. You take responsibility, make it right if you can, and move forward.

You just need to say it and trust that clarity is never cruelty.

Vulnerability as Power Not Weakness

Vulnerability has been sold as the ultimate relationship tool. Just open up, share your feelings, and watch connection deepen. But most women have tried that and ended up feeling exposed, dismissed, or used. Because vulnerability without discernment is just oversharing. Vulnerability without strength is just emotional dumping. Real vulnerability is strategic. It's a choice you make with people who have earned the right to see that part of you.

You don't hand your soft underbelly to everyone who asks. You pay attention to how people respond when you share something real. Do they hold it carefully? Do they use it against you later? Do they meet your honesty with their own, or do they stay closed off while expecting you to stay open? These patterns tell you who deserves access to your inner world and who doesn't.

Vulnerability becomes power when it's grounded in self-awareness. You're not opening up because you're desperate for connection or validation. You're opening up because you've chosen this person as someone safe enough to let in. That's a very different energy. One comes from lack. The other comes from strength.

When you share something vulnerable, you're not performing. You're not crafting the story to get a specific reaction. You're just telling the truth about your experience. If your chest tightens, take one breath before speaking. Calm breath gives your truth steadiness. "This is what I'm feeling." "This is what scared me." "This is where I struggled." No drama. No need to make it bigger or more tragic than it was. Just the facts of your emotional reality, delivered clearly.

The mistake most women make is thinking vulnerability means you have to share everything. It doesn't. You get to choose what you reveal and when. You get to keep some things private. You get to decide that certain parts of your story aren't for public consumption, and that doesn't make you closed off or inauthentic. It makes you boundaried.

Real intimacy happens when both people are willing to be seen. Seeing and being seen are equal acts of courage. Not just you doing all the emotional labor while someone else stays guarded. If you're always the one being vulnerable and the other person never reciprocates, that's not intimacy. That's an imbalanced dynamic, and you should notice it.

Vulnerability also means admitting when you don't have it all together. When you're scared. When you don't know what to do. When you need support. High value women don't pretend to be invincible. They're honest about their humanity. But they're honest from a place of self-possession, not collapse. There's a difference between "I'm struggling with this and I could use your perspective" and "I'm falling apart and I need you to fix me."

One invites partnership. The other creates caretaking, which isn't sustainable. You want people in your life who can hold space for your struggles without needing to rescue you. People who trust that you're capable of handling your own life but are willing to support you when you ask.

The deepest vulnerability isn't sharing your trauma. It's sharing your desires. Telling someone what you actually want, what you dream about, what you hope for, that's riskier than telling them what you've survived. Because when you share what you want, you're exposing yourself to judgment, rejection, or ridicule. You're saying "This matters to me," and that's a much softer target than "This hurt me."

High value communication means you're willing to say what you want anyway. Not apologetically. Not prefaced with "I know this sounds silly but..." You just say it. And if the person you're with can't honor that, can't take your desires seriously, can't meet you with curiosity instead of criticism, then you know they're not your person.

Vulnerability paired with boundaries is what creates safety. You can be open and protected at the same time. You can share deeply and still maintain your sense of self. You're not merging with the other person. You're letting them see you while staying intact. That's the balance that allows intimacy without loss of identity.

Practice this in low-stakes situations first. Share something small with someone you trust and see how they handle it. Do they listen? Do they respond with care? Do they remember it later and check in? That's how you build confidence in your ability to be vulnerable without it backfiring. You test the waters before diving in.

When someone meets your vulnerability with their own, that's when you know you've found something real. That's when connection stops being one-sided and becomes mutual. That's when you can relax into the relationship instead of constantly managing how much of yourself to show. Vulnerability offered wisely becomes shared strength.

Expressing Needs Without Neediness

There's a specific tone that happens when you don't believe you deserve what you're asking for. Your voice goes up at the end like you're asking permission instead of stating a need. It is the vocal equivalent of shrinking, a quiet question mark at the end of every sentence. You apologize before you even finish the sentence. You frame it as an imposition instead of a reasonable request. That's neediness, and people can hear it instantly.

Neediness isn't about what you're asking for. It's about the energy you bring to the ask. You can request something completely reasonable and still sound desperate if you don't believe you're entitled to it. Conversely, you can ask for something significant and have it received well if you ask from a place of self-worth.

The difference lives in whether you believe you deserve a yes. If you think you're lucky to even be considered, that desperation leaks into your words. If you know your needs are valid and you're simply communicating them to see if this person can meet them, that confidence changes everything.

High value communication means you state your needs as facts, not favors. Fact: I need follow-through. Favor: Could you maybe, if it's not too much. Choose the first. "I need this to feel secure in this relationship." "I need more support with this." "I need you to follow through when you say you'll do something." These aren't requests for permission. They're information about what has to happen for you to stay engaged.

You're not demanding that the other person comply. You're letting them know what the terms are. They get to decide if they can meet those terms. But you're not negotiating your core needs down to make it easier for them to stay. If your needs are too much for them, they're not your person. That's not a tragedy. That's clarity.

The trap is thinking that having needs makes you high-maintenance. It doesn't. Everyone has needs. The low-value move is pretending you don't have any and then silently resenting the other person for not reading your mind. The high-value move is naming what you need clearly and allowing the other person to either step up or step back.

When you express a need, keep it simple. Don't bury it in a ten-minute preamble about why you shouldn't have to ask or how you wish things were different. Just state it. "I need more quality time." "I need you to communicate when plans change." "I need physical affection to feel connected." Direct. Clean.

No apology attached.

If their first reaction is defense or dismissal, that is all the information you need. Someone who values you will want to understand your needs, even if they can't meet all of them immediately. They'll ask questions. They'll work with you to find solutions. They won't make you feel bad for having needs in the first place.

Neediness also shows up in how often you check in. If you're constantly seeking reassurance, constantly asking if everything's okay, constantly needing confirmation that the other person still cares, that's a signal that you don't trust the foundation of the relationship. And if you don't trust it, either the foundation isn't solid or your own insecurity is louder than the evidence in front of you.

Secure communication means you ask once, clearly, and then you trust the answer. You don't keep poking at it to see if it changes. You don't test the other person by asking the same question in different ways. You take them at their word unless their actions prove otherwise.

If their actions don't match their words, you address the discrepancy directly. "You said this mattered to you, but your behavior suggests otherwise. Which one is true?" Then you listen. And you decide based on what they do next, not what they promise.

The goal isn't to eliminate needs. The goal is to express them from a place of self-possession instead of desperation. You're not begging. You're informing. You're not hoping they'll choose to meet your needs out of pity. You're expecting that if they want to be in your life, they'll show up in ways that matter to you. If they don't, you're prepared to walk.

Once you know that staying unseen is worse than being alone, your voice changes and every response to it changes too.

Listening With Intuition and Holding Space

Most people don't listen. They wait for their turn to talk. They're already formulating their response while you're still speaking. They're scanning for the parts they agree or disagree with instead of actually absorbing what you're saying. That's not listening. That's verbal chess. Real listening begins when you stop preparing your next move.

Real listening is rare. It's when you're fully present with what the other person is saying without rushing to fix it, correct it, or top it with your own story. It's when you're hearing not just the words but the emotion underneath them. The need that's being expressed even if they don't name it directly. The fear or hope or anger that's shaping the message.

Women grounded in self-worth listen this way because they know that being heard is one of the deepest human needs. When you give someone your full attention, when you let them speak without interrupting, when you reflect back what you heard to make sure you got it right, you're offering something most people never experience. And that creates trust faster than almost anything else.

Listening with intuition means you're tuning into what isn't being said as much as what is. You notice body language. Tone shifts. The moments where someone pauses or looks away. The places where their words don't quite match their energy. You're paying attention to the full picture, not just the script.

This doesn't mean you interrogate them or call them out on every inconsistency. It means you hold the awareness quietly and use it to guide how you respond. If someone says they're fine but their entire body is tense, you don't just accept "fine" and move on. You offer space for them to share more if they want to. "You seem like something's weighing on you. I'm here if you want to talk about it."

Sometimes they'll take that opening. Sometimes they won't. Either way, you've signaled that you're paying attention beyond the surface level, and that matters.

Holding space is not fixing. It is witnessing. When someone shares something difficult with you, your instinct might be to jump in with solutions, reassurance, or stories about how you handled something similar. Resist that. Most of the time, people don't need you to fix it. They need you to witness it. To let them feel what they're feeling without trying to talk them out of it or make it better. Holding space means you stay present with their discomfort without needing to resolve it. You don't rush them through their emotions. You don't minimize what they're going through with platitudes like "Everything happens for a reason" or "It could be worse." You just listen. You acknowledge what they're feeling. You let them know they're not alone in it.

This is one of the most powerful things you can do for someone, and most people never learn how. They think love means fixing problems or cheering people up. Love that fixes drains both people. Love that listens restores them. But real love is being able to sit with someone in their pain without needing to make it go away. It's trusting that they're strong enough to feel their feelings and that your job isn't to rescue them but to be present while they move through it.

You can tell when someone is truly listening because their presence feels different. They're not fidgeting or checking their phone. They're not rushing you. They're not making it about them. They're just there, fully, giving you their attention like it's the most important thing happening in that moment. That's the kind of listening you want to offer, and it's the kind you should expect in return.

If you're always the one holding space and no one ever does it for you, that's a problem. Relationships require reciprocity. You shouldn't be the only one doing the emotional labor, the only one listening deeply, the only one making space for difficult conversations. If you notice this pattern, name it. "I feel like I'm always the one listening, and I need that to be mutual."

Intuitive listening also helps you spot manipulation. When someone's words sound good but something feels off, trust that feeling. Maybe they're saying all the right things but their energy is incongruent. Maybe they're using emotional language to bypass accountability. Maybe they're testing to see if you'll accept a non-answer as closure. Your intuition picks up on these patterns faster than your conscious mind does.

You don't need proof to trust your gut. If something feels off, it probably is. You can listen fully and still hold your discernment. You can be compassionate and still notice when someone isn't being truthful. The two aren't mutually exclusive.

Practice listening without planning your response. Let the other person finish completely. Take a breath before you speak. Make sure you actually heard what they said instead of what you expected them to say. This one shift will change the quality of every conversation you have. When you listen this way, people exhale. They feel safe enough to tell you the truth, and that is the language of real connection.

Key Takeaways

- Communicate directly without softening your truth or apologizing for your needs; clarity builds trust more than cushioning your words ever will.

- Speak simply and decisively; avoid burying your real message under disclaimers or nervous laughter.

- Vulnerability is powerful only when shared consciously and selectively, not when used as a tool for validation or attention.

- Real intimacy arises from mutual openness—share deeply only when the other person consistently meets you halfway.

- Express your needs plainly as facts rather than favors; you deserve clarity about whether someone can meet them or not.

- Asking clearly is never demanding; it's setting transparent terms that prevent future resentment.

- Secure communication requires stating a need once clearly, then believing the response without repeatedly seeking reassurance.

- True listening means fully absorbing what's said without immediately planning your reply, offering solutions, or interrupting.

- Holding space means allowing others to express themselves without trying to fix, change, or hurry their emotional experience.

- Trust your intuition during conversations; when words and energy don't match, believe your instincts over explanations.

Chapter 11:
Your Body Is Your Temple Not Your Enemy

"And I said to my body softly, 'I want to be your friend.' It took a long breath and replied, 'I have been waiting my whole life for this.'" — Nayyirah Waheed

Most women spend their entire lives at war with their bodies. The mirror becomes a battlefield and the scale a daily verdict. Too soft here. Not toned enough there. Wrong shape. Wrong size. Wrong everything. You've been taught to see your body as a project that needs fixing, a problem that needs solving, a constant source of disappointment that requires management, control, and apology.

This chapter is about ending that war. Not by forcing yourself to love every inch of your body when you don't. Not by pretending you have no preferences or desires about how you look. But by fundamentally shifting your relationship with your physical form from one of hostility to one of respect. From seeing your body as an enemy to seeing it as the home you live in, the vehicle that carries you through this life, the only physical space that is truly yours.

High value women don't punish their bodies into submission. They don't starve themselves thin or exercise themselves into exhaustion to meet some external standard of worthiness. They understand that their body is not separate from them. It is them. And the way they treat it reflects how they believe they deserve to be treated in every other area of their lives.

When you spend years hating your body, criticizing it, depriving it, ignoring its signals, that hatred doesn't stay contained. It leaks into how you let others treat you. It informs what you think you deserve. It shapes your entire sense of self-worth. You cannot feel powerful in a body you're ashamed of. You cannot feel grounded in a body you're constantly trying to escape.

This chapter will teach you how to listen to your body instead of overriding it. How to work with your menstrual cycle instead of fighting against it. How to nourish yourself from a place of care instead of punishment. And how to reclaim beauty rituals as acts of self-reverence instead of desperate attempts to be acceptable to others.

Your body has been waiting for you to come home. Start now.

Healing Your Relationship With Your Physical Form

The first step is awareness. Start noticing how you talk to your body, about your body, inside your own mind. The running commentary that plays every time you look in the mirror. The comparisons you make. The judgments you pass. The disgust you feel. The shame you carry.

Most women would never speak to another person the way they speak to themselves about their bodies. You'd never look at a friend and say "Your thighs are disgusting" or "You don't deserve to eat that" or "No one will ever want you looking like this." But you say these things to yourself constantly. And your body hears every word.

Your body is not stupid. It knows when you hate it. It flinches under criticism the same way a person would. It feels the resentment in every punishing workout, every meal you force yourself to skip, every mirror you avoid. And it responds accordingly. It holds tension. It stores stress. It shuts down. Because it's trying to survive in an environment where even you, its only inhabitant, have turned against it.

Healing begins when you stop treating your body like the enemy. You don't have to love it yet. You don't have to think it's perfect. But you do have to stop waging war against it. You start by introducing neutrality where there used to be hatred.

Begin with language. Instead of "I hate my stomach," try "This is my stomach." Instead of "My arms are disgusting," try "These are my arms." Remove the judgment. Just observe. This is the body you have. This is the form you're living in. It's not good or bad. It just is.

Neutrality is the bridge to acceptance. And acceptance is the bridge to care. You can't care for something you're actively rejecting. But once you accept that this is your body, that it's the only one you get, that hating it won't change it but will absolutely damage your relationship with yourself, then you can start treating it with the respect it deserves.

Start small. One shift at a time. Look at your body in the mirror once a day without judgment. Just breathe and look. Instead of skipping meals to punish yourself for eating "too much" yesterday, eat when you're hungry. Instead of forcing yourself through workouts you hate because you think you have to earn your body, move in ways that feel good. Instead of criticizing every perceived flaw when you look in the mirror, find one thing you appreciate. Even if it's just "My body got me through today."

Your body has carried you through everything you've survived. Every heartbreak. Every loss. Every moment of joy. It's held your grief. It's metabolized your stress. It's healed itself from injuries you didn't even notice. It's kept you breathing, kept your heart beating, kept you alive through all of it. And you've spent that entire time telling it that it's not good enough.

That ends now.

You start thanking your body for what it does instead of punishing it for what it looks like. Thank your legs for carrying you. Thank your arms for holding the people you love. Thank your lungs for breathing. Thank your heart for beating. Thank your hands for creating. Thank your stomach for digesting. Thank your skin for protecting you.

This isn't abstract spirituality. This is recognizing that your body is a living system that works for you every single day without you even asking. And the least you can do is stop treating it like it owes you something.

One of the deepest shifts happens when you realize that your body's worth is not determined by how it looks. Your body's worth is inherent. It exists because you exist. It doesn't need to be smaller, firmer, younger, or different to deserve care, rest, nourishment, and respect. It deserves those things right now, exactly as it is.

Most women have been conditioned to believe they'll care for their bodies once they reach a certain weight, once they fit into a certain size, once they look a certain way. But that day never comes. Because even when you reach the goal, you just set a new one. The goalposts keep moving. The body is never good enough. And meanwhile, you've spent decades withholding care from yourself as punishment for not being perfect.

Women rooted in self-worth don't wait. They care for their bodies now. They rest when they're tired. They eat when they're hungry. They move in ways that feel good. They dress in clothes that fit and feel comfortable instead of keeping a wardrobe full of sizes they hope to fit into someday. They honor their bodies as they are instead of waiting for permission to exist fully in the world.

This doesn't mean you can't have goals. You can want to build strength, improve your health, change your shape. But the energy behind it matters. Are you doing it because you hate your body and want to escape it? Or are you doing it because you respect your body and want to take care of it?

One is rooted in shame. The other is rooted in love. And your body knows the difference.

When you start treating your body with care instead of contempt, everything shifts. You stop seeking validation from others because you're no longer trying to prove that your body is acceptable. You stop comparing yourself to other women because you're no longer measuring your worth by your appearance. You stop tolerating relationships where your body is criticized, objectified, or treated as something that needs improvement.

Your body becomes sacred ground. And you protect it accordingly.

This doesn't happen overnight. You've spent years, maybe decades, learning to hate your body. Unlearning that takes time. But every day that you choose neutrality over hatred, every day that you choose care over punishment, every day that you speak to your body with respect instead of contempt, you are healing.

Your body has been waiting for peace. Begin giving it what it always gave you: life.

Understanding Your Menstrual Cycle as Wisdom

Your menstrual cycle is not a flaw. It's not an inconvenience. It's not something to suppress, hide, or push through. Your cycle is a monthly blueprint for how to live in alignment with your body's natural rhythms. And most women have never been taught to read it.

You've been taught to function the same way every day. Same energy. Same productivity. Same availability. As if your body operates on a flat line instead of a wave. But your body doesn't work that way. Your hormones fluctuate throughout the month, and those fluctuations affect everything. Your energy levels. Your emotional capacity. Your creativity. Your need for rest. Your tolerance for stress. Your desire for connection or solitude.

When you ignore these fluctuations and try to force yourself to perform at the same level every single day, you're working against your body instead of with it. You exhaust yourself. You burn out. You wonder why some weeks you feel unstoppable and other weeks you can barely function. It's not random. It's your cycle.

There are four phases to your menstrual cycle, and each one has its own energy, strengths, and needs. When you understand these phases, you can plan your life around them instead of fighting against them. You can honor your body's natural rhythm instead of trying to override it.

Menstrual Phase is when you're bleeding. This is your winter. Your body is shedding. Your energy is low. Your tolerance for stress is minimal. This is not the time to push yourself. This is the time to rest. To turn inward. To move slowly. To say no to everything that isn't essential.

Most women try to power through this phase because they've been taught that rest is laziness. But rest during your menstrual phase isn't optional. Your body is doing significant biological work. It needs your cooperation, not your resistance. Give yourself permission to do less. Cancel plans if you need to. Sleep more. Move gently or not at all. Eat warm, nourishing foods. Let yourself be soft.

Follicular Phase is the week after your period ends. This is your spring. Your energy is rising. Your mood is lifting. Your creativity is sparking. This is the time to start new projects, make plans, schedule social events, take risks. Your body is building toward ovulation, and that rising energy wants to be channeled into action.

Use this phase to tackle the things that require focus, problem-solving, and innovation. Your brain is sharper. Your communication is clearer. Your confidence is higher. This is when you pitch ideas, have difficult conversations, push your limits. You have the energy for it.

Ovulatory Phase is mid-cycle, usually around day fourteen. This is your summer. You're at peak energy. Peak attractiveness. Peak social capacity. This is when you feel most magnetic, most confident, most connected to others. Your body is biologically primed for connection, which is why you're more outgoing, more expressive, more interested in being seen.

This is the time to schedule important meetings, go on dates, show up in public spaces, collaborate with others. You're at your most charismatic. Use it. But also recognize that this phase is short. A few days at most. Don't expect yourself to feel this way all month. You won't.

Luteal Phase is the week or two before your period starts. This is your autumn. Your energy is declining. Your tolerance for nonsense is low. You're more introspective, more critical, more aware of what isn't working in your life. This phase gets a bad reputation because women experience PMS here, but PMS isn't just random irritability. It's your body amplifying the truths you've been ignoring all month.

If something bothers you during your luteal phase, it probably bothered you during the rest of your cycle too. You just didn't have the emotional bandwidth to acknowledge it. Now you do. Your body is turning down the volume on everything else so you can hear what needs your attention. Listen. When fatigue hits mid-cycle, place a hand on your lower belly and pause. That is the body speaking.

This is also the time to complete projects, tie up loose ends, organize, clean, clear out what's no longer serving you. Your body is preparing to shed, and that includes energetic and emotional clutter. Let it go.

The mistake most women make is expecting themselves to feel the same way all month. You won't. You shouldn't. Your body is designed to cycle. When you work with your cycle instead of against it, you stop feeling like something is wrong with you. You stop wondering why you can't maintain the same energy level every single day. You stop judging yourself for needing more rest some weeks than others.

You start planning around your cycle. You schedule your most demanding work during your follicular and ovulatory phases when your energy is high. You protect your menstrual and late luteal phases for rest and reflection. You stop saying yes to things during your low-energy weeks just because you said yes during your high-energy weeks.

This requires tracking your cycle. Not just the days you bleed, but how you feel throughout the entire month. What your energy is like. What your mood is like. What you're drawn to. What you're avoiding. After a few months of tracking, patterns emerge. You start to predict when you'll feel expansive and when you'll need to contract. And you can plan accordingly.

Self-aware women honor their cycles. They don't apologize for needing rest during their period. They don't force themselves to be social when their body is asking for solitude. They don't override their intuition during the luteal phase when their body is showing them what needs to change. They listen. They adjust. They work with their body instead of against it.

Your cycle is a map. Learn to navigate it.

Nourishment Over Punishment

Food is not the enemy. Your appetite is not the enemy. Hunger is not something to suppress, ignore, or feel ashamed of. Hunger is your body communicating a need, and when you respond to that need with care instead of punishment, you begin to heal your relationship with food.

Most women have been taught to see food as something that must be earned, controlled, or restricted. You've been told that eating is something you should feel guilty about unless you've exercised enough to "deserve" it. You've been taught that your worth is tied to how little space you take up, and that eating less is morally superior to eating enough.

This is a lie. And it's a lie that keeps you small, weak, and obsessed with control in an area of your life that should be simple. Eating is a basic biological need. It's not a moral decision. It's not a character flaw. It's not something you need to earn permission for.

High value women eat when they're hungry. They don't wait until they're starving. They don't skip meals to punish themselves for eating "too much" the day before. They don't label foods as good or bad. They just eat. They choose foods that make them feel good, nourished, energized. And sometimes they choose foods just because they taste good. Both are valid.

Nourishment is not about perfection. It's not about eating clean all the time or never having sugar or only consuming organic vegetables. Nourishment is about fueling your body in a way that supports how you want to feel. Do you want energy? Do you want mental clarity? Do you want to feel grounded and steady? Then eat foods that give you those things.

But nourishment is also about pleasure. Food is one of life's great joys. Eating should feel good. It should taste good. It should be something you enjoy, not something you endure. When you remove pleasure from eating, when you turn every meal into a calculation of calories or macros or whether you "earned" it, you strip away the humanity of the act. You turn something sacred into something mechanical.

Your body knows what it needs. You've just been taught not to trust it. You've been taught that your body's signals are wrong, that your cravings are weaknesses, that your hunger is something to be controlled. But your body is not trying to sabotage you. It's trying to keep you alive. And when you ignore its signals long enough, those signals get louder, more urgent, more difficult to ignore.

Start by listening. When you're hungry, eat. Not in an hour when it's more convenient. Not after you've done enough to deserve it. Now. When your body asks for food, give it food. This is the first step toward trust.

Notice what your body is asking for. Are you craving something warm and grounding? Your body might need comfort. Are you craving something fresh and light? Your body might need cleansing. Are you craving something rich and dense? Your body might need energy. Stop overriding these signals with what you think you should eat and start honoring what your body is actually asking for.

This doesn't mean you eat everything you crave without discernment. It means you stop treating your cravings as evidence that you're broken or out of control. You treat them as information. Sometimes your body is asking for nutrients. Sometimes it's asking for emotional comfort. Sometimes it's asking for pleasure. All of these are valid needs.

The problem is when you try to meet every emotional need with food because you've been taught that eating is the only acceptable way to self-soothe. When you're sad, you eat. When you're stressed, you eat. When you're bored, you eat. Not because you're hungry, but because you don't know what else to do with the feeling.

Nourishment is about giving your body what it actually needs. Sometimes that's food. Sometimes that's rest. Sometimes that's movement. Sometimes that's connection. Sometimes that's solitude. When you start meeting your needs appropriately instead of using food as a catch-all solution, your relationship with eating becomes simpler.

You also stop using food as punishment. You don't starve yourself to make up for eating. You don't exercise yourself into exhaustion because you ate something you "shouldn't" have. You don't weigh yourself every morning to determine whether you're allowed to eat that day. You stop treating your body like it needs to be controlled and start treating it like it needs to be cared for.

One of the most powerful shifts is removing moral language from food. Food is not good or bad. You are not good or bad based on what you eat. A salad doesn't make you virtuous. A cookie doesn't make you weak.

When you stop labeling foods, you stop creating forbidden categories that make you want them even more. You stop bingeing on the "bad" foods because you've finally given yourself permission to have them. You stop cycling between restriction and overindulgence because you're no longer operating from a place of deprivation.

You just eat. Some days you eat more. Some days you eat less. Some days you want salads. Some days you want pizza. And none of it means anything about your worth, your discipline, or your value as a person. It just means you're a human being with a body that has needs and preferences that change.

Nourishment also means feeding yourself regularly. Not waiting until you're so hungry that you'll eat anything in sight. Not skipping meals because you're too busy or don't feel like you deserve to eat. You prioritize feeding yourself the same way you prioritize everything else that matters. Because if you don't eat, you can't function. And a body that isn't fed can't show up fully for anything.

High value women don't play games with their hunger. They don't test how long they can go without eating. They don't pride themselves on their ability to ignore their body's signals. They eat. They nourish themselves. They fuel their lives. And they do it without guilt, without apology, without needing anyone's permission.

Before each meal, take one breath, notice the colors on your plate, and silently thank your body for asking.

Your body is not your enemy. Your hunger is not your enemy. Food is not your enemy. The only enemy is the belief that you need to earn the right to take up space, to have needs, to be nourished. You don't. You already deserve it, simply because you exist.

Beauty Rituals That Connect You to Divinity

Beauty rituals are not about fixing what's broken. They are about remembering what is sacred. When you approach beauty from a place of self-reverence instead of self-improvement, the entire experience changes. You're no longer trying to make yourself acceptable to the world. You're connecting to the part of yourself that is already divine.

Most women have a complicated relationship with beauty. You've been taught that caring about how you look makes you vain, shallow, or insecure. But you've also been taught that not caring about how you look makes you lazy, sloppy, or undesirable. You can't win. So you end up stuck in a cycle of performing beauty for external validation while simultaneously resenting the performance.

High value women don't perform beauty. They practice it. Not for anyone else. For themselves. Because they understand that the way they adorn their body, the care they put into their appearance, the rituals they create around grooming and dressing, all of these are acts of self-worship. They're saying "This body matters. This life matters. I matter."

Beauty rituals are most powerful when they're done slowly. When you're fully present. When you're not rushing through your skincare routine while thinking about everything else you need to do. When you're not throwing on makeup in the car. When you're not getting dressed in five minutes because you hate everything in your closet and don't feel like dealing with it.

Slow down. Turn your beauty rituals into meditation. Let every touch be a reminder that you belong in this skin. When you wash your face, feel the water on your skin. When you apply lotion, thank your body for holding you. When you brush your hair, honor the softness of the act. When you choose your clothes, dress yourself the way you'd dress someone you love. With care. With intention. With respect.

This doesn't mean you need to spend hours getting ready. It means the time you do spend is sacred. You're not just going through the motions. You're connecting to your body. You're grounding yourself in your physical form. You're reminding yourself that you deserve beauty, softness, care.

Your beauty rituals should feel good. If they don't, change them. If your skincare routine feels like a chore, simplify it. If your makeup routine makes you feel like you're hiding, stop wearing it or wear less. If your clothes don't fit right or don't reflect who you are, get rid of them. Every part of your beauty practice should make you feel more like yourself, not less.

Adornment is ancient, a language older than words. Women have been decorating their bodies for thousands of years. It's not vanity. It's ritual. It's honoring the feminine. It's expressing identity. It's claiming space. When you wear something that makes you feel powerful, when you apply makeup that makes you feel confident, when you style your hair in a way that feels aligned, you're tapping into something deeper than aesthetics. You're embodying your essence.

But adornment is only powerful when it's chosen, not performed. If you're dressing for someone else's approval, if you're wearing makeup because you're afraid of being seen without it, if you're following trends that don't resonate with you just to fit in, you're not adorning yourself. You're hiding.

High value women know the difference. They dress for themselves first. They choose styles, colors, textures that make them feel alive. They don't follow fashion rules that were designed to sell them things they don't need. They don't shrink themselves to fit into boxes created by industries that profit from their insecurity. They wear what makes them feel like themselves. And if that's sweatpants and no makeup, fine. If that's silk and red lipstick, also fine. There's no right way to do this.

Your beauty rituals can also be spiritual. Anointing your body with oils. Lighting candles while you bathe. Speaking affirmations while you look in the mirror. Dressing with intention for the energy you want to embody that day. These are not superficial acts. They're acts of devotion. You're treating your body like the temple it is.

When you care for your body in this way, when you slow down and make beauty a sacred practice instead of a rushed obligation, you start to feel different in your skin. You stop seeing yourself as an object to be improved and start seeing yourself as a being to be honored. You stop comparing yourself to other women because you're no longer trying to meet an external standard. You're creating your own.

This is where true beauty lives. Not in perfection. Not in youth. Not in meeting someone else's criteria. But in the quiet confidence that comes from knowing you've cared for yourself well. In the glow that comes from being fully present in your body. In the power that comes from adorning yourself as an act of self-love instead of a bid for approval.

Your beauty rituals are yours. They don't need to look like anyone else's. They don't need to follow trends or meet standards. They just need to make you feel connected to yourself. Grounded in your body. Present in your life. That is all beauty has ever been: a practice of returning to yourself. And that return is sacred.

Key Takeaways

- Your body hears every thought you have about it—shift your internal dialogue from criticism to acknowledgment.
- Respect for your body begins by removing moral judgments about its shape, size, or appearance.
- Healing happens when you replace hostility toward your body with simple neutrality and acceptance.
- Your menstrual cycle isn't an inconvenience; it's an intuitive guide teaching you when to push forward and when to rest.
- Honoring your body's natural rhythms prevents burnout and keeps you aligned with your own energy.
- Hunger is not a weakness but a signal—respond to it with nourishment rather than punishment or restriction.
- Food is neither reward nor enemy; it is fuel, comfort, pleasure, and care all at once.
- Beauty rituals, when practiced intentionally, become sacred acts of self-devotion rather than acts of self-correction.
- Dressing, grooming, and caring for yourself with presence communicates self-worth to your subconscious.
- Your body is the only physical home you'll ever have—start treating it as sacred ground, not something to conquer.

Step 4:
RELATING - Creating Love and Connection on Your Terms

Here's where it gets personal. Healing yourself, building confidence, embodying feminine power... all of that progress can feel like it's slipping through your fingers the moment you step into a relationship with someone who doesn't match your growth.

The pattern is familiar. Meeting someone. Chemistry. Feeling seen, wanted, chosen. And before long, back in the same dynamics you swore you'd never repeat again. Giving too much. Ignoring red flags. Making excuses for behaviour that would make you furious if it was happening to your best friend.

Six months later, sitting there wondering how this happened again. How you ended up with someone who's emotionally unavailable, inconsistent, or just not showing up the way you need them to.

The problem isn't choosing wrong. The problem is choosing from an old blueprint, one that was written when worth wasn't clear, when love meant sacrifice, and when being picked felt more important than being cherished.

But that woman doesn't exist anymore. And the relationships you used to settle for don't fit who you're becoming.

This part is about learning to recognize the difference between a trauma bond and real love. Between chemistry and compatibility. Between someone who wants you when it's convenient and someone who chooses you consistently, even when it's hard.

High standards aren't about being difficult or high-maintenance. They're about refusing to betray yourself just to keep someone else comfortable.

These chapters will show you what it feels like to be in a relationship where sacrifice isn't required for love. Where feeling safe enough to be soft, strong enough to hold boundaries, and clear enough to walk away from anything that asks you to be less than whole becomes the standard.

Chapter 12:
Recognizing Love From Trauma Bonds

"We accept the love we think we deserve." — Stephen Chbosky

It starts like a spark and ends like a knot in the stomach. You meet someone who makes you feel alive in ways you haven't felt in years. The connection is immediate, intense, overwhelming. You tell yourself this must be it. This must be love. Because nothing this powerful could be anything else.

But intensity feels like intimacy until it doesn't. And by the time you realize the difference, you're already tangled in patterns you can't seem to escape. You wonder why you keep attracting the same type of person in different packaging. Why every relationship starts with chemistry and ends in the same painful cycles. Why you can't seem to find someone who treats you well without it feeling flat.

The problem isn't bad luck. The problem is that you've been conditioned to confuse volatility with passion. Drama as passion. Uncertainty as excitement. You've learned to associate love with struggle, and when a relationship feels easy, you think something's missing. What's missing is the chaos you've been taught to mistake for connection.

This chapter is about learning to tell the difference between real love and trauma bonds. Between chemistry that leads somewhere healthy and chemistry that keeps you stuck in cycles you can't escape. Between relationships that challenge you to grow and relationships that just hurt. Most women have never been taught to recognize the difference, which is why they keep choosing the same painful dynamic over and over, hoping this time will be different.

Women rooted in self-worth do not audition for toxic patterns. They refuse the role. They know what real love looks like, and they don't settle for anything that requires them to abandon themselves to keep it. They understand that the right relationship won't feel like a constant battle for security, validation, or proof that they matter.

This chapter will teach you how to identify the patterns you've been unconsciously recreating. How to spot red flags you've been trained to ignore or rationalize. How to distinguish between chemistry and compatibility. And how to know when a relationship is worth working on and when it's time to walk away. Because staying in the wrong relationship doesn't make you loyal. It makes you unavailable for the right one.

Why You Keep Attracting the Same Toxic Patterns

You do not attract your wish list. You attract your baseline. And if you believe, even subconsciously, that love has to be earned through suffering, through proving your worth, through tolerating behavior that hurts you, then you'll keep finding people who confirm that belief.

This isn't about blame. It's about awareness. Most women who end up in toxic relationships aren't choosing them consciously. They're following patterns established long before they ever started dating. Patterns learned in childhood. Patterns reinforced by every relationship where love felt conditional, where approval had to be earned, where closeness came with a cost.

If you grew up with a parent who was emotionally unavailable, inconsistent, or controlling, you learned to associate love with uncertainty. You learned that affection is something you have to work for. That connection requires constant effort. That being loved means figuring out what someone else needs and becoming that, even if it means losing yourself in the process.

You carry that template into adulthood. And when you meet someone who mirrors that dynamic, someone emotionally unavailable, hot and cold, withholding, your nervous system recognizes it as familiar. It is not safety. It is familiarity, and the body mistakes familiar for right. It feels like home, even when home was never secure.

This is why you're drawn to people who are hard to reach. Who pull away when you get close. Who make you feel like you have to prove yourself. It's not because you're self-destructive. It's because you're trying to resolve an old wound. You're trying to finally be chosen by the person who never chose you consistently. Except this time, it's not your parent. It's your partner. And the outcome will be the same.

You will not resolve an old wound by replaying it. You interrupt it by choosing a different template.

The first step is noticing what you're attracted to. Not what you say you want, but what you actually pursue. Do you feel most alive when someone is pulling away? Do you lose interest once someone is fully available? Do you confuse anxiety with attraction? Do you stay in relationships where you're constantly trying to earn love instead of just receiving it?

If the answer is yes, you're not attracted to love. You're attracted to the familiar feeling of trying to win it. And that's a game you'll never stop playing until you realize the only person who needs to choose you is you.

Toxic patterns also persist because of intermittent reinforcement. When someone treats you well inconsistently, when affection is unpredictable, your brain gets hooked. Notice the rush after a breadcrumb of affection and the crash that follows. That is the hook. You stay because you remember the good moments and believe if you just do the right thing, you'll get them back. This is the same mechanism that makes gambling addictive. The unpredictability keeps you engaged, hoping the next interaction will be the one where they finally show up the way you need them to.

But intermittent reinforcement isn't love. It's manipulation, whether intentional or not. Real love is consistent. It doesn't make you beg for scraps of attention. It doesn't make you feel like you're always one mistake away from losing everything. It doesn't require you to perform or prove yourself to keep it.

Another reason you keep attracting the same patterns is that you haven't fully processed the last relationship. You left physically, but you're still carrying the emotional residue. The unresolved anger. The unanswered questions. The belief that if you had just done something differently, it would have worked. So you enter the next relationship still trying to fix the last one. Still proving you're worthy of the love you didn't get. Still operating from a deficit instead of a full cup.

You have to close the door completely before you can walk through a new one. That means grieving what didn't work. Releasing the fantasy of who you thought that person could be. Accepting that the relationship is over, not because you failed, but because it wasn't aligned. And choosing not to carry the weight of that failure into the next connection.

The pattern also repeats because you don't trust yourself. You override your instincts. You talk yourself out of red flags. You give people the benefit of the doubt long after they've shown you who they are. You stay because you don't want to be wrong about them. But staying doesn't prove you were right. It just proves you were willing to ignore yourself to avoid discomfort.

Self-respecting women trust their instincts. When something feels off, they don't need proof to walk away. They don't need the other person to admit they're wrong. They don't need permission to leave. They just go. Because they know that staying in a relationship that feels wrong is worse than being alone.

When the pull toward the unavailable appears, text a friend and delay any reply by twenty-four hours. Distance creates clarity.

Become the consistent presence you needed. Consistency breaks the loop.

Red Flags You've Been Trained to Ignore

Red flags aren't always obvious. They don't show up as cruelty or violence on the first date. They show up as small inconsistencies. Subtle boundary violations. Patterns that don't quite add up. And most women have been trained to explain them away, to give people the benefit of the doubt, to believe that noticing these things makes them judgmental or demanding.

But noticing red flags doesn't make you difficult. It makes you discerning. And ignoring them doesn't make you open-minded. It makes you vulnerable.

One of the earliest red flags is how someone responds when you set a boundary. A boundary respected once is respect. A boundary tested twice is data. A boundary ignored three times is a decision. A person who respects you will honor your boundaries without making it a negotiation. A person who doesn't will test them repeatedly, slowly eroding your sense of what's acceptable until you're tolerating things you never thought you would.

Another red flag is inconsistency between words and actions. Words are intention. Behavior is proof. They say they care about you, but they don't follow through. They say they want a relationship, but they won't commit to plans. They say you matter, but they disappear for days without explanation. Pay attention to what people do, not what they say. Actions reveal truth.

Watch how they talk about their exes. If every ex is the villain, you are next. If they take no responsibility for how those relationships ended, if they vilify everyone they've been with, that's a red flag. It means they lack self-awareness. It means they don't learn from their mistakes. And it means one day, you'll be the villain in their story too.

Notice how they handle conflict. Do they shut down? Do they blow up? Do they deflect blame? Do they gaslight you into questioning your own perceptions? Conflict is inevitable in relationships. What matters is how people move through it. If they can't have a difficult conversation without making you the problem, they're not safe.

Love bombing is a red flag. Grand declarations on day fourteen are performance. Real connection reveals itself over time. When someone comes on too strong too fast, when they're calling you their soulmate after two weeks, when they're making promises before they even know you, that's not romance. That's a warning sign.

Pay attention to how they treat people who can't do anything for them. Waiters. Cashiers. Customer service workers. If they're rude, dismissive, or condescending to people they perceive as beneath them, that's how they'll eventually treat you once the honeymoon phase ends.

Another red flag is isolation. Healthy love expands your world. If your life is shrinking, pay attention. If they're slowly pulling you away from your friends, your family, your support system, that's not love. That's control. If you find yourself making excuses for why you haven't seen your friends, why you're not close with your family anymore, why your world has become smaller since this relationship started, notice it.

Notice if they take responsibility for their actions or if everything is always someone else's fault. If they blame their ex for their trust issues. If they blame their boss for their anger. If they blame you for their reactions. People who refuse to take accountability will never change because they don't believe they're the problem.

Watch for patterns of guilt and obligation. If they make you feel like you owe them for basic decency. If they bring up everything they've done for you whenever you express a need. If they make you feel guilty for having a life outside the relationship. That is control, not care.

Red flags also show up in how they respond to your success. Do they celebrate you? Do they diminish your accomplishments? Do they compete with you? A secure person is happy when you win. An insecure person feels threatened by your growth and will subtly undermine it to keep you small.

Another red flag is secrecy. If they're vague about where they've been, who they're with, what they're doing. If they guard their phone like it contains classified information. If you're not integrated into their life in any meaningful way. If you feel like a secret instead of a priority. That's not privacy. That's hiding.

If your stomach tightens when their name appears, pause. The body is voting before the mind explains. If you feel anxious around them, if you're walking on eggshells, if you're constantly bracing for the next blow-up or silent treatment, your body is telling you something your mind is trying to rationalize. Listen to it.

The biggest red flag of all is when you find yourself changing who you are to keep the peace. When you're editing your thoughts, suppressing your feelings, shrinking your personality to avoid conflict. When you're constantly wondering if you're too much or not enough. When you've lost touch with who you were before this relationship started. That's not growth. That's erasure.

Write one sentence of behavior, one of impact, one of boundary. If the list grows, your answer is in the list.

Discerning women don't ignore red flags. They don't wait for the red flags to turn into deal-breakers. They don't hope the person will change or that they misread the situation. They trust their instincts. They honor their discomfort. And they walk away before the red flags become scars.

Red flags do not turn green with effort. They only become clearer with time.

The Difference Between Chemistry and Compatibility

Chemistry is the spark. Compatibility is the structure. Chemistry is easy to feel. It's the attraction. The way your body responds when they walk into a room. It's exciting. It's intoxicating. It feels like destiny. And most women mistake it for love.

But chemistry without compatibility is just tension without resolution. It's volatility without depth. It's the beginning of something that has no sustainable middle or end. You can have incredible chemistry with someone who is completely wrong for you. And when you build a relationship on chemistry alone, you end up in a cycle of passion and pain that never stabilizes into something real.

Compatibility is different. Compatibility is about alignment. Shared values. Similar life goals. Complementary communication styles. The ability to navigate conflict in ways that bring you closer instead of tearing you apart. Compatibility is what makes a relationship last after the chemistry fades. And chemistry always fades.

Chemistry builds the first three months. Compatibility builds the next three years. Chemistry makes you want someone. Compatibility makes you able to build a life with them. You need both. But if you have to choose, choose compatibility. Chemistry can be rekindled. Misaligned values cannot.

Most women choose chemistry. They meet someone who makes them feel alive, who gives them butterflies, who occupies every thought. And they convince themselves that the incompatibilities don't matter. That love will be enough. That they can compromise on the big things because the connection feels so strong. But you can't compromise on core values. You can't compromise on whether you want children, where you want to live, how you handle money, what kind of life you're building. These aren't small details. They're the foundation of a shared life.

Chemistry often feels strongest with people who are emotionally unavailable. The push and pull. The uncertainty. The intermittent reinforcement. Uncertainty amplifies arousal. Anxiety is not attraction. Your nervous system interprets volatility as excitement. But it's not excitement. It's stress. And stress is not the same as connection, even though your body experiences them similarly.

When you feel instant, overwhelming chemistry with someone, slow down. Don't let the intensity override your discernment. Ask yourself: Are they available. Are they consistent. Do our values align. Can we repair conflict. Or am I just addicted to the uncertainty?

Compatibility shows up in how you handle the mundane parts of life together. Not the vacations or the date nights. The grocery shopping. The cleaning. The bill paying. The conversations about whose family to visit for the holidays. The compromises you make when you want different things. Compatibility is whether those compromises feel fair or whether one person is always bending.

It shows up in how you communicate. Can you talk about difficult things without it becoming a fight? Can you express needs without feeling like you're asking for too much? Can you hear feedback without it feeling like an attack? Do you feel safe being vulnerable with this person, or do you have to protect yourself?

Compatibility is also about pace. Are you both moving in the same direction at the same speed? Or is one person always dragging the other along, and the other person always pulling away? Compatibility means you're matched in your level of commitment, your desire for depth, your willingness to invest in the relationship.

Another aspect of compatibility is how you spend your time together. Do you enjoy the same things? Can you be bored together and still feel connected? Or do you need constant stimulation, constant novelty, constant drama to feel engaged? Sustainable relationships require the ability to be together in silence, in stillness, in the ordinary moments that make up most of life.

You also need to look at how this person fits into your life, not just how they make you feel when you're alone together. Do your friends like them? Does your family respect them? Do they enhance your life or do they isolate you from it? You don't need everyone's approval, but if the people who know you best are concerned, it's worth asking why.

Compatibility feels like steady breath, unhurried plans, quiet relief. Chemistry feels like adrenaline. Both matter. But only one sustains.

Wait two normal life cycles together before big decisions: a busy week and a boring week. See how they handle both.

Self-aware women don't choose relationships based on chemistry alone. They wait for someone who checks both boxes. Someone who makes them feel alive and also makes them feel safe. Someone who excites them and also respects them. Someone who offers both passion and peace.

Seek passion and peace in the same person.

When to Stay and When to Walk Away

One of the hardest things about relationships is knowing when to keep trying and when to let go. Most women stay too long, hoping things will change. Hoping the person will finally see their worth. Hoping the relationship will eventually become what it was in the beginning. But hope is a feeling. Strategy is behavior. And staying in a relationship that isn't working doesn't make you loyal. It makes you stuck.

You stay when the foundation is solid but the circumstances are hard. When you're both committed to growth, to communication, to working through the difficult seasons. When conflict brings you closer instead of tearing you apart. When you're arguing about how to solve problems together, not whether the relationship should exist.

You stay when growth is mutual. When both people are willing to look at their patterns, their wounds, their contributions to the problems. When they take responsibility instead of deflecting blame. When they're doing the work, not just promising to change.

You stay when repair is possible and practiced. When mistakes are acknowledged. When apologies are followed by changed behavior. When you can move through conflict and come out stronger on the other side.

You stay when boundaries are honored without penalty. When you can express needs without being made to feel guilty. When you're seen as a partner, not a project. When you can be fully yourself without fear of judgment or rejection.

You stay when effort flows both ways. When both people are investing equally. When you're not the only one initiating, planning, compromising, apologizing. When the relationship feels balanced instead of one-sided.

You stay when you feel more yourself, not less. When the relationship enhances your life instead of consuming it. When your world expands instead of contracts. When you're growing together instead of one person constantly sacrificing for the other.

You leave when you explain your needs and nothing changes. When you've communicated what you need and it's ignored. When your requests for change are met with defensiveness or dismissal. When you're expected to tolerate things that harm you just to keep the peace.

You leave when your boundaries are tested on repeat. When you've set a boundary and it's violated again and again. When you're constantly having to defend your right to have limits. When maintaining your boundaries feels like a battle instead of a baseline.

You leave when their words and actions do not match. When they make promises they don't keep. When they disappear and reappear based on their convenience, not your needs. When they treat you like an option instead of a priority.

You leave when your world is smaller and you are smaller in it. When you can't remember who you were before this relationship. When you're constantly editing your thoughts, suppressing your feelings, making yourself smaller to fit into someone else's version of who you should be. When you've sacrificed your identity to maintain the relationship.

You leave when your body lives in dread, not calm. When you're constantly walking on eggshells. When you're bracing for conflict instead of looking forward to connection. When seeing their name on your phone makes your stomach drop instead of your heart lift.

You leave when the relationship requires you to betray yourself. When staying means abandoning your values, your dreams, your boundaries. When keeping the relationship intact is more important than keeping yourself intact. When you're sacrificing your well-being for someone who wouldn't do the same for you.

You leave when there's a pattern of disrespect. When they speak to you in ways they'd never tolerate from anyone else. When they criticize, belittle, or demean you. When they make you feel like you're never good enough. When they blame you for their feelings, their reactions, their choices.

Believe the pattern, not the promise. You leave when you've given them time, space, second chances, and the patterns persist. When you're making excuses for behavior you'd never accept from anyone else. When you're hoping they'll become someone they've shown you they're not.

You leave when love feels like suffering. When the hard days outnumber the good ones. When you're crying more than you're laughing. When you're defending the relationship to everyone around you because even you can see it's not working. When you're holding on to who they used to be instead of accepting who they are now.

The hardest part of walking away is accepting that love isn't always enough. You can love someone deeply and still know they're not right for you. You can love someone and still choose yourself. Walking away doesn't mean you failed. It means you finally valued yourself enough to stop accepting less than you deserve. Before deciding, place a hand on your chest and ask: peace or panic. Choose in favor of peace. Draft the goodbye message without sending it. If you feel relief in your body, treat that as data.

Women grounded in self-worth don't stay in relationships out of fear or obligation. They stay because the relationship adds to their life in meaningful ways. And when it stops doing that, when it starts taking more than it gives, when it requires them to abandon themselves to keep it, they leave. Not with anger. Not with bitterness. But with clarity. Because they know their worth, and they refuse to settle for anything less than a love that honors it.

Love is not proved by suffering. Choose the bond that honors your self-respect.

Key Takeaways

- Real love brings a quiet sense of security rather than a constant need to prove your worth.
- Trauma bonds feel intense and chaotic, whereas true intimacy makes you feel safe and genuinely seen.
- You're drawn to familiar relationship patterns, even when they hurt, because your body mistakes familiarity for safety.
- Healthy relationships don't leave you guessing about your value—they consistently affirm it through actions, not just words.
- You cannot heal past wounds by recreating them; changing your relationships requires consciously choosing new patterns.
- Red flags ignored early become the same reasons relationships eventually fail, so trust your instincts from the beginning.
- Chemistry without compatibility creates excitement but never deep connection; lasting relationships are built on shared values.
- Mutual willingness to grow and take responsibility is a sign you're in a relationship worth keeping.
- Staying in a relationship should never mean betraying yourself, minimizing your needs, or compromising your boundaries.
- Walking away from a toxic relationship doesn't indicate failure; it reflects a powerful choice to honor your own self-worth.

Chapter 13:
Dating as a High Value Woman

"Never allow someone to be your priority while allowing yourself to be their option." — Mark Twain

Dating has become a performance. Women are told to be available but not too available. Interested but not intimidating. Confident but not threatening. The rules change depending on who's giving them, and many women end up exhausted trying to figure out the right way to act instead of simply being themselves.

High value dating isn't about following a script. It's about embodying a set of principles that naturally filter out the wrong people and attract the right ones. It's about understanding your worth so deeply that you don't need to convince anyone of it. It's about creating space for a man to step into instead of filling every gap with your effort. And it's about holding standards that protect your peace instead of lowering them to keep someone interested.

Plenty of women approach dating from a place of deficit. They meet someone with potential and immediately start investing as if this is their only chance. They initiate. They plan. They chase. They ignore red flags because they're afraid of being alone. They tolerate lukewarm effort because they think that's all they deserve. And then they wonder why the relationship never stabilizes into something real.

Women rooted in self-worth date differently. They don't chase. They don't perform. They don't bend themselves into shapes that feel unnatural just to keep someone's attention. They show up as themselves and let that be enough. And if it's not enough for someone, they don't try to convince them otherwise. They simply move on.

This chapter will teach you how to date from a place of fullness instead of desperation. How to maintain your feminine energy without losing your power. How to let a man lead without abandoning yourself in the process. And how to set standards that immediately filter out men who aren't serious, who aren't ready, or who just want to waste your time.

Dating should feel like discovery, not audition. When you approach it correctly, you're not trying to win someone over. You're deciding if they're worthy of your time.

The Energy That Attracts Quality Not Quantity

The energy you bring to dating determines the caliber of person you attract. If you show up desperate, anxious, or trying too hard, you'll attract people who feed on that energy. If you show up grounded, self-assured, and selectively interested, you'll attract people who respect boundaries and value substance.

Most women think they need to be more available to attract quality men. They:

- Respond immediately to every message.
- Rearrange their schedules for last-minute plans.
- Make themselves easy to reach, easy to impress, easy to keep.

Access signals value only when your life is already full. This doesn't mean playing games or pretending you're busier than you are. It means actually having a life that doesn't revolve around dating. When you have hobbies, friendships, goals, routines that matter to you, you naturally become less available. And that unavailability signals worth. It tells a man that your time is precious, that access to you is earned, not given freely to anyone who asks.

The energy that attracts quality men looks like:

- Calm confidence.
- A life that feels full before love arrives.
- Interest without attachment to outcome.
- Warmth that invites, not effort that persuades.

When you're anxious, you leak energy. You over-text. You overexplain. You seek reassurance. You need constant confirmation that the person is still interested. That anxiety is palpable, and it repels serious men. Not because they're cruel, but because they're looking for a partner who is secure in herself. Someone they can add to, not someone they have to constantly validate.

Quality men are attracted to women who are at peace with themselves.

Women who don't need a relationship to feel complete. Women who have standards and enforce them without apology. Women who can walk away if something doesn't feel right. That level of self-possession is magnetic because it's rare.

Abundance mentality shifts everything. When you believe there are multiple people who could be right for you, you stop clinging to the first person who shows interest. You stop tolerating mediocre effort because you're afraid you won't find anyone better. You invest slowly until worth is demonstrated. You stay in your power because you know that if this person isn't the one, someone else will be.

This doesn't mean you're cold or detached. It means you're discerning. You're warm and open with people who earn it. But you're not pouring energy into connections that aren't reciprocal. You're not chasing potential. You're responding to reality.

One of the most attractive qualities you can have is the ability to be alone without being lonely. When you genuinely enjoy your own company, when your life is rich and fulfilling without a partner, that shows. You're not dating from lack. You're dating from overflow. And that energy attracts people who are also operating from a place of fullness, not need.

Pay attention to how you feel when you're getting ready for a date. Are you anxious? Are you rehearsing what you'll say? Are you worried about whether he'll like you? Or are you curious? Excited to meet someone new but not attached to the outcome? If you catch yourself rehearsing, pause and ask: What would presence choose right now.

Pre-date reset:

- Take three slow breaths.
- Feel your feet on the ground.
- Remind yourself that you are already whole.
- Let curiosity replace pressure.

Quality men feel the difference between being assessed and being impressed. When you're assessing, you're evaluating whether they meet your standards. When you're trying to impress, you're trying to prove you meet theirs. The first is attractive. The second is not.

Your job on a date is not to be perfect. It's to be present. To listen. To observe. To notice how this person makes you feel. Do they ask questions? Do they listen to your answers? Do they make an effort? Do they respect your boundaries? These are the things that matter, not whether you said the right thing or laughed at the right time.

The energy that attracts quality is also consistent. You don't shift depending on who you're with. You're the same version of yourself whether you're on a first date or a tenth date. You don't perform to keep someone interested. You just exist as you are, and if that's not enough for someone, you recognize it as incompatibility, not inadequacy.

Mini-check pre-date:

- Am I curious or attached to outcome?
- What standard will I quietly observe tonight?
- What is one boundary I will keep if tested?

Stop trying to attract everyone. Start being the version of yourself that naturally attracts the right person.

Why Chasing Destroys Polarity and Attraction

Polarity is what creates attraction. Masculine energy and feminine energy, when balanced, create a magnetic pull. When that polarity collapses, attraction fades. And one of the fastest ways to collapse polarity is by chasing.

Chasing happens when a woman steps into masculine energy in a relationship. When chasing, you:

- Initiate the contact.
- Plan the dates.
- Keep the connection alive.
- Manage the pace of the relationship.

While this might feel like showing interest, what you're actually doing is removing the man's opportunity to lead. You're filling a role that he should be filling, and in doing so, you eliminate the tension that keeps attraction alive.

Masculine energy moves toward. Feminine energy attracts. When you chase, you're moving toward instead of allowing him to come to you. You're pursuing instead of being pursued. Some men will accept that dynamic, but few sustain attraction within it. Because deep down, they know that if they had to put in no effort to win you, your value must not be that high.

When grounded in your feminine energy, you:

- Respond to effort instead of creating it.
- Allow him to pursue at his own pace.
- Match consistency, not intensity.

This doesn't mean you sit back and do nothing. It means you respond to effort, but you don't create it. If a man is interested, he will show it. He will text. He will ask you out. He will make plans. He will find ways to see you. Your job is to notice whether he's doing these things and respond accordingly. If he's not, you have your answer.

Many women chase because they're afraid of losing someone they've decided is valuable. But here's the truth: if effort must be one-sided to keep it, it cannot last. And even if you manage to hold on through constant effort, you'll exhaust yourself maintaining a connection that was never reciprocal.

Chasing also communicates that you don't believe you're enough. It says "I need to convince you to choose me." And men pick up on that. They sense the desperation, the lack of self-worth, the willingness to accept crumbs. And instead of stepping up, they step back. Because a woman who doesn't value herself won't inspire a man to value her either.

When you stop chasing, one of two things happens. Either the man steps up and starts pursuing you, which tells you he was interested but got comfortable with you doing all the work. Or he fades away, which tells you he was never that interested to begin with. Either way, you get clarity. And clarity is more valuable than false hope.

Feminine energy is magnetic, but only when it's allowed to be. When you're in your feminine presence, you're open, receptive, responsive. You're not controlling the outcome. You're not managing the pace of the relationship. You're allowing things to unfold naturally while staying rooted in your worth. You're saying "I'm here, I'm available to someone who values me, and if that's you, show me."

Masculine energy respects feminine energy when it's grounded. But if your feminine energy is desperate, anxious, or needy, it doesn't attract. It repels. Because masculine energy is designed to protect and provide for something it perceives as valuable. If you're giving yourself away for free, there's nothing to protect or provide for.

This is why standards matter. When you have clear boundaries about what you will and won't accept, you naturally stop chasing. Because you know that chasing someone who isn't pursuing you is a violation of your own standards. You're teaching them that your interest is more important than their effort. And that's a lesson no high-value woman should be teaching.

If you find yourself always initiating texts, always making plans, always being the one to reach out, stop. Pull back. See what happens. Notice the urge in your fingers to text first. Wait fifteen minutes and re-check the evidence. If he doesn't notice or doesn't care, you have all the information you need. If he does notice and steps up, then you've just reset the dynamic to something healthier.

Before texting first, ask:

- Am I seeking connection or reassurance?
- Has he already shown effort worth reciprocating?
- Would I still send this message if I felt secure?

Chasing also keeps you in a state of anxiety. You're constantly wondering if you're doing enough, saying the right things, being interesting enough. That mental loop is exhausting, and it keeps you from being present. When you stop chasing and allow him to lead, you relax. You become more of yourself. And that version of you is far more attractive than the one trying to hold his attention through effort.

Investment creates attachment. When you chase, you remove his reason to invest. You're doing the work for him. And without that investment, he has no skin in the game. He can walk away without losing anything because he never had to earn you in the first place.

Stop chasing. Start choosing:

- Choose effort over potential.

- Choose calm over anxiety.
- Choose clarity over confusion.

Polarity grows in response, not in pursuit. Be present. Be open. Be yourself. And let him do the rest.

If you need to communicate boundaries around texting or consistency, keep it simple and direct. If he texts rarely, you might say: "I enjoy plans made in advance. If that works for you, let me know a day and time." If he mirrors your effort and you had a good time, keep it light: "I had a good time. Reach out when you want to plan the next." And if you pulled back and nothing changed, you have your answer. You can say: "I'm looking for consistency. Since this isn't aligning, I'm going to pass."

Letting Him Lead Without Losing Yourself

Letting a man lead does not mean becoming passive, submissive, or voiceless. It means allowing him to take initiative in the relationship while you remain grounded in who you are. It means creating space for him to show up without abandoning your needs, your boundaries, or your sense of self.

Many women resist the idea of letting a man lead because they associate it with losing power. They think that if they're not in control, they'll be taken advantage of. But leadership and control are not the same thing. Leadership includes your needs. Control deletes them.

You can tell the difference by how you feel:
- When a man leads, you feel cared for, protected, and considered.
- When a man controls, you feel small, silenced, and erased.

One expands you. The other diminishes you. And you should never tolerate the second.

Letting him lead looks like:
- Allowing him to plan or initiate while you stay receptive.
- Expressing preferences without dictating the outcome.
- Saying yes when it feels right and no when it doesn't.
- Appreciating his effort instead of managing it.

But receiving doesn't mean accepting anything he offers. You still have standards. You still have preferences. You still have boundaries. Let him plan. If it misfits your needs, name the adjustment. You let him take initiative, but if his initiative disrespects your time or boundaries, you address it.

Feminine energy is not weak. It's discerning. It knows what it wants and what it doesn't want. It can say no just as easily as it says yes. It doesn't bend itself into uncomfortable shapes to accommodate someone else's vision. It simply responds to what's offered and decides whether it's acceptable.

One of the biggest mistakes women make is thinking that letting a man lead means suppressing their own desires. It doesn't. You still voice what you want. You still express your needs. You still communicate your boundaries. But you do it from a place of invitation rather than demand. You're saying "Here's what I need to feel good in this relationship. Can you meet me there?" And then you pay attention to whether he tries.

For example, if you need plans set in advance to feel secure, you might say: "I feel best with plans by midweek. Can you set something for Thursday." You're expressing your need clearly while inviting him to meet it. You're not demanding. You're not nagging. You're simply stating what works for you and giving him the opportunity to show up.

If he consistently ignores your needs while expecting you to follow his lead, that's not leadership. That's selfishness. Do not follow a man who cannot consider you.

Letting him lead also means trusting him to handle things without jumping in to fix or manage. If he's planning a date and it's not going the way you would have planned it, resist the urge to take over. Let him figure it out. If he makes a mistake, let him learn from it. If you are correcting details all night, you are managing, not relating. And that kills attraction.

Masculine energy wants to provide, protect, and solve. But it can't do that if you're always doing it first. You have to create space for him to step up. And that means being okay with things not being done exactly the way you would do them. It means trusting that he's capable, even if his approach is different from yours.

This doesn't mean you ignore genuine incompetence or disrespect. If he's consistently failing to show up, if his leadership feels careless or dismissive, if you're constantly disappointed by his lack of effort, that's not a man worth following. That's a man who isn't ready to lead. And you shouldn't wait around for him to figure it out.

Letting him lead without losing yourself also means staying connected to your own life. You don't abandon your friends, your hobbies, your goals just because you're in a relationship. You don't make him the center of your world. You have your own center, and he complements it. You're not following him blindly. You're walking beside him, each of you contributing to the direction of the relationship.

When decisions need to be made, you have a voice. You share your perspective. You offer your input. But you're not demanding that everything goes your way. You're willing to compromise when it makes sense, and you're willing to defer to him when he's better equipped to lead in a particular area. That's partnership. That's balance.

Before you step in to manage or control, exhale. Unclench your shoulders. Ask yourself: Is my input needed or is this discomfort with not being in charge.

If a man is leading well, you'll feel it. You'll feel lighter. You'll feel more feminine. You'll feel cherished and considered. You'll trust him to handle things because he's proven he can. You won't feel the need to control everything because you know he's got it. And that trust is what allows you to relax into your feminine energy.

But if a man is not leading well, you'll feel it too. You'll feel anxious. You'll feel like you have to manage everything. You'll feel like you can't rely on him. And when that happens, you don't force it. You don't try to teach him how to lead. You simply recognize that he's not the right person to follow, and you move on.

If his leadership feels like:

- Care → stay open.
- Neglect → step back.
- Control → walk away.

Let him lead, but never at the expense of your peace. Let him lead, but never into places that compromise your values. Let him lead, but only if his leadership makes you feel more like yourself, not less. That's the balance. That's how you stay powerful while staying feminine.

When you need to set boundaries around his leadership, be clear and direct. If late-night invitations don't work for you, say so: "Late-night invitations do not work for me. I prefer plans set earlier." And when he does lead well, acknowledge it. Appreciation reinforces the behavior you want to see more of: "I liked that you booked and confirmed. Thank you."

Standards That Filter Out Men Who Waste Your Time

Standards are not about being difficult. They're about being clear. When you know what you will and won't accept, you immediately filter out men who aren't serious, who aren't ready, or who just want to waste your time. And that clarity saves you months, sometimes years, of investing in the wrong person.

Many women are afraid to have standards because they think it will limit their options. But the men you're filtering out with standards are not men you want anyway. You're not narrowing your pool of quality men. You're eliminating the men who would have hurt you, disappointed you, or drained your energy. Standards protect your peace.

Core Standards for Dating:

Consistency: He shows up regularly, communicates clearly, and follows through.

Effort: He invests time and thought, not just words.

Respect: He honors your boundaries and never makes you feel guilty for having them.

Intentionality: He's clear about his goals and where the relationship is heading.

Emotional availability: He engages in real conversations and shares feelings.

Conflict skills: He resolves issues instead of avoiding them.

Integration: He includes you in his world.

Money hygiene: He's responsible and reliable in how he manages his life. Chronic chaos with money spills into the relationship.

Kindness: He treats everyone, not just you, with respect.

Net effect: Time with him leaves you peaceful, not depleted.

The first standard is consistency. A man who is serious about you will show up consistently. He will text regularly. He will make plans in advance. He will follow through on what he says he'll do. He won't disappear for days and then reappear with excuses. He won't leave you guessing about where you stand. Consistency is the baseline. If he can't meet that, he's not serious.

Another standard is effort. A man who values you will put in effort. He will plan dates. He will ask you questions about your life. He will remember details. He will make you feel like spending time with you matters to him. If you're always the one making plans, if he's only reaching out when it's convenient for him, if he's putting in the bare minimum and expecting you to accept it, he's wasting your time.

Respect is non-negotiable. A man who respects you will honor your boundaries. He won't pressure you into things you're not ready for. He won't dismiss your feelings or make you feel like your needs are unreasonable. He won't speak to you in ways that make you feel small. If he violates your boundaries, if he disrespects your time, if he makes you feel less than, he doesn't meet your standards. Walk away.

Intentionality is another standard. A man who is serious about building something with you will be intentional. He will talk about the future. He will introduce you to important people in his life. He will make it clear that he's not just passing time with you. If he's vague about what he wants, if he won't define the relationship, if he keeps you in limbo for months, he's not serious. And you don't wait for him to become serious. You move on.

Emotional availability is essential. A man who is ready for a relationship will be emotionally present. He will share how he's feeling. He will be curious about how you're feeling. He will engage in meaningful conversations. He won't shut down when things get uncomfortable. If he's emotionally distant, if he can't or won't open up, if he's still hung up on his ex, he's not available. And you can't build a relationship with someone who isn't there. Your standards should also include how he handles conflict. Does he communicate when something bothers him, or does he shut down? Does he take responsibility for his actions, or does he deflect? Does he work to resolve issues, or does he avoid them? A man who can't handle conflict maturely is not ready for a serious relationship. And you shouldn't have to teach him.

Another standard is integration. A man who is serious about you will want to integrate you into his life. You'll meet his friends. You'll meet his family. You'll be included in his plans. If he's keeping you separate, if you're not part of his world in any meaningful way, if he's treating you like a secret, he's not serious. He's keeping his options open. And you don't compete for a man's attention. You move on to someone who is certain about you. Financial responsibility matters. You're not looking for someone to support you financially, but you should be looking for someone who is responsible with money. Someone who has goals. Someone who can manage their life. If he's constantly in financial crisis, constantly borrowing, constantly making poor decisions, that's a red flag. It signals a lack of maturity and planning, and those issues will affect the relationship. Standards also include how he treats others. Does he speak respectfully about his family? Does he have healthy friendships? Does he treat service workers kindly? How a man treats others when there's nothing to gain is how he'll eventually treat you. If he's rude, dismissive, or unkind to people around him, don't expect that you'll be the exception forever.

Finally, your standard should be that he adds to your life, not drains it. After spending time with him, do you feel energized or exhausted? Do you feel more like yourself or less? Do you feel better about your life or worse? A relationship should enhance your life, not complicate it. If being with him feels like more work than joy, he's not the one.

Red flags within standards:

- Vague about plans signals low intentionality
- Apologies without change signals no repair
- Warm texts but cold actions signals misaligned signals

When you set these standards, some men will walk away. Let them. They were never going to meet your needs anyway. The right man won't be intimidated by your standards. He'll respect them. He'll rise to meet them. Because he knows that a woman with standards is a woman who values herself. And that's exactly the kind of woman a quality man wants.

Holding your standards means:

- Communicating them clearly.
- Enforcing them consistently.

- Walking away when they're violated.
- Refusing to negotiate your self-respect.

Hold your standards without apology. Communicate them clearly. Enforce them consistently. And never lower them to keep someone interested. The moment you compromise on your standards, you teach people that your boundaries are negotiable. They're not. Your standards are the floor, not the ceiling. And anyone who can't meet them doesn't deserve access to you.

After the date, ask yourself:

- Did I feel relaxed or anxious?
- Did I feel seen or scanned?
- Did the conversation flow naturally?
- Would I want to repeat this energy, not just the evening?

If you need to define the relationship, be direct. You can say: "I am looking for an exclusive relationship. Is that what you want too." If he's keeping things vague and you need clarity, set a boundary: "I do not stay in undefined dynamics. If you want to continue, let's define this." And if it becomes clear that he's not meeting your standards, exit with grace: "This has been clarifying. I'm looking for consistency and intention, so I'm going to step back."

Dating Toolkit

Pre-date reset:

- Breathe three times.
- Feel your feet on the ground.
- Set one standard to observe tonight.

First three dates evidence list:

- Did he plan and confirm.
- Did he ask and remember something about you.
- Did you feel calm in your body.

Texting cadence:

- Match pace for the first week, then let him lead frequency.

- If you catch yourself double-texting, wait one sleep cycle.

Green flags:

- Consistency, curiosity, care in small details.
- Repairs small misses quickly.
- You feel like yourself.

Personal boundary:

"If I feel anxious after each interaction, I slow down or step back."

Key Takeaways

- Dating from a place of worth means being selective rather than desperate, inviting genuine effort instead of chasing attention.
- When you know your value, you don't try to convince anyone of it—you allow people to recognize it and respond accordingly.
- Chasing a man shifts you out of your feminine energy, reducing attraction and removing his motivation to pursue.
- Real attraction grows from consistent effort over time, not from dramatic gestures or intense starts followed by uncertainty.
- Letting him lead means trusting him to initiate plans and actions, while clearly communicating your needs and boundaries.
- Healthy leadership in dating makes you feel calm, considered, and respected—not anxious or controlled.
- Holding clear standards filters out men who aren't serious, available, or respectful, saving you from investing in connections that drain your energy.
- Having an abundant life outside of dating naturally increases your value, making access to your time and energy something special.
- High value dating isn't about performing the right role but about being authentic and trusting that the right person will recognize and appreciate that authenticity.
- When you stop trying to impress and start assessing whether someone is truly compatible, you attract relationships that enhance your life rather than complicate it.

Chapter 14:
Creating Relationships Where You Feel Safe

"To love someone long-term is to attend a thousand funerals of the people they used to be." — Heidi Priebe

Safety is not something you hope someone gives you. It's something you create together. Most women spend years in relationships where they feel like they're tiptoeing around truth, carefully curating words before they leave their mouth, managing someone else's emotions, suppressing their own needs to keep the peace. They confuse this state of hypervigilance with love, thinking that if they just get better at anticipating problems, things will stabilize. But that's not safety. That's survival.

Real safety in a relationship means you can speak your truth without fear of punishment. You can express a need without being made to feel demanding. You can have a bad day without worrying that your partner will withdraw love or turn it into a conflict about them. Safety means you don't have to perform, pretend, or reduce yourself to be acceptable. You can just be. And in that space of being fully yourself, intimacy actually becomes possible.

Many women don't know what emotional safety feels like because they've never experienced it. They've been in relationships where love was conditional, where closeness required sacrifice, where being vulnerable meant being hurt. So they've learned to protect themselves by staying surface-level, by never asking for too much, by keeping their deepest needs hidden. And then they wonder why their relationships feel hollow.

High value relationships are built on a foundation of safety. Not the illusion of safety that comes from avoiding conflict or pretending everything is fine. Safety is the rhythm your body recognizes when conflict no longer threatens connection. When you know you can bring your whole self to the relationship and be met with respect, curiosity, and care. Safety that allows both people to grow instead of shrinking to fit into roles that don't serve them.

This chapter will teach you what emotional safety actually looks and feels like.

How to recognize it when it's present and notice when it's missing. How to build the kind of closeness that deepens over time instead of fading after the honeymoon phase. How to communicate your needs in ways that bring you closer instead of creating distance. And how to create partnerships based on mutual growth instead of codependency disguised as love.

You deserve a relationship where you feel safe. Not just physically safe, but emotionally safe. Where you can lower your guard and trust that you won't be punished for being human. That kind of safety doesn't happen by accident. It's built intentionally, brick by brick, through how you show up and what you accept. And it starts with knowing what you're building toward.

What Emotional Safety Actually Looks and Feels Like

Emotional safety is not the absence of conflict. It's the presence of trust. Knowing that when things get hard, your partner won't abandon you, attack you, or use your vulnerability against you. Knowing you can have a difficult conversation without the entire relationship being threatened.

Most people mistake comfort for safety. Comfort is easy. Comfort is predictable. Comfort is staying surface-level so nothing ever gets disrupted. But comfort without depth is just two people coexisting, not connecting. Safety allows for discomfort because it's rooted in something deeper than convenience. It's rooted in commitment to working through things together instead of running when it gets hard.

You notice emotional safety when you can express a feeling without it being dismissed, minimized, or turned into a debate. When you say "I felt hurt when this happened," and your partner's first response is curiosity, not defense. When they ask questions to understand instead of immediately explaining why you're wrong to feel that way.

In a safe relationship, emotion lands softly instead of being deflected. You can cry without being told you're too sensitive. You can express anger without being labeled as dramatic. You can say "I need space" without your partner taking it personally or punishing you with silence. There's room to be fully human, with all your emotions, without being made to feel like any of them are too much.

Safety reveals itself in how your partner responds when you set a boundary. Do they respect it? Do they ask clarifying questions? Do they adjust their behavior? Or do they push back, make you feel guilty, or treat your boundary like an attack on them? A healthy partner reads boundaries as direction, not criticism.

Another marker of emotional safety is steadiness. You don't have to guess what mood your partner will be in. You don't have to brace yourself wondering if something you say will trigger an explosion or cold withdrawal. Even when things are tense, there's a baseline of respect that doesn't disappear. Steadiness means you can relax into the relationship instead of constantly preparing for impact.

Emotional safety also means your partner takes responsibility for their actions. When they hurt you, they don't deflect blame or make excuses. They don't turn it around and make themselves the victim. They acknowledge the impact, apologize sincerely, and make an effort to repair. They understand that intent doesn't erase impact, and they're more interested in making things right than in being right.

You recognize safety when your needs are treated as valid, not inconvenient. When you ask for something and your partner doesn't make you feel like you're asking for too much. They might not always be able to meet every need in the exact moment you express it, but they take it seriously. They work with you to find solutions. They don't make you feel like having needs is a character flaw.

Safety shows itself when you can share your fears, your insecurities, your past wounds without them being used against you later. Trusting that what you share in a vulnerable moment won't be thrown back at you during an argument. Knowing your partner is a safe place to land, not another source of stress you have to manage.

Another aspect of emotional safety is knowing you can make mistakes without being punished indefinitely. Everyone messes up. Everyone has bad days. Everyone says things they regret. In a safe relationship, mistakes are addressed, repaired, and released. They're not stored up as ammunition. They're not brought up repeatedly to keep you in a state of guilt or shame. There's room for growth, for learning, for being imperfect.

Safety appears when you're celebrated, not competed with. When your partner is genuinely happy for your wins instead of threatened by them. When your success doesn't make them feel small. When they encourage your growth instead of subtly undermining it to keep you dependent or manageable.

Emotional safety shows up in the small moments. The way your partner listens when you talk about your day. The way they check in when they notice you're quiet. The way they remember things that matter to you. The way they make space for your feelings even when they don't fully understand them. Safety isn't one grand gesture. It's a thousand small acts of attentiveness and care.

Place your hand on your chest and take a slow breath. Does the relationship make your body tighten or soften? That's the fastest way to know whether safety is present.

If you're in a relationship and you constantly feel anxious, you're not safe. If you're rehearsing sentences in your head before speaking them, you're not safe. If you're afraid to ask for what you need, you're not safe. If you feel like you have to be perfect to be loved, you're not safe. And no amount of chemistry, history, or hope will change that unless the foundation itself shifts.

Emotional safety is not something you can create alone. It requires both people to be committed to it. But you can recognize when it's absent. And you can decide whether you're willing to stay in a relationship where safety is constantly compromised, or whether you'll wait for something better. Once you've known steadiness, the noise of chaos stops sounding like love.

The Foundation of True Intimacy

Intimacy is not sex. Intimacy is being known. It's letting someone see the parts of you that you usually keep hidden and trusting that they won't use that knowledge to hurt you. It's the slow revelation of who you are beneath the surface, and the willingness to witness someone else do the same.

Most people confuse physical closeness with intimacy. They think that because they share a bed, share a home, share a life logistically, they're intimate. But you can share a home yet feel like a visitor inside it. You can sleep next to someone every night and still feel completely alone. Physical proximity doesn't create intimacy. Emotional transparency does.

Genuine intimacy requires vulnerability, but not the performative kind. Not the rehearsed story you tell on dates to seem deep. Steady vulnerability is messy. It's admitting you don't have it all figured out. It's sharing the things you're ashamed of. It's letting someone see you when you're not at your best and trusting they won't leave.

But vulnerability without safety is just exposure. You can't build intimacy in a relationship where your honesty is met with judgment, dismissal, or weaponization. Intimacy grows in the soil of emotional safety. When you know that what you share will be held with care, you can risk revealing more. And that revealing is what deepens the bond.

Intimacy doesn't arrive. It's maintained through daily micro-adjustments. It's not the big declarations of love or the grand romantic gestures. It's the quiet conversations late at night where you share something you've never told anyone. It's the way your partner notices when you're off and creates space for you to talk about it. It's the inside jokes, the shared history, the way you can communicate with a look across a crowded room.

One of the foundations of intimacy is curiosity. A partner who is genuinely curious about you will ask questions. Not surface-level questions, but questions that get to the core of who you are. What shaped you. What scares you. What you dream about. What you're working through. And they'll listen to the answers without trying to fix you or change the subject to themselves.

Attention renews intimacy. It's how long-term love stays awake. When you stop being curious about your partner, when you assume you already know everything about them, closeness stagnates. People change. They grow. They evolve. And if you're not paying attention, you'll wake up next to a stranger because you stopped asking questions years ago.

Honesty, presence, and reciprocity weave intimacy into daily life. Not brutal honesty that's just cruelty disguised as truth-telling. But gentle, consistent honesty about how you're feeling, what you're thinking, what you need. When you hide parts of yourself to keep the peace, you create distance. When you pretend everything is fine when it's not, you erode trust. Intimacy can only exist where there's truth.

Another foundation of intimacy is presence. Presence in intimacy isn't about your body being still. It's about your mind staying here when emotion gets uncomfortable. You can't build intimacy while scrolling your phone, half-listening to your partner talk about their day. You can't create connection when you're physically there but mentally somewhere else. Presence means putting down distractions and actually being with the person in front of you. It means eye contact. It means active listening. It means making the other person feel like they matter more than whatever else is competing for your attention.

Closeness deepens when you share not just the highlights of your life but the struggles. When you let your partner see you in pain and allow them to comfort you. When you admit you're scared or confused or overwhelmed and trust that they won't see you as weak. Strength in intimacy isn't pretending you have it all together. It's being honest about when you don't.

But intimacy is also reciprocal. If one person is always the one being vulnerable, always the one sharing, always the one reaching for connection, that's not intimacy. That's one person performing emotional labor while the other stays protected behind walls. Intimacy requires both people to be willing to be seen. Both people taking turns being vulnerable. Both people investing in knowing and being known.

Intimacy also grows through repair. Every relationship has ruptures. Moments where you hurt each other, intentionally or not. Moments where you disconnect. The intimacy isn't destroyed by these ruptures. It's destroyed by the refusal to repair them. When you can come back after a fight, acknowledge what happened, take responsibility, and reconnect, intimacy actually deepens. You learn that the relationship can survive conflict. That you're safe even when things get messy.

Physical intimacy is part of this, but it's the result of emotional intimacy, not a substitute for it. When you feel emotionally safe and connected, physical intimacy becomes an extension of that. It's not performative. It's not transactional. It's a natural expression of the closeness you've built. When connection thins, touch becomes choreography instead of communion.

Whole intimacy also means you don't lose yourself in the relationship. You remain an individual with your own interests, your own friendships, your own goals. And your partner does the same. Intimacy isn't enmeshment. It's not two people merging into one and losing their separate identities. Two complete lives choosing to intersect rather than overlap.

The deepest intimacy happens when you can be completely yourself and feel completely loved. Not loved despite who you are, but because of who you are. When you don't have to perform or pretend or reduce yourself to be acceptable.

When you can show up exactly as you are and know that's enough. That's when closeness stops feeling earned and starts feeling lived.

Communicating Needs in Ways That Bring You Closer

Most women have been taught that expressing needs is needy. That asking for what they want makes them demanding. That good partners should just know what you need without you having to say it. So they stay silent, hoping their partner will read their mind, and then feel hurt and resentful when that doesn't happen.

But unexpressed needs don't disappear. They accumulate. They turn into bitterness. They create distance. And eventually, they destroy the relationship. Not because the needs were unreasonable, but because they were never communicated clearly enough for the other person to even know they existed.

Women grounded in self-worth state their needs directly. Not as complaints. Not as accusations. Not buried in passive-aggressive comments. You say "I need this" and you give your partner the opportunity to show up or show you who they are. Either way, you get clarity.

The way you communicate a need determines whether it brings you closer or creates defensiveness. When you frame it through blame, the wall goes up. When you frame it through experience, the space between you opens. There's a difference between "You never make time for me" and "I feel disconnected when we don't spend quality time together. Can we prioritize that this week?"

Anchor your words in emotion, not accusation. Take ownership of your emotional experience instead of making your partner defend themselves against exaggerations. "I feel unheard when I'm talking and you're on your phone" is different from "You never listen to me." The first gives specific, actionable information. The second is a character assassination that puts your partner on the defensive.

Be specific about what you need. Vague requests don't help anyone. "I need more attention" doesn't tell your partner what to actually do. "I need us to have one night a week where we put our phones away and just talk" gives them something concrete to work with. The clearer you are, the easier it is for them to meet you where you are.

In lasting relationships, clarity invites trust and timing keeps it intact. Don't bring up a need in the middle of an argument about something else. Don't ambush your partner with a serious conversation when they just walked in the door after a long day. Choose a time when you're both calm, when you have space to talk without distractions. "I want to talk about something that's been on my mind. Is now a good time, or should we set aside time later?" This shows respect for their capacity and increases the likelihood they'll actually hear you.

Also, frame needs as invitations to connect, not ultimatums. "I need physical affection to feel close to you. Can we find ways to build more of that into our routine?" opens a door. "If you don't touch me more, I'm going to feel unloved" creates pressure. One invites partnership. The other demands compliance.

When you express a need, give your partner room to respond. Don't pile on five different issues at once. Don't list every time they've failed to meet this need in the past. Stay focused on the present and the future. "Here's what I need going forward. Can you do that?" And then listen to their response without interrupting, defending, or dismissing.

If they can't meet the need, you've learned enough to choose accordingly. Maybe they're not capable. Maybe they don't want to. Maybe the need is incompatible with who they are. That's disappointing, but it's clarifying. You can't force someone to meet a need they're unwilling or unable to meet. But you can decide whether you're willing to stay in a relationship where that need remains unmet.

Sometimes your partner will have questions. They'll want to understand better. Let them ask. Don't assume questions are resistance. Sometimes people need more information to fully grasp what you're asking for. Be patient. Be willing to clarify. The goal is mutual understanding, not winning the conversation.

Also, be open to feedback. Communication that sustains love is rhythmic: one speaks, one listens, both adjust. If you're expressing a need, your partner might have needs too. They might share something that helps you understand why meeting your need has been difficult for them. This isn't an excuse, but it might reveal a dynamic neither of you had fully seen. When both people can share needs and work together to meet them, that's when you build partnership.

Another key to communicating needs is follow-through. If your partner agrees to meet a need and then doesn't follow through, address it. Not with "I knew you wouldn't do it" but with "We agreed on this, and it didn't happen. What got in the way?" Give them a chance to course-correct. But if it becomes a pattern, if they keep agreeing and not following through, that tells you they're not actually committed to meeting the need. And you have to decide what to do with that understanding.

Communicating needs also means appreciating when they're met. If your partner makes an effort to show up in the way you asked, acknowledge it. "I really appreciated that you planned a date night this week. It made me feel valued." Positive reinforcement encourages more of the behavior you want. It also shows your partner that their effort matters, which motivates them to keep trying.

The biggest mistake women make is waiting until they're so frustrated that the need comes out as an explosion. By the time you finally say something, you're angry, your partner is blindsided, and the conversation becomes about the delivery instead of the actual issue. Don't wait until resentment has built up. Address needs when they first arise, before they turn into resentment.

You also have to accept that some needs are your responsibility to meet. Not every need can or should be met by your partner. If you need creative fulfillment, find an outlet for that. If you need deep friendships, invest in those relationships. If you need alone time, carve it out. Your partner can't be everything to you. And expecting them to be sets both of you up for failure.

But the needs that are about how you want to feel in the relationship, those are worth communicating. And if your partner consistently dismisses those needs, makes you feel guilty for having them, or refuses to engage with them, that's not a communication problem. That's a compatibility problem. And no amount of better communication will fix someone who doesn't want to meet you halfway.

When dialogue turns into rhythm, love steadies itself. It's because both people are committed to understanding each other and working together. It's because both people value the relationship more than being right. It's because both people are willing to stretch, to grow, to meet each other where they are.

Building Partnerships Based on Growth Not Codependency

Most people think love means needing each other. That the more dependent you are on someone, the stronger the bond. But dependence isn't love. It's fear. Fear that you can't be okay without them. Fear that if they leave, you'll fall apart. And that fear keeps you trapped in relationships that stop serving you, because leaving feels like losing yourself.

Codependency often wears devotion's mask. It looks like putting your partner's needs above your own. Like sacrificing your goals for theirs. Like making them the center of your world and feeling lost when they're not around. It feels like love because it's intense. But intensity isn't intimacy. And codependency isn't partnership.

Healthy love is co-created, not co-owned. Two whole people who choose to share their lives, who support each other's growth, who enhance each other without needing each other to function. Two complete lives choosing to intersect rather than overlap. You're both already complete on your own. The relationship is the bonus, not the foundation of your existence.

Codependency shows up in a lot of ways. When you can't make decisions without consulting your partner first. When you lose yourself in their problems and neglect your own life. When their mood determines your mood. When you feel responsible for their happiness and guilty when you can't fix their pain. When your identity becomes so enmeshed with theirs that you don't know who you are anymore.

It also shows up as needing constant reassurance. Constantly checking in. Constantly needing to know where they are, what they're doing, who they're with. Not because you don't trust them, but because their presence is what regulates you. You've made them your source of stability instead of cultivating your own.

In a grounded partnership, both people maintain their individuality. You have your own friends. Your own hobbies. Your own goals. Your own sense of self that exists independently of the relationship. You don't lose yourself when you're together. You bring your full self to the relationship and your partner does the same.

Growth-based partnerships are built on mutual encouragement. You want your partner to succeed, to evolve, to pursue their dreams, even if that means they're busy sometimes. Even if that means they need time away from you to focus on their goals. You're not threatened by their growth. You celebrate it. Because you're secure enough in yourself and in the relationship to know that their success doesn't diminish you.

Codependent relationships resist growth. Because growth means change. And change threatens the dynamic you've built. If one person starts setting boundaries, starts pursuing their own interests, starts prioritizing their own needs, the other person panics. They feel abandoned. They pull harder. They try to bring the person back into the old dynamic where everything revolved around keeping the relationship stable, even at the cost of individual fulfillment.

In a partnership based on growth, change is expected. You're not trying to keep each other the same. You're evolving together. Sometimes that means you grow in parallel, pursuing different interests but coming back together to share what you've learned. Sometimes it means you grow through challenges together, becoming stronger as a unit. But there's always room for both people to expand, not contract.

Another marker of healthy partnership is that you can be apart without falling apart. You miss each other, but you don't spiral. You can spend time with friends, focus on work, enjoy your own company without feeling incomplete. Your sense of security doesn't evaporate the moment your partner isn't physically present. You trust the relationship enough to function independently within it.

Codependency also creates an unhealthy dynamic around conflict. In codependent relationships, conflict feels catastrophic. Every disagreement feels like the relationship might end. So you avoid conflict at all costs. You suppress your needs. You monitor your words. You prioritize keeping the peace over being honest. And that suppression builds resentment that eventually erupts or quietly kills the relationship from the inside.

In growth-based partnerships, conflict is seen as an opportunity to understand each other better. It's not fun, but it's not catastrophic. You can disagree without the relationship being threatened. You can have hard conversations without one person shutting down or storming out. You work through things together because you're both committed to the health of the relationship, not just the comfort of avoiding discomfort.

Healthy partnerships also have clear boundaries. You don't have access to every part of each other's lives. You respect each other's privacy. You don't go through each other's phones. You don't demand to know every detail of every conversation. You trust that your partner is making choices that honor the relationship, and you give them the space to be their own person.

Codependency blurs boundaries. Everything is shared. Everything is enmeshed. You stop knowing where you end and they begin. And while that might feel romantic in theory, in practice it's suffocating. It creates a dynamic where neither person can breathe without permission from the other.

Another aspect of growth-based partnership is that both people take responsibility for their own healing. You don't expect your partner to fix your childhood wounds. You don't make them responsible for your emotional regulation. You do your own work. You go to therapy. You address your patterns. You show up as the healthiest version of yourself instead of expecting the relationship to heal you.

This doesn't mean you can't lean on your partner for support. You can. But support is different from repair. You listen to their problems, but you don't cancel your plans to fix them. You offer comfort, but you don't take on their emotions as your own. You're present without becoming responsible for their well-being. The first is partnership. The second is codependency.

Healthy partnerships also require both people to contribute. You're not carrying the relationship alone. You're not the only one planning, initiating, compromising, sacrificing. The effort is mutual. The investment is mutual. The commitment is mutual. When one person is doing all the work, that's not partnership. That's one person in a relationship and the other person along for the ride.

Finally, growth-based partnerships are rooted in choice, not need. You're not with your partner because you can't survive without them. You're with them because you choose them. Every day. Even when it's hard. Even when you're frustrated. You choose them because the relationship adds value to your life, because you respect who they are, because you want to build something together. That choice is what makes the relationship sustainable.

Codependency feels like you have no choice. Like you're stuck. Like leaving would destroy you. And that feeling of being trapped is what erodes the relationship over time. Because love that feels like a prison isn't love. It's fear dressed up as devotion.

In a safe relationship, tension leaves the room before words do. In that kind of love, expansion feels natural. You both keep becoming.

Key Takeaways

- True emotional safety means you can show your authentic self without fear of rejection, criticism, or abandonment.
- In healthy relationships, conflicts deepen trust rather than threaten the bond between you.
- Feeling safe means knowing your vulnerability won't be weaponized or dismissed, but respected and held with care.
- Real intimacy grows when you're able to reveal yourself without constantly worrying about being misunderstood or judged.
- A safe partner respects your boundaries and sees them as guidance, not as personal attacks.
- Intimacy isn't built by avoiding discomfort, but by trusting that difficult moments won't destroy your connection.
- Clearly communicating your needs invites closeness; suppressing them creates resentment and emotional distance.
- Healthy partnerships are built on mutual growth, not on sacrificing your individuality to maintain harmony.
- Safety appears when you both can admit mistakes, apologize sincerely, and work together on repairs.
- Choosing yourself first is not selfish; it's foundational to creating relationships that honor your worth.

Chapter 15:
The Sacred Feminine in Sisterhood

"We rise by lifting others." — Robert Ingersoll

Women have been taught to compete with each other. For gatekeeping access. For referral circles. For the one-token slots at tables designed to keep women divided. You've been conditioned to see other women as threats instead of allies, rivals instead of mirrors, competitors instead of collaborators. And that conditioning keeps you small, isolated, and easier to control.

The truth is that women are most powerful when they're connected. When they support each other. When they celebrate each other's wins instead of feeling diminished by them. When they share resources, wisdom, and strength instead of hoarding them out of fear that there isn't enough to go around. Sisterhood is infrastructure. Without it, growth is brittle.

But most women carry deep wounds around female friendship. Betrayals from childhood. Jealousy disguised as friendship. Women who smiled to your face and undermined you behind your back. Cliques that excluded you. Friendships that ended in ways that left scars. These experiences taught you to be cautious around women, to keep your guard up, to never fully trust that another woman has your best interests at heart.

High value women understand that those wounds were learned in environments where zero-sum thinking was the operating system. Where there was only one spot for the pretty girl, the smart girl, the successful girl. Where women were pitted against each other instead of taught to lift each other up. And they refuse to perpetuate that dynamic. They heal their competition wounds. They build genuine sisterhood. They rise together because they know that one woman's success expands what's possible for all of them.

This chapter will teach you how to heal the competition wounds you carry from other women. How to recognize when you're operating from a zero-sum script instead of collective upside in your female friendships. Why sisterhood is not just nice to have but essential for your growth, your sanity, and your power. How to build a circle of women who genuinely support you. And how to rise together through collaboration instead of trying to climb alone.

Isolation is an artifact of design, not a measure of strength. The feminine thrives in connection, in community, in circles of women who see each other clearly and choose to support each other anyway. When women stop competing and start collaborating, everything changes. Not just for you, but for every woman watching.

Healing Competition Wounds With Other Women

Almost every woman carries wounds from other women. The colleague who took credit for your idea in the meeting. The friend who excluded you from the group chat. The coworker who passed your work up the chain without mentioning your name. The woman who appropriated your pitch on a call and presented it as her own. These experiences leave marks that shape how you relate to women for the rest of your life.

The wound manifests as hypervigilance disguised as detachment, as perfectionism in public and silent comparison in private. You cancel invitations at the last minute. You scroll past other women's wins looking for the flaw. You withhold congratulations because celebrating her feels like diminishing yourself. That reflex is learned. And it can be unlearned.

It also shows up as self-protection disguised as judgment. Devaluing is an anesthetic: it works for an hour and isolates for months. When you criticize another woman's choices, her appearance, her life, what you're really doing is distancing yourself from the threat you perceive she represents. If you can find something wrong with her, she's not someone you need to compare yourself to. She's not someone who makes you question your own worth. But that judgment keeps you isolated. It keeps you from connecting with women who could actually support you.

Healing competition wounds starts with awareness. Notice when you feel threatened by another woman. Notice when you feel the impulse to compete, to compare, to criticize. Don't judge yourself for it. Just notice it. That impulse is a learned response from a system that taught you there wasn't room for all women to win. But you don't have to keep believing that story.

The next step is recognizing that the women who hurt you were operating from their own wounds. They were taught the same scarcity mindset. They were competing because they believed they had to. They were protecting themselves the only way they knew how. This doesn't excuse the harm they caused, but it helps you understand that it was never really about you. It was about their pain, their fear, their survival mechanisms.

Once you see that, you can start to release the grip those experiences have on you. You can decide that one woman's betrayal doesn't mean all women are untrustworthy. That one painful friendship doesn't define what female connection has to be. That you get to choose differently now.

Healing also requires ritual. Not abstract grief, but concrete action. Write a post-mortem of the friendship with three specific lessons you're taking forward. Return any borrowed items, books, or photos as a gesture of closure. Define a personal no-gossip clause and enforce it with yourself first. These small acts create boundaries between old patterns and new possibilities.

Another part of healing is learning to celebrate other women without feeling diminished by their success. When a woman you know achieves something significant, notice your first reaction. Is it genuine happiness? Or is it tinged with envy, with a quiet voice asking "Why her and not me?" That voice is the wound talking. And you can choose not to listen to it.

Practice celebrating women, especially women who intimidate you. Women who are further along in their journey. Women who have what you want. Instead of seeing them as competition, see them as proof that what you want is possible. Their achievement expands the perimeter of what you can reach.

You also heal by being the kind of woman you wish you had encountered earlier. Be the woman who shows up for other women without keeping score. Who celebrates their wins genuinely. Who offers support without expecting anything in return. Who creates space for other women to shine without needing to dim yourself. When you become that woman, you start attracting women who operate the same way.

Healing competition wounds also means addressing the internalized misogyny you carry. The ways you've been taught to devalue femininity, to see women as less than, to prioritize male approval over female connection. The tendency to reward male-pleasing compliance as social currency. The belief that distancing yourself from other women somehow elevates your status. All of this is learned. And all of it can be unlearned.

Start paying attention to how you speak about women, both to their faces and behind their backs. Do you use language that diminishes them? Do you engage in gossip that harms their reputation? Do you participate in conversations where women are reduced to their appearance, their relationship status, their perceived failures? If you do, stop. Refuse to participate in dynamics that tear women down. Be the one who redirects the conversation, who defends the woman who isn't there to defend herself, who chooses solidarity over complicity.

Another aspect of healing is learning to apologize when you've been the one who caused harm. If you've betrayed a friend, excluded someone, or competed in ways that hurt another woman, own it. Reach out if it's possible and appropriate. Acknowledge what you did. Apologize without making excuses. And commit to doing better. Not everyone will accept your apology, and that's okay. The point is to take responsibility for your part in perpetuating the dynamics you now want to heal.

Healing is not linear. You'll have moments where you slip back into old patterns. Where you feel competitive. Where you judge another woman harshly. When that happens, notice it. Acknowledge it. And choose again. Healing is about choosing differently more often than you used to. It's about building new patterns slowly, over time, until connection becomes more natural than competition.

The deepest healing happens when you realize that another woman's light is a route, not a spotlight to measure yourself against. That there's room for all women to be powerful, beautiful, successful, loved. That you're not in a zero-sum game with other women. You're in collaboration with them, building a world where all women can thrive. When you internalize that truth, the wounds lose their power. And sisterhood becomes possible.

Why Sisterhood Is Your Secret Weapon

Sisterhood is not about having a lot of female friends. It's about having a few women who see you, support you, and hold you accountable. Women who celebrate your growth and call you out when you're self-sabotaging. Women who remind you of your worth when you forget. Women who show up when things fall apart and don't leave when it gets messy. That kind of connection is rare, and it's powerful.

Women who try to do everything alone burn out. They carry the weight of their struggles in silence because they've been taught that asking for help is weakness. They push through exhaustion, isolation, overwhelm because they believe they have to prove they can handle it all. But that's not strength. That's survival. And survival is not the same as thriving.

Your network of close women is your multiplier. When you have a circle of women who genuinely support you, you have a safety net. They text you the morning of the interview. They pass you the contact that matters. They catch you when you fall and remind you who you are when you lose yourself. That support is not a sign of weakness. It's a source of power.

In the presence of trusted women, breathing slows and perspective widens. The stress you carry alone feels lighter when it's shared. The problems that seem insurmountable when you're isolated become manageable when you have women who can help you see solutions you couldn't see on your own. This is not theory. This is lived experience. Connection regulates. Isolation amplifies.

Sisterhood also amplifies your voice. When you have women who believe in you, who champion your ideas, who amplify your message, you reach further than you ever could alone. Women who support each other create opportunities for each other. They open doors. They make introductions. They share resources. They recommend each other for opportunities. This is how women rise. Not by climbing over each other, but by lifting each other up.

Another reason sisterhood is powerful is that women who are connected stop settling for less. When you're surrounded by women who know their worth, who hold high standards, who refuse to tolerate disrespect, you start holding yourself to the same standard. You stop accepting treatment that diminishes you because you see other women refusing to accept it. You raise your expectations because you're in an environment where high standards are normal, not exceptional.

Sisterhood also protects you from gaslighting. When you're in a situation where someone is trying to make you doubt your own reality, having women who can validate your experience is critical. Create pacts for reality-checking.

Before responding to a manipulative message, share the screenshot with your circle. Get their read. Let them reflect back what they see. That external validation helps you trust yourself when you're being told not to. It helps you hold your ground when you're being pressured to back down.

Women in sisterhood also hold each other accountable. Real friends don't just support your dreams. They call you out when you're not living up to them. They notice when you're making excuses, when you're playing small, when you're settling for less than you deserve. And they tell you. Not to criticize, but because they believe in you too much to let you waste your potential. Rotate facilitation of difficult conversations. Share that responsibility. That kind of accountability is priceless.

Sisterhood is also where you learn to receive. Many women are excellent at giving, at supporting others, at showing up for everyone else. But they struggle to let others do the same for them. They can't receive help without feeling guilty. They can't accept compliments without deflecting. They can't let someone care for them without feeling like they owe something in return. Sisterhood teaches you that receiving is just as important as giving. That it's not weak to need support. That letting someone help you is not a burden. It's a gift you give them by trusting them with your vulnerability.

Another aspect of sisterhood is that it creates a space where you can be fully yourself. You don't have to perform. You don't have to be impressive. You don't have to have it all together. You can show up messy, confused, struggling, and still be loved. That kind of unconditional acceptance is healing. It allows you to drop the masks you wear in other areas of your life and just be human.

Sisterhood also reminds you that you're not alone in your struggles. When you hear other women share their fears, their failures, their dark moments, you realize that the things you thought made you uniquely flawed are actually part of the shared human experience. That realization is liberating. It releases the shame you've been carrying in isolation and replaces it with connection.

Women in sisterhood also model what's possible. When you see a woman in your circle do something you thought was impossible, it expands your sense of what you can do. When you watch her navigate a challenge you're facing, you learn strategies you wouldn't have thought of on your own. When you witness her success, you see a path you can follow. Sisterhood is not just emotional support. It's practical wisdom shared between women who are committed to each other's growth.

Build mechanics into your circle. A monthly resource swap hour. A referral chain where you track who connected whom. A shared win log where everyone posts their achievements. These structures keep sisterhood active, not abstract.

Finally, sisterhood creates legacy. When women support each other, they're not just changing their own lives. They're changing the lives of the women who come after them. They're modeling a different way of relating to other women. They're breaking cycles of competition and creating new patterns of collaboration. They're showing the next generation of women that they don't have to fight each other for scraps. They can build tables together where everyone has a seat.

Your strength grows through rebound, not through isolation.

Building Your Soul Tribe of Empowered Women

Not every woman you meet will be part of your inner circle. And that's okay. You're not looking for a large network of surface-level friendships. You're looking for a small cohort of women who genuinely see you, who share your values, who are committed to growth, and who will show up when it matters. A few deeply maintained relationships outperform vast, noisy networks.

Your circle is made up of women who are on a similar path. Not identical, but aligned. Women who are doing their own work. Who are healing their wounds. Who are building lives they're proud of. Who are committed to living with integrity. Deep fellowship requires reciprocal responsibility. Where that's absent, connection stays surface-level.

Start by getting clear on what you need in friendship. What kind of support are you looking for? Do you need women who will challenge you intellectually? Women who will hold space for your emotions? Women who will help you strategize and problem-solve? Women who will celebrate your wins and mourn your losses? Different friendships serve different purposes, and that's fine. But be clear about what you're building so you can recognize it when you find it.

Pay attention to how you feel in a woman's presence. Do you feel lighter or heavier? Do you feel inspired or depleted? Do you feel like you can be yourself or like you have to perform? Do you leave the conversation feeling energized or drained? Your body will tell you whether a friendship is nourishing or not. Trust that information.

Test slowly. Use situational heuristics, not declarations of intent. Here are ways to assess without announcing:

Trust deposits: Ask for a small practical exchange with a near deadline and observe punctuality and care.

Joy thermometer: Share a minor success and measure the quality of her response within twenty-four hours.

Light stress test: Propose a mutual favor at low cost. Notice if balance emerges or if there are infinite delays.

Availability thresholds: Offer an invitation with a clear window. Observe whether she respects your time.

Your circle will include women who are genuinely happy for your success. Women who don't feel threatened when you grow. Women who cheer you on without secretly hoping you'll fail so they don't have to confront their own stagnation. If you share good news and a woman's response feels flat, forced, or quickly redirected back to her, pay attention. Real friends celebrate your wins as if they're their own.

Another marker of circle women is reciprocity. The friendship flows both ways. You're not always the one reaching out, making plans, offering support. She shows up for you the way you show up for her. There's balance. There's mutual investment. If you find yourself doing all the emotional labor in a friendship, that's not inner circle. That's a one-sided dynamic that will exhaust you over time.

Circle women also respect your boundaries. They don't guilt you for saying no. They don't pressure you to show up in ways that don't feel good. They understand that your time, your energy, your capacity are limited, and they honor that. They trust that your boundaries aren't rejection. They're self-care. And they want you to take care of yourself.

Look for women who are secure in themselves. Women who don't need constant reassurance. Women who aren't looking for you to fix them or save them. Women who take responsibility for their own healing and growth.

Secure women make better friends because they're not using the friendship to fill voids that only they can fill. They're coming to the friendship whole, looking to share, not to take.

Another quality to look for is honesty. Circle women will tell you the truth even when it's uncomfortable. They'll let you know when you're making excuses. They'll call out patterns they see you repeating. They'll challenge you when you're playing small. And they'll do it with love, not judgment. They're not afraid of conflict if it means helping you grow. They value your potential more than your comfort.

Your circle will also include women at different stages of life and different areas of expertise. Some will be ahead of you in career. Some will understand legal structures. Some will know financial planning. Some will be versed in mental health. Some will bring creative vision. This diversity of competence strengthens the circle. Everyone has something to offer. Everyone has something to learn.

You build your circle slowly. You don't force it. You meet women in spaces where like-minded people gather. Book clubs. Workshops. Fitness classes. Volunteer work. Online communities centered around shared interests or values. You show up consistently in these spaces. You start conversations. You take small risks by being authentic. You see who responds to that authenticity with their own.

When you meet a woman you connect with, invest in the friendship. Make plans. Follow up. Be consistent. Don't wait for her to do all the initiating. Show her that you value the connection. Friendships, like any relationship, require effort. If you want deep sisterhood, you have to be willing to invest in building it.

Your circle will also include women who respect your other commitments. Women who understand that you have a partner, a family, a career, other friendships. They don't expect you to prioritize them above everything else. They understand that healthy friendships exist within the context of a full life, not as a replacement for one.

Another important aspect of your circle is shared values. You don't have to agree on everything, but you need to be aligned on the core things that matter to you. Integrity. Growth. Respect. Kindness. Accountability. If your values are fundamentally misaligned, the friendship won't sustain itself. You'll constantly be navigating differences that create friction instead of flow.

Circle women also give you space to evolve. They don't hold you to who you used to be. They don't make you feel guilty for outgrowing old patterns or leaving behind dynamics that no longer serve you. They celebrate your evolution. They grow with you. And if there comes a time when you grow in different directions, they release you with love instead of resentment.

Finally, you recognize your circle in the mutual gaze, even when you disagree. Not in the sense that it's always comfortable, but in the sense that it's safe. You can show up as you are. You can be seen in your fullness. You can be vulnerable without fear of judgment. You can be powerful without being dimmed. You can be human without being rejected.

Rising Together in Collaboration Not Isolation

No one arrives alone. The map has been drawn by many hands. Behind every woman who has achieved something significant, there are other women who supported her, guided her, opened doors for her, believed in her when she didn't believe in herself. Success is not a solo journey. It's a collective effort.

But many women have been conditioned to compete rather than collaborate. They see other women in their field as threats instead of potential partners. They hoard resources, connections, knowledge because they believe that sharing diminishes their advantage. They operate from resource hoarding, convinced that there's only room for one woman to succeed, so it better be them. This mindset keeps everyone small.

Collaboration begins with rejecting that zero-sum reflex. Recognizing that another woman's success doesn't limit yours. That there's room for all women to thrive. When one opens a door, the hinge turns for all of them. Her success expands what's possible for everyone. It doesn't diminish the opportunities available to you. It increases them.

When women collaborate, they multiply their impact. Two women working together can achieve more than two women working separately. Not just because there are two sets of hands, but because collaboration creates synergy. Different perspectives. Different strengths. Different networks. When you combine those, you create something neither of you could have created alone.

Here are two examples of collaboration in practice:

Case A: Two consultants co-pitch a project to a client, split the fee equally, and each bring their unique expertise. The client gets better service. Both women get paid. The collaboration creates a model they can repeat.

Case B: A circle of five women creates a rotating micro-grant fund. Each contributes a small amount monthly. Every quarter, one woman receives the pooled amount to invest in her business, education, or project. The fund cycles through all five over time.

Collaboration also means celebrating other women publicly. Promoting their work. Recommending them for opportunities. Sharing their content. Introducing them to people who can help them. Amplifying their voices. When you do this, you're not diminishing yourself. You're demonstrating that you're secure enough in your own value to shine a light on someone else. That confidence is magnetic. It attracts more opportunities to you, not fewer.

Another form of collaboration is mentorship. If you're further along in your journey, reach back and pull someone forward. Share what you've learned. Offer guidance. Open doors. Be the woman you wish you had when you were starting out. And if you're earlier in your journey, seek out women who are where you want to be. Ask questions. Learn from their experience. Let them invest in you. Mentorship creates a chain of support that lifts entire communities of women.

Collaboration also happens through co-creation. Partnering with other women on projects, businesses, creative endeavors. Combining your skills and resources to build something together. This requires trust, clear communication, and shared vision. But when it works, it's powerful. You're not just building something together. You're modeling a different way of working. You're showing that women don't have to compete for limited resources. They can create abundance together.

Establish clear protocols before you begin:

Credit protocol: Decide how you'll name contributions publicly before starting any shared project.

Amplification calendar: Each woman takes a monthly turn to boost another's work with a specific call to action.

Anti-gossip charter: A group agreement on what stays private and how to interrupt harmful conversations.

Reciprocity index: For every request for help, one reciprocal action within thirty days.

Women who collaborate also share resources. If you learn something valuable, share it. If you find a tool that helps you, tell other women about it. If you have access to opportunities, information, or connections, pass them along. Hoarding resources doesn't make you more successful. It just keeps everyone at the same level. Sharing resources raises the entire community.

Another key to collaboration is honoring different approaches. Not every woman will do things the way you do them. Not every woman will have the same priorities, the same strategies, the same goals. That's okay. You don't have to agree with every choice another woman makes to support her. You just have to respect her right to make her own choices and live her own life.

Collaboration also means showing up for other women's launches, events, celebrations. Being present. Offering genuine support. Not because you want something in return, but because rising together means you celebrate each other's milestones. You show up when it matters. You let her know she's not alone in her efforts.

Women who collaborate also practice accountability. They hold each other to high standards. They don't let each other make excuses or play small. They challenge each other to keep growing. But they do it with love. They're not tearing each other down. They're pushing each other toward their potential. That kind of accountability is a gift.

Another aspect of collaboration is being willing to ask for help. Many women struggle with this because they've been taught that needing help is weakness. But asking for help is how collaboration begins. It's how you let other women know what you need. It's how you create opportunities for them to contribute. When you ask for help, you're not being a burden. You're inviting someone into partnership with you.

Collaboration also means being generous with your praise. Compliment other women. Acknowledge their hard work. Recognize their achievements. Tell them specifically what you admire about them. Women are starved for genuine recognition from other women. Be the one who gives it freely. That generosity creates a culture where all women feel valued.

Women who rise together also protect each other. They defend other women when they're not in the room. They refuse to participate in gossip or character assassination. They speak up when they see another woman being treated unfairly. They use whatever power or platform they have to make space for women who don't have the same access. That protection creates safety for all women to take risks and be visible.

Finally, collaboration means understanding that your success is tied to other women's success. When women are thriving collectively, doors open for all of you. When women are divided and competing, everyone suffers. When one creates a path, the others find less friction.

Collaboration requires vulnerability. It requires trust. It requires releasing the belief that you have to do everything alone. It requires being willing to share credit, to lift others up, to celebrate wins that aren't your own. But when you do that, you become part of something bigger than yourself. You become part of a movement of women who are rewriting the rules, creating new systems, building a world where all women can thrive.

Count how many you bring with you, not how many follow you.

Key Takeaways

- True sisterhood replaces competition with genuine support, knowing that one woman's success expands possibilities for all.
- • Healing from competition wounds with other women begins by recognizing scarcity thinking and replacing it with collaboration.
- • Sisterhood provides the strength of community, helping you grow further than you ever could alone.
- • Instead of seeing other women as threats, view them as mirrors, mentors, and allies whose growth enhances your own.
- • High-value women understand that sharing resources, connections, and knowledge doesn't diminish their power—it multiplies it.
- • Real friendships among women involve mutual respect, honest accountability, and a willingness to show up authentically.

- • Sisterhood protects you from isolation, allowing you to thrive by being fully seen, supported, and celebrated.
- • Women who collaborate rather than compete create a collective strength that is far greater than individual achievement.
- • Building a supportive circle of women around you is an intentional choice to surround yourself with those who celebrate your growth, not those who undermine it.
- • Your power multiplies when you actively lift other women up; genuine sisterhood is the foundation of lasting empowerment.

Step 5:
THRIVING - Manifesting and Creating Your Reality

The wounds have been healed. The confidence has been built. Relating to yourself and others from wholeness instead of woundedness has been learned.

Now it's time to ask the question that matters most: What do you actually want?

Not what you think you should want. Not what would make your family proud or your friends impressed. Not the safe, small version of dreams that fear has talked you into because the big ones feel too scary, too selfish, too far out of reach.

What do you want?

Most women can't answer that question. Not because desires don't exist, but because managing other people's needs, proving worth through productivity, and keeping small to stay safe has completely severed the connection to what lights them up.

And when they do let themselves want something, really want it, sabotage happens before it even has a chance to materialize. Through patterns so deeply ingrained that they feel like truth: I'm not ready yet. I'm not good enough yet. People like me don't get things like that.

Abundance isn't something to chase or earn or work yourself into the ground trying to deserve. It's your natural state. The only reason it's not present is because somewhere along the line, blocking it got learned.

These final three chapters are about stepping into the version of yourself who doesn't just survive, but thrives. Who builds a life so aligned with truth that success doesn't feel like a constant uphill battle. Who understands that receiving isn't selfish, that rest isn't lazy, and that joy isn't something to earn through suffering first.

The work has been done. Now it's time to claim the life that work has earned.

Chapter 16:
Abundance Is Your Natural State

"Abundance is not something we acquire. It is something we tune into." — Wayne Dyer

Most women live in a state of perpetual lack. Not because resources aren't available, but because they've been conditioned to believe that wanting more is selfish, that having enough is greedy, that receiving without earning is undeserved. You've been taught to shrink your desires, to apologize for your needs, to make yourself small so others feel comfortable. And that conditioning keeps you trapped in cycles that have nothing to do with what's actually possible and everything to do with what you've been taught to accept.

Abundance is operating from the certainty that there's enough: love, money, opportunity, recognition. It's the opposite of the logic where one person's gain means another's loss, the mindset that keeps women competing, hoarding, and living in fear that if they take up space, someone else will lose theirs.

But most women don't believe in this. They've seen too many examples of gatekeeping and invisible quotas. They've watched opportunities be distributed unevenly. They've experienced what it's like to go without. They've been disappointed too many times to trust that good things will keep coming. So they grip tightly to what they have, push away what they want, and stay stuck in patterns that confirm their belief that there isn't enough.

Women rooted in their own worth know that abundance is not something you chase. It's something you embody. It's a state of being that starts with how you see yourself and what you believe you deserve. When you operate from this place, you stop blocking your own opportunities. You stop sabotaging what shows up because you don't think you're worthy. You stop rejecting love, money, and success because you've been taught that wanting these things makes you shallow or selfish.

This chapter will teach you why you block your own opportunities and how to stop. How to release the programming that keeps you small and step into the overflow that's always been available to you. How to receive without guilt, without feeling like you owe something in return, without diminishing yourself to make others comfortable. And how to understand that money, love, and success are not rewards for being good enough. They're reflections of the worth you already carry.

You were not born to live in lack. Abundance is native to you. Remember it.

Why You Block Your Own Blessings

You say you want more, but every time an opportunity shows up, you find a reason it's not right. You say you're ready for love, but when someone treats you well, you pull away because it feels too easy. You say you want financial security, but when money comes in, you immediately find ways to give it away or spend it on things that don't serve you. This isn't bad luck. This is you pulling the emergency brake one meter from the finish line. And it's rooted in beliefs you don't even know you're carrying.

The first way you block your own opportunities is by believing you don't deserve them. Somewhere along the way, you internalized the message that you have to earn good things through suffering. That struggle is proof of worthiness. That if something comes easily, it can't be valuable. So when support shows up without the struggle, you reject it. You tell yourself it's provisional and prepare for the backlash. You create problems where there aren't any just to confirm your belief that nothing good lasts.

This belief often comes from childhood. If you grew up watching your parents struggle, you learned that life is hard. If you were praised for being selfless and criticized for having needs, you learned that wanting things for yourself is bad. If you saw love being withheld as punishment, you learned that good things are conditional. These lessons didn't come with words. They came through observation. And now they run in the background of your life, blocking every opportunity that doesn't fit the narrative you were taught.

Another way you block yourself is through guilt. You feel guilty for having when others don't. You feel guilty for succeeding when people you love are struggling. You feel guilty for being happy when the world is full of pain. So you dim your light. You downplay your wins. You reject opportunities because accepting them feels like betraying the people who didn't get the same chances. But your dimming doesn't help anyone. It just keeps everyone in the dark.

Guilt is often tied to loyalty. You think that staying small keeps you connected to the people you came from. That if you rise, you'll lose them. That success will create distance between you and the people who knew you before you had anything. Sometimes that fear is valid. Some people will resent your growth. Some people will try to pull you back down. But staying small to keep them comfortable is not loyalty. It's self-abandonment. And it doesn't serve anyone.

Here's what it looks like in practice. You refuse a raise because accepting it would mean earning more than your partner. You reimburse a client beyond what's owed because you don't want to create an enemy. You don't publish a result because you worry it will irritate your team. These aren't acts of humility. They're acts of self-rejection disguised as consideration.

You also block yourself by refusing to receive. Someone offers to help you, and you say "I'm fine." Someone compliments you, and you deflect. Someone wants to give you something, and you immediately think about how you can repay them. You've been taught that receiving makes you indebted, that accepting help makes you weak, that letting someone give to you without giving back means you're taking advantage. So you push away every offering, every kindness, every opportunity that requires you to simply receive.

But receiving is not taking. Receiving is allowing. It's trusting that you're worthy of support, of love, of generosity without having to earn it first. It's understanding that when you refuse to receive, you're not being humble. You're blocking the flow. You're communicating that there isn't space, and the systems around you respond to that posture. You end up not seeing what's actually there.

Try this: For one week, accept any help or compliment with only "thank you." No counter-gift. No explanations. If you feel the urgent need to balance the ledger, that's loyalty to debt talking. Notice it. Don't act on it.

Another way you block yourself is through comparison. You look at what other people have and decide that if they have it, there isn't enough left for you. You see someone else's success and feel like it's proof that you're behind, that you're not doing enough, that your time has passed. So instead of celebrating their win and staying open to your own, you close down. You tell yourself it's not fair. You resent them for having what you want. And that resentment creates a barrier between you and the provision you're seeking.

Comparison also makes you question your own desires. You see what other people value and start wanting those things even if they don't align with what you actually need. You chase external markers of success because you think they'll make you feel worthy. But chasing someone else's version of fullness will never satisfy you. You'll get the thing and realize it doesn't fill the void because it was never your thing to begin with.

You also block yourself through fear. Fear that if you get what you want, you'll lose it. Fear that if you're happy, something bad will happen to balance it out. Fear that if you succeed, people will expect more from you than you can give. Fear that if you have plenty, you'll become the kind of person you've been taught to judge. So you stay safe in shortage. You keep yourself just below the level of success that would require you to change, to grow, to step into a version of yourself you're not sure you're ready to be.

Fear also shows up as perfectionism. You tell yourself you'll pursue the opportunity when you're more prepared. You'll accept love when you're healed. You'll ask for the raise when you've proven yourself beyond doubt. But that day never comes. You raise the bar every time you're about to clear it. There's always one more thing you need to fix, one more qualification you need to earn, one more way you're not ready. And it keeps you stuck in waiting instead of living.

Another way you block yourself is by staying loyal to old identities. You've spent years being the struggling one, the responsible one, the one who doesn't ask for much. That identity feels safe. It's familiar. People know how to relate to you when you're in that role. But if you step into fullness, you have to let go of that identity. You have to become someone new. And that feels like a loss even when it's growth. So you sabotage yourself to stay who you've always been instead of becoming who you're meant to be.

Try this: List three identity roles you repeat. "The one who fixes everything." "The one who never complains." "The one who stays small." Then cut one action that's consistent with that role in the next week. Notice what happens when you don't perform it.

Finally, you block yourself by not asking. You wait to be chosen. You wait to be noticed. You wait for someone to offer instead of stating what you need. You think that if you have to ask, it doesn't count. That real support should come without effort. But clarity draws response. Intention creates movement.

Women who know what they want and aren't afraid to name it create the conditions for receiving. When you don't ask, you're not being humble. You're hiding. And what's hidden can't be given.

Before every important conversation, write one concrete request of value. "Can we revisit the fee?" If you don't speak it, write down why. The pattern is there.

Try this barrier test: Before an important call, write the exact phrase you'll use to say yes to an advantageous proposal. If during the call you avoid it or postpone it, note the thought that made you deviate. That's your shortage script talking.

Stop blocking your own opportunities. Start noticing the ways you reject, deflect, postpone, or dismantle good things when they show up. Start asking yourself what you're afraid will happen if you actually let yourself have what you want. And then choose differently. Because the only thing standing between you and the overflow you desire is the belief that you're not allowed to have it.

Releasing Scarcity and Embracing Overflow

Scarcity is a learned belief. You weren't born thinking there isn't enough. You were taught it. Through messages about money being tight. Through watching adults stress about bills. Through being told no more often than yes. Through environments where resources were limited and competition was necessary. Through cultures that value sacrifice over pleasure, shortage over plenty, struggle over ease. All of that taught you to expect less, to settle for less, to believe that wanting more is unrealistic or wrong.

Releasing scarcity starts with recognizing it. Notice when you operate from lack. When you hoard instead of share. When you panic at the thought of spending money even when you have it. When you stay in situations that drain you because you're afraid nothing better exists. When you reject opportunities because you don't believe you're worthy of them. These are signs of design oriented toward lack. And they keep you trapped in cycles that confirm the very shortage you fear.

Scarcity also shows up in how you relate to time. You say you don't have enough time. You rush through your days. You overcommit because you're afraid of missing out. You sacrifice rest because you think productivity is the only way to prove your value. But time scarcity is often a symptom of misaligned priorities.

Try this: Audit your week using three categories. Earning time. Nourishing time. Empty space. If empty space is less than ten percent, you're in time scarcity by definition. Not because you're busy, but because you've designed a life with no room to breathe.

Another way scarcity shows up is in your relationships. You tolerate poor treatment because you think this is the best you can get. You stay in friendships that drain you because you're afraid of being alone. You settle for partners who don't meet your needs because you don't believe someone better will come along. Scarcity in relationships makes you cling to people who aren't right for you out of fear that no one else will want you. That fear keeps you small and keeps you stuck.

Apply a no-limbo rule. Every uncertain connection requires a concrete request with a deadline. If there's no response, close it. This protects your capacity for connections that reciprocate.

Releasing scarcity requires shifting your focus from what's missing to what's present. Not as toxic positivity that ignores real problems. But as a practice of noticing what's already working. What you already have. What's already sufficient in your life. When you train your brain to see enough instead of lack, you start attracting more of it. Not because the universe magically provides, but because you stop filtering out the good things that are already there.

Start a daily practice of noticing sufficiency. Not just material things, but the full spectrum of wealth in your life. The people who love you. The skills you've developed. The body that carries you. The home that shelters you. The food that nourishes you. The opportunities that have shown up. The challenges you've survived. All of this is wealth. And when you acknowledge it, you create space for more.

Releasing scarcity also means releasing the belief that you have to struggle to deserve good things. You've been taught that ease equals laziness. That if something comes easily, it's not valuable. That suffering is noble and pleasure is indulgent. These beliefs keep you grinding, overworking, sacrificing your well-being to prove you're worthy. But worthiness is not earned through pain. It's inherent. You're worthy because you exist. And the sooner you believe that, the sooner you stop creating unnecessary struggle.

Embracing overflow means allowing things to be easy. When a path is clear, take it. Don't construct obstacles to feel legitimized. When someone offers help, accept it. When money comes in, receive it without immediately looking for the catch. When love feels good, trust it. You don't have to make everything hard to prove it's real. Sometimes the best things in life come easily. And your job is to let them.

Overflow also requires trust. Trust that if you spend money, more will come. Trust that if you give love, you won't run out. Trust that if you share your knowledge, it won't diminish your value. Trust that there's enough for you and for everyone else. This doesn't mean being reckless. It means operating from confidence instead of fear. It means making decisions based on possibility instead of shortage.

Identify your spend triggers. List three situations that make you spend against your values. Late-night scrolling. Stress after difficult calls. Comparison after social media. Then create wealth alternatives. A walk. A call to an ally. A playlist. This redirects the impulse before it drains you.

Another aspect of embracing overflow is generosity. Give without expecting anything in return. Tip well. Share resources. Support other people's work. Celebrate other people's wins. When you give freely, you signal to yourself that you trust there's more where that came from. And that trust creates the energetic space for more to flow in. Establish a circulation threshold. Five to ten percent of your time, money, or contacts automatically enters the shared commons.

Every month, circulate one key contact, one template, and one introduction. Mark the date and track the pattern. Measurement is the antidote to "me first" thinking.

Embracing overflow also means raising your standards. Stop settling for less than you want because you're afraid to ask for more. Stop accepting mediocre treatment because you think that's all you deserve. Stop de-pricing your work, your expectations, your needs to make other people comfortable. Overflow is available, but you have to believe you're worthy of it. And belief shows up in the standards you hold.

Turn standards into protocols, not abstract values. Set a pricing floor for new work. Require minimum advance notice for appointments. Write your yes-and-no conditions before the decision arrives. This removes the emotional negotiation in the moment.

Another way to embrace overflow is to practice receiving. Let someone buy you dinner without immediately offering to pay next time. Accept a compliment without deflecting. Let someone help you without feeling guilty. Say thank you instead of I'm sorry. Receiving is a skill. And the more you practice it, the more natural it becomes. The more you receive, the more you signal that you're open to plenty. And the more plenty flows your way.

Overflow also requires letting go of what's no longer serving you. The job that drains you. The relationship that depletes you. The habits that keep you small. The beliefs that limit you. You can't embrace overflow while gripping tightly to lack. You have to release what's not working to create space for what will. And that release often feels scary because letting go means trusting that something better is coming. But almost always, there's a better substitute if you free the space.

Finally, embracing overflow means redefining what sufficiency looks like for you. Not chasing someone else's version of success. Not accumulating things you don't need to prove you've made it. But building a life that feels full. A life where you have enough time for rest. Enough love to feel supported. Enough money to feel secure. Enough space to breathe. Enough joy to feel alive. That's overflow. And it's available to you right now. Not someday when you've earned it. Now. Because you already have.

The Art of Receiving Without Guilt

Receiving is one of the hardest things for women to do. You've been trained to give, to serve, to prioritize everyone else's needs above your own. You've been praised for being selfless and shamed for being selfish. You've learned that your value comes from how much you do for others, not from who you are. So when someone tries to give to you, your first instinct is to refuse. To deflect. To minimize. To find a way to give back immediately so you don't feel indebted.

But this refusal to receive keeps you stuck in shortage. When you can't receive, you can't be filled. You can't build reserves. You can't accumulate the resources, the love, the support you need to thrive. You stay in a constant state of output with no input. And eventually, you burn out. Not because you gave too much, but because you refused to receive enough.

Receiving without guilt starts with understanding that receiving is not taking. Taking is forceful. It's extracting something from someone who doesn't want to give it. Receiving is allowing. It's accepting what's freely offered. It's trusting that the person giving to you wants to, that it brings them joy, that it's not a burden. When you refuse to receive, you're not protecting them. You're rejecting their generosity. And that rejection creates distance.

The guilt you feel when receiving often comes from the belief that you have to earn everything. That nothing should be given freely. That if you didn't work for it, you don't deserve it. But love, support, kindness, generosity, these aren't things you earn. They're things people choose to give because they care about you. Your job is not to earn them. Your job is to receive them with grace.

Another source of guilt is the belief that receiving creates debt. That if someone gives to you, you owe them. That accepting help means you're obligated to return the favor in equal measure. But a bond is a resonance chamber, not a spreadsheet. Sometimes you give more. Sometimes you receive more. It balances out, but not in a ledger. In a living, breathing dynamic where both people contribute what they can when they can.

Practice receiving in three levels:

Words: Accept compliments without refuting them. Close with "Thanks for seeing that."

Time and service: When someone offers practical help, respond with "Yes, that would help. Thursday works." No apology. No counter-offer of equal labor.

Compensation and money: When someone proposes a rate higher than expected, don't counter-offer downward in the first twenty-four hours. Let it sit. Let yourself hold it.

When they propose a project advance, accept it and immediately allocate thirty percent to tools or freed time. Don't convert it into a discount.

Receiving without guilt also means allowing yourself to be supported. When you're going through something hard, let people help. Don't pretend you're fine when you're not. Don't isolate yourself because you don't want to be a burden. Let people show up for you. Let them bring you meals. Let them watch your kids. Let them sit with you while you cry. That's not weakness. That's trust. And trust deepens relationships in ways that independence never can.

Another aspect of receiving is accepting provision when it shows up. When you get a raise, receive it without immediately thinking about all the ways you still don't have enough. When someone loves you well, receive it without waiting for them to disappoint you. When an opportunity comes your way, receive it without questioning whether you deserve it. Just take it. Say yes. Trust that it's yours because it showed up for you.

Receiving also requires releasing the need to be the strong one all the time. The one who has it together. The one who doesn't need help. The one who can handle everything alone. That identity might feel safe, but it's lonely. It keeps people at arm's length. It shuts down closeness. Because closeness requires vulnerability. And vulnerability requires admitting you need things. That you can't do it all. That you want support. That you're human.

One of the blocks to receiving is the fear that if you let yourself have what you want, it will be taken away. So you don't let yourself fully enjoy it. You don't let yourself relax into it. You keep one foot out the door, ready to leave before you're left. But that self-protection keeps you from ever fully experiencing the provision. You're so busy guarding against loss that you never fully receive what's being given.

Another block is the belief that you'll be judged for having. That people will think you're spoiled, entitled, or ungrateful if you accept too much. So you perform humility. You downplay your wins. You reject gifts. You make yourself smaller so others feel comfortable. But that performance doesn't serve you. It just keeps you stuck in a version of yourself that's more concerned with other people's comfort than your own fulfillment.

When you refuse to receive, you also make worse decisions. Receiving is maintenance that preserves clarity and margin. You operate on a low battery. Your discernment weakens. Your patience thins. Your creativity dulls. Receiving isn't indulgence. It's how you stay sharp enough to contribute meaningfully.

Receiving also means letting yourself want things. Declaring a desire is not a demand. It's a specification. Not apologizing for your desires. Not pretending you don't care. Not acting like you're above material things or romantic love or success. You're allowed to want. You're allowed to have preferences. You're allowed to go after what lights you up. Wanting is not shallow. It's human. And when you own your wants without guilt, you give yourself permission to receive them.

Practice speaking your desires out loud. Tell people what you want. Not in a demanding way, but in an honest way. "I want to travel more." "I want a partner who values me." "I want financial security." "I want to feel appreciated." When you name what you want, you create the possibility for it to be given. When you hide your wants, you guarantee they won't be met.

Finally, receiving without guilt means trusting that you're worthy of good things simply because you exist. Not because you worked hard. Not because you sacrificed. Not because you earned it. But because you're here. And being here is enough. You don't have to prove your worthiness. You don't have to justify your existence. You're allowed to receive love, money, success, joy, rest, support, kindness, and every other good thing without feeling like you owe the world an explanation. That's the art of receiving. And it starts with believing you deserve it.

Money, Love and Success as Reflections of Worth

Most women have a complicated relationship with wanting. They want money but feel guilty for caring about it. They want love but feel ashamed for needing it. They want success but worry it makes them selfish. This internal conflict keeps them stuck in patterns where they sabotage the very things they desire because they haven't reconciled the belief that wanting these things is wrong.

But money, love, and success are not superficial desires. They're reflections of worth. When you believe you're worthy, you allow yourself to have financial security. You allow yourself to be loved well. You allow yourself to succeed without diminishing it. And when you don't believe you're worthy, you block all of it. You settle for less. You tolerate poor treatment. You stay small. Not because you're not capable, but because you don't believe you deserve more.

Money is one of the most loaded topics for women. You've been taught that caring about money makes you materialistic. That wanting financial security means you're shallow. That good women don't prioritize wealth. So you undercharge for your work. You don't negotiate. You give your time and energy away for free. You let others profit from your labor while you struggle. And you tell yourself that's noble. But it's not. It's self-betrayal.

Money is infrastructure and options. It provides security, freedom, choices. It funds margin: a cash reserve of six months, targeted training, unbillable time to build pipeline. It allows you to take care of yourself and the people you love. It gives you the ability to make decisions based on what you want, not just what you can afford. And when you reject money because you think it's virtuous to struggle, you're not being humble. You're staying stuck. You're limiting your ability to show up fully in the world. You're making yourself dependent on others instead of building your own foundation.

Your relationship with money reflects your relationship with yourself. If you don't value your time, you won't charge appropriately for it. If you don't believe you're worth investing in, you won't spend money on things that support your growth. If you think you have to earn every dollar through suffering, you'll create a life of struggle even when easier paths are available. But when you know your worth, you price based on the outcome you deliver, not the hours you spend. You invest in yourself. You make financial decisions from confidence instead of fear.

Love is another area where worth shows up. Women who don't believe they're worthy of love settle for relationships that don't meet their needs. They tolerate disrespect because they think that's all they deserve. They stay with partners who don't value them because they're afraid no one else will want them. They convince themselves that love is supposed to be hard, that sacrifice is proof of devotion, that if they just give more, the other person will finally see their value.

But a bond that asks you to reduce yourself reduces the bond too. Love is not supposed to require you to abandon yourself. Love is not supposed to feel like you're constantly proving you're enough. When you know your worth, you don't settle for relationships that diminish you. You don't tolerate poor treatment. You don't stay where you're not valued. You walk away from situations that require you to shrink, and you wait for someone who sees you clearly and loves you fully. Not someday when you've fixed all your flaws. Now. As you are.

Your relationship with love reflects how you feel about yourself. If you don't love yourself, you won't trust that anyone else can. If you don't think you're valuable, you'll stay with people who confirm that belief. If you think you have to earn love through service, sacrifice, or perfection, you'll never feel secure in any relationship. But when you know your worth, you stop accepting minimum entry points disguised as care. You stop begging for bare minimum. You start expecting love that feels good. And you refuse anything less.

After ninety days, list three moments when you expanded because of the relationship. If you can't find concrete examples, there's an issue of worth or direction.

Success is the third area where worth plays out. Women who don't believe they deserve success sabotage themselves. They don't apply for the promotion. They don't launch the business. They don't share their work publicly. They stay in roles where they're underutilized because stepping into their power feels dangerous. They tell themselves they're not ready, not qualified, not experienced enough. But readiness is not the issue. Worthiness is.

The sequence that works: sense of value, then aligned choice, then measurable performance. Not the reverse. Success is not a reward for being good enough. It's a natural result of believing you deserve to be seen, valued, and compensated for your contributions. When you know your worth, you stop waiting for permission. You stop downplaying your abilities. You stop making yourself small to avoid threatening others. You own your talent, your intelligence, your skills. And you pursue opportunities that match your value.

Build visibility infrastructure. A calendar with twelve annual public outputs. A quarterly win dossier for compensation negotiations. Three documented attempts per hypothesis, then iterate the message or the offer. This removes the emotional volatility from being seen.

Your relationship with success reflects how much space you believe you're allowed to take up. If you think visibility is dangerous, you'll hide. If you think ambition is unfeminine, you'll stay small. If you think successful women are threatening, you'll sabotage yourself to stay safe. But when you know your worth, you stop apologizing for your ambition. You stop pretending you don't want recognition. You stop shrinking to make others comfortable. You claim your space. And you let your success be visible.

All three of these areas, money, love, and success, are interconnected. When you heal your relationship with one, the others shift too. Because at the core, they're all about the same thing. Worth. Do you believe you deserve to be financially secure? Do you believe you deserve to be loved well? Do you believe you deserve to succeed? If the answer to any of those questions is no, you'll keep creating patterns that confirm that belief. But if the answer is yes, everything changes.

Choose three decisions aligned with your worth in the next four weeks. One financial. One relational. One around visibility. Verification date in thirty days: write the outcome of each decision in one paragraph. Let the evidence confirm the rest.

Key Takeaways

- Abundance isn't something you earn through struggle; it's your natural state when you stop believing you must suffer first.
- • You block your blessings by believing you must earn good things through sacrifice instead of simply receiving them because you're worthy.
- • Scarcity is a learned mindset that makes you view other people's success as proof there's not enough for you.
- • Real abundance begins when you trust that receiving doesn't make you selfish; it aligns you with your inherent worthiness.
- • Rejecting help or support doesn't prove strength; it signals that you don't feel deserving of what's offered.
- • Money, love, and success are not rewards for good behavior but natural reflections of your sense of self-worth.
- • If you believe abundance must be earned through pain, you'll unconsciously create obstacles rather than allowing ease and flow.
- • Embracing overflow means recognizing that accepting support, success, and love does not diminish anyone else's opportunities.
- • Real abundance isn't about accumulation, it's about knowing you're already enough and allowing yourself to be fully supported.
- • Stop waiting for permission to claim abundance; start living as if your desires are already deserved.

Chapter 17:
Manifestation Without Spiritual Bypassing

"You do not attract what you want, you attract what you are." — Neville Goddard

Manifestation has been sold as magic. Think positive thoughts, visualize what you want, raise your vibration, and outcomes will materialize. Just believe hard enough and everything you desire will appear. This oversimplified version of manifestation has created a generation of women sitting on their couches affirming abundance while their bank accounts drain, visualizing love while tolerating poor treatment, and outsourcing decisions to omens instead of setting criteria and choosing.

Manifestation is disciplined alignment between belief, choice, and execution. It's the process of bringing your internal beliefs into coherence with your external actions so that what you say you want matches what you're actually creating. It's about identifying the subconscious patterns that sabotage your stated desires and reprogramming them. It's about taking strategic, aligned action and tracking weekly inputs against the outcomes you intend to create. And it's about understanding that timing doesn't mean sitting back and hoping. It means preparing yourself so that when opportunity arrives, you're ready to receive it.

But most women use manifestation as spiritual bypassing. They avoid doing the hard work of healing by slapping affirmations over wounds. They blame their lack of results on their vibration instead of examining their choices. From there you stop blocking opportunities, you quit sabotaging what arrives, and you let love, money, and recognition in without labeling them as guilt. They confuse surrender with passivity, faith with avoidance, and trust with inaction. And then they wonder why nothing changes.

Women rooted in self-respect act before they affirm. They understand that manifestation without action is just wishful thinking. That you can't affirm your way out of patterns you're not willing to confront. That outcomes respond to who you're being, not what you're saying. That timing works in partnership with human responsibility, not as a replacement for it.

This chapter will teach you what manifestation actually is beyond the Instagram quotes and the vision boards. How to align your subconscious beliefs with your conscious desires so they're working together instead of against each other. How to take aligned action that moves you toward what you want instead of just visualizing and hoping. And how to trust the timing of your life while taking full responsibility for the role you play in creating it.

Manifestation is real. But it's not what you've been sold. Scarcity is a learned habit. Abundance is home. Return to it.

What Manifestation Really Is Beyond the Hype

Manifestation is not about outcomes delivering your wishes like a cosmic vending machine. It's about becoming the version of yourself who already has what you want. It's about embodying the beliefs, the behaviors, the standards of the person who lives the life you're trying to create. And then taking action from that place.

Most people approach manifestation backward. They think "I'll believe it when I see it." But manifestation works in reverse. You have to believe it before you see it. Not blind belief. Not delusional positivity. But a deep, embodied knowing that what you want is possible for you. And that knowing shifts how you show up. It changes the decisions you make. The opportunities you notice. The risks you take. The people you attract. The signals you bring into every room.

This is not mysticism. It is disciplined attention and decision hygiene. Call it attentional budgeting: choose the signals you'll fund, then design cues that make the chosen behaviors cheaper than the old reflex. When you believe something is possible, your brain starts filtering reality to find evidence that supports that belief. You notice opportunities you would have missed. You take actions you wouldn't have taken. You say yes to things you would have said no to. And those small shifts compound over time into the life you were visualizing.

But if you don't actually believe what you're affirming, your subconscious will sabotage it. You can say "I am worthy of love" a thousand times, but if you don't believe it, you'll keep choosing people who confirm your unworthiness. You can visualize financial abundance, but if you don't believe you deserve it, you'll find ways to push money away as fast as it comes in. Manifestation doesn't work if your conscious desires and your subconscious beliefs are in opposition.

Unrevised defaults keep steering until you install a different route.

This is why affirmations often fail. You're speaking to your conscious mind, but your subconscious isn't listening. And your subconscious is running the show. It's the part of you that's been programmed by every experience, every message, every wound you've accumulated over a lifetime. It operates below your awareness, driving decisions that feel automatic. And unless you reprogram it, it will keep creating the same patterns no matter what you're consciously affirming.

Real manifestation starts with examining your assumptions. Not the beliefs you say you have, but the ones you're actually operating from. If you say you want a relationship but you're not dating, what's the assumption underneath that? "No one will want me." "I'll get hurt." "All the good ones are taken." If you say you want financial security but you're not saving or investing, what's the belief? "I'm bad with money." "I'll never have enough." "Money is the root of all evil."

These beliefs are not abstract. They show up in your behavior. And your behavior creates your results. So if you want different results, you have to change the beliefs that are driving the behavior. That's the real work of manifestation. Not visualizing. Not affirming. But excavating the beliefs that are keeping you stuck and replacing them with beliefs that support what you actually want.

Another aspect of manifestation that gets ignored is identity. You can't manifest something that's incongruent with your identity. If you see yourself as someone who struggles, you'll manifest struggle. If you see yourself as someone who never gets picked, you'll manifest rejection. If you see yourself as someone who's always broke, you'll manifest financial instability. Because your identity is the lens through which you interpret every experience and the filter through which you make every decision.

Manifestation requires you to shift your identity before the external circumstances change. You have to start seeing yourself as the person who has what you want. Not in the future. Now. How does that person think? How does that person act? What choices does that person make? What does that person tolerate? What does that person refuse? When you start embodying that identity, your external reality begins to shift to match it.

Try this identity alignment check:

Name three non-negotiables of the identity you are enacting.

Log one confirming choice per day for seven days.

Remove the most frequent blocker you logged.

This doesn't mean pretending to be someone you're not. It means stepping into the version of yourself that already exists but has been suppressed by fear, by conditioning, by old patterns. That version is real. You're not creating it. You're uncovering it. And the more you embody it, the more your life reflects it.

Manifestation is also about signals. Not in the mystical sense, but in the practical sense. People register your pacing, posture, and congruence before they parse sentences. If you walk into a job interview vibrating with desperation, people feel it. If you walk into a date feeling unworthy, the other person senses it. If you approach opportunities from scarcity, you repel them. But if you walk into those same situations grounded, confident, expectant, you attract different responses. Your signals are a direct reflection of your internal state.

Try the signal budget: Define three "green-light" signals you want to emit this month (prepared, punctual, decisive). Each morning pick one and decide one behavior that broadcasts it in the next meeting. Log whether it was visible to others.

So manifestation is not just about thinking positive thoughts. It's about doing the internal work to shift your state so that your signals naturally align with what you want. It's about healing the wounds that keep you vibrating at a frequency of fear, doubt, or unworthiness. It's about building genuine confidence, not performing it. It's about becoming so solid in who you are that your presence alone starts opening doors.

Finally, manifestation is about focus. What you review grows. If you're constantly focused on what you don't have, you'll create more lack. If you're constantly focused on what's wrong, you'll find more problems. But if you train your focus on what you want, on what's working, on what's possible, you start creating momentum in that direction.

This is not toxic positivity. You're not ignoring real problems. You're just not giving them all your attention. You acknowledge what's not working, you address it, and then you redirect your focus to what you're building. Set a review rhythm and judge yourself by inputs shipped, not by mood.

Try: Cap daily inputs at three sources, schedule two forty-five minute output blocks, then review weekly for signal-to-noise.

Manifestation is bringing all of your internal resources, your assumptions, your stance, your behaviors, into alignment with what you're consciously trying to create. And when those things align, when there's no internal conflict, when you're moving in one clear direction, that's when you start seeing results. Not because context handed them to you. But because you became the person who naturally attracts them.

Aligning Subconscious Beliefs With Conscious Desires

Your conscious mind is the part of you that sets goals, makes plans, and decides what you want. But your subconscious mind is the part that actually runs your life. It controls your habits, your reactions, your automatic behaviors. And if your subconscious doesn't believe what your conscious mind is trying to create, it will sabotage you every single time.

This is why you can know what you need to do and still not do it. Why you can want something desperately and still push it away. Why you can set the same goal year after year and never achieve it. It's not a lack of willpower. It's a lack of alignment. Your conscious and subconscious minds are working against each other. And unrevised scripts keep driving. Rewrite the script and the steering changes.

The first step to aligning your subconscious with your conscious desires is identifying the conflicting beliefs. These beliefs usually sound like: "I want love, but I don't trust anyone." "I want money, but rich people are greedy." "I want success, but I don't want to be seen as threatening." These are contradictions. And contradictions create stagnation.

To uncover these beliefs, look at your results. Today's results reveal which belief drove your last ten choices. Your results are a reflection of what you actually believe, not what you say you believe. If you say you want a relationship but you're single, there's a belief underneath that's blocking it. If you say you want financial freedom but you're in debt, there's a belief keeping you there. Your job is to find it.

Start by asking yourself: What would I have to believe to create this result? If the result is being single, the belief might be "Relationships are painful" or "I'm better off alone" or "No one will accept the real me." If the result is financial struggle, the belief might be "I'm not good with money" or "Money is hard to come by" or "Wanting money makes me shallow."

Once you identify the belief, you can start dismantling it. Ask yourself: Is this belief actually true? Where did I learn it? Is it mine, or did I inherit it from someone else? Does this belief serve me, or is it keeping me stuck? Many beliefs were signed on your behalf. Unsigned ones can be voided. They're hand-me-downs from your parents, your culture, your religion, your past experiences. And you've been running them on autopilot without ever questioning whether they're accurate or useful.

The next step is replacing the limiting belief with an empowering one. But you can't just slap a new belief on top of the old one and expect it to stick. You have to find evidence that supports the new belief. Your subconscious needs proof. It needs to see that the new belief is more true than the old one.

If the old belief is "I'm bad with money," find evidence to the contrary. Times you saved. Times you made a smart financial decision. Times you managed resources well. Start building a case for the new belief: "I'm learning to manage money effectively." The more evidence you accumulate, the more the new belief becomes embedded.

Try this belief swap check:

Current result → operative belief → credible counter-belief (≥7/10) → two proof actions in seventy-two hours.

If it never reaches 8/10 by week four, rewrite the statement rather than forcing it.

This process takes time. You're not going to reprogram decades of conditioning in a week. But every time you choose the new belief over the old one, you're strengthening the new neural pathway. Every time you act in alignment with the new belief, you're proving to your subconscious that it's real. And over time, the new belief becomes automatic. It becomes the lens through which you see the world. And your behavior shifts to match it.

Another way to align your subconscious with your conscious desires is through repetition. Your subconscious learns through repetition. This is why affirmations can work, but only if they're backed by feeling and action. If you're just repeating words without any emotional resonance or behavioral change, you're wasting your time. But if you're saying the affirmation, feeling the truth of it in your body, and taking actions that reinforce it, you're creating real change.

Try this: Instead of saying "I am wealthy" when you're broke and don't believe it, say "I am becoming financially secure." That feels more true. Your subconscious can accept it. And then take one action that a financially secure person would take. Open a savings account. Track your spending. Read a book on investing. Each action sends a signal to your subconscious that this identity is real. And the more signals you send, the more the identity solidifies.

Use the credibility ladder: phrase the new belief in three levels. Use only the version you rate at least seven out of ten believable, then escalate after two weeks.

Visualization is another tool for aligning your subconscious with your desires, but most people do it wrong. They visualize the end result, the big house, the perfect partner, the dream job, and then they stop. But visualization without embodiment is just fantasy. You have to visualize in a way that engages your nervous system, that makes your body believe it's already happening.

When you visualize, don't just see the images. Feel the emotions. Hear the sounds. Smell the scents. Engage all your senses. Make it as real as possible. And then notice how your body responds. If you're visualizing success but your body is tense, there's a conflict. Your subconscious doesn't believe it. So you adjust. You visualize smaller milestones that your body can accept. You build the belief incrementally.

Another powerful method for subconscious reprogramming is working with your nervous system. Your nervous system holds your trauma, your fears, your limiting beliefs in your body. Talk therapy can help you understand these beliefs intellectually, but it doesn't always release them from your nervous system. Somatic practices, breathwork, movement, these modalities help your body let go of what your mind is trying to release.

When you feel the fear, the doubt, the resistance in your body, don't just think your way through it. Feel it. Breathe into it. Move through it. Let your body process the emotion instead of suppressing it. This releases the stored energy and makes room for new beliefs to take root.

You also align your subconscious through environment. If you're trying to embody abundance but your environment reflects scarcity, there's a mismatch. Your subconscious is constantly taking in information from your surroundings. If your space is cluttered, chaotic, neglected, your subconscious interprets that as a reflection of your internal state. Clean it up. Organize it. Make it feel like a place where the version of yourself you're becoming would live.

This doesn't mean you need to buy expensive things you can't afford. It means taking care of what you have. Treating your space with respect. Creating an environment that supports who you're becoming, not who you've been. Small changes in your environment send signals to your subconscious that things are shifting. And those signals accumulate.

Try context tags: apply small identity tags to three daily objects that force a micro-action on contact. For example, "Send one pitch" sticker on laptop lid.

Finally, aligning your subconscious with your conscious desires requires consistency. You can't do this work for a week and expect permanent change. You have to commit to the process. Every day, you're either reinforcing the old patterns or building new ones. Every choice is a vote for the identity you're creating. And the more votes you cast for the new identity, the more it becomes your default.

This is not about perfection. You'll slip back into old patterns. You'll have days where the old beliefs feel more true than the new ones. That's normal. The point is not to never falter. The point is to notice when you do and choose again. To keep coming back to the new belief, the new identity, the new way of being. That's how you align your subconscious with your conscious desires. Not through one big shift, but through a thousand small ones.

Try the seventy-two hour counter-belief sprint: For any stubborn belief, schedule two concrete micro-acts within seventy-two hours that only the opposite belief would perform. If you miss the window, shrink the act and try again immediately. Do not let the sprint lapse.

Taking Aligned Action Not Just Visualizing

Visualization without action is daydreaming. You can spend hours imagining your perfect life, but if you're not doing anything to create it, nothing will change. Outcomes accrue to traction, not daydreams. And not just any movement. Aligned action. Action that's consistent with the outcome you're trying to create.

Most people confuse activity with progress. They stay busy to avoid the discomfort of doing the thing that would actually move them forward. In relationships, they draft a reconciliation letter instead of actually scheduling the conversation. In health, they color-code a workout plan instead of walking twenty minutes today. In finance, they read about investing instead of setting a one percent auto-transfer tonight. This is not aligned action. This is avoidance disguised as productivity.

Aligned action is strategic. It's taking the next right step, even when you don't have the whole staircase mapped out. It's doing the thing that scares you because that's the thing that will create the shift. It's prioritizing impact over comfort. It's asking yourself: What's the one action that would move me closest to what I want? And then doing that, even if it's uncomfortable.

The reason most people don't take aligned action is fear. Fear of failure. Fear of rejection. Fear of being seen. Fear of succeeding and having to live up to it. So they stay in the visualization stage because it feels safe. They can imagine the life they want without risking anything. But risk is required for growth. And growth is required for manifestation.

Aligned action also means taking action from the identity you're embodying, not from your old patterns. If you're trying to manifest financial abundance, you don't act from scarcity. You don't hoard every dollar. You don't make decisions from fear of loss. You act from abundance. You invest in yourself. You spend money on things that align with your goals. You make choices that a financially secure person would make, even before the bank account reflects it.

This doesn't mean being reckless. It means making intentional choices that reinforce the identity you're building. If you're trying to manifest love, you don't act desperate. You don't tolerate poor treatment. You don't settle for less than what you want. You act from the belief that you're worthy of healthy love. You set boundaries. You walk away from situations that don't serve you. You make space for the right person by refusing to fill that space with the wrong one.

Aligned action is also about consistency. You can't take one aligned action and then go back to your old patterns and expect results. You have to keep taking aligned action, day after day, even when you don't see immediate results. Because manifestation is not linear. You don't take action and immediately see the outcome. There's often a lag time. You're planting seeds, and seeds take time to grow.

Most stop in the silent stretch between sowing and harvest, exactly when compounding is about to become visible. They take action for a week, a month, maybe even a year, and when they don't see the results they want, they give up. They assume it's not working. But the work you do today might not show up as results until months from now. And the work you did months ago is showing up in your life today. You just don't see the connection because you're focused on immediate gratification.

Another aspect of aligned action is course correction. You're not going to get it right the first time. You're going to take actions that don't work. You're going to make mistakes. That's part of the process. But instead of seeing failure as evidence that manifestation doesn't work, see it as feedback. What did I learn? What can I adjust? What do I need to do differently?

Aligned action is not rigid. It's responsive. You try something. You see what happens. You adjust. You try again. This is how you refine your approach. This is how you get closer to what you want. But you have to stay in motion. Stopping because something didn't work the first time is not manifestation. It's giving up.

Try the execution cadence:

24 hours: schedule one slot.

48 hours: ship first version.

10 days: complete a three-rep sprint; then decide persist, pivot, or park.

Run a three-rep sprint: three distinct attempts in ten days, each with one variable changed. Only then decide to persist, pivot, or park.

You also have to be willing to take action before you feel ready. Most people wait until they feel confident, prepared, certain. But confidence comes from action, not the other way around. You take the action, you see that you survived, and that builds confidence. Waiting to feel ready is just another form of procrastination.

Ask yourself: What's one action I could take today that would move me toward what I want? Not next week. Not when conditions are perfect. Today. And then do it. Even if it's small. Even if it's imperfect. Because small, imperfect action beats perfect inaction every time.

Aligned action also means saying no. No to opportunities that don't align with where you're going. No to people who drain your energy. No to commitments that keep you stuck in old patterns. Manifestation is as much about what you remove from your life as what you add. You have to create space for what you want. And that means letting go of what's in the way.

This is where most people struggle. They want to add the new life on top of the old one. But you can't do that. You have to release the old to make room for the new. You have to say no to the familiar to say yes to the unknown. And that's terrifying. But it's also necessary.

Try the one-three-one cadence: per week pick one high-leverage move, three supports, one obstacle to remove. Tackle the obstacle first.

Finally, aligned action requires you to make your calendar mirror your identity. If sixty percent of your future self's week is deep work and care, block that now. Review compliance on Fridays. Not in a fake-it-till-you-make-it way. But in a genuine embodiment of the person who has that life. How does that person spend their time? What do they prioritize? How do they treat themselves? How do they show up in the world? When you start acting from that place, you become that person. And when you become that person, the external results follow.

Try the action pairing map: For each visualization artifact (vision board item, written goal), attach exactly one recurring calendar block labeled "Input that makes this inevitable." Review completion rate weekly.

Manifestation is not passive. It's not about sitting back and waiting. It's about becoming so clear on what you want, so aligned in your beliefs and your identity, that your actions naturally create the life you're envisioning. No context can compensate for inaction. But you have to take the first step. And the second. And the third. You have to keep moving. And that movement, when it's aligned, is what creates the life you want.

Trusting Divine Timing While Taking Responsibility

One of the most misunderstood concepts in manifestation is divine timing. People use it as an excuse to avoid taking action. "It's not the right time." "I'll know when." "If it's meant to be, it will happen." But divine timing is not an excuse for passivity. It's a partnership between surrender and responsibility.

Divine timing means trusting that things will unfold when they're supposed to, but only if you're doing your part. You can't sit waiting for a sign and expect opportunities to fall into your lap. You have to be preparing, building, moving, creating. And when the timing is right, when you've done the internal and external work, the opportunity will arrive. But if you haven't been preparing, you won't be ready to receive it.

Think of it this way. You can plant a seed and trust that it will grow. But you still have to water it. You still have to make sure it gets sunlight. You still have to protect it from pests. The timing of the growth is not entirely in your control. But your role in creating the conditions for growth absolutely is. Divine timing works the same way. You create the conditions. You do the work. And then you trust the process.

Before calling it "timing," run this timing versus preparation gate:

Prepared artifacts exist.

At least three quality reps executed.

External feedback gathered from a qualified source.

If one is missing, the blocker is preparation, not timing. Plan the next rep within forty-eight hours.

Most people want guarantees. They want to know that if they take action, it will work out. But life doesn't offer guarantees. Manifestation doesn't offer guarantees. What it offers is probability. The more aligned your beliefs, your identity, your signals, and your actions, the more likely you are to create what you want. But there's still uncertainty. There's still risk. And you have to be willing to move forward anyway.

Trusting divine timing also means releasing attachment to how things unfold.

You can have a clear vision of what you want, but you can't control the path to get there. You can't dictate the timeline. You can't force the sequence to move at your pace. Sometimes things take longer than you want. Sometimes they happen faster than you expected. Sometimes they show up in ways you didn't anticipate. Your job is to stay flexible. To trust that if something doesn't work out the way you planned, it's because something better is coming.

Not blind faith, but a track record you can point to. You build trust in divine timing by looking back at your life and seeing all the times things didn't go according to plan and ended up working out better than you could have imagined. All the times a door closed and a better one opened. All the times you were rejected and later realized it was protection. When you see that pattern, you start to trust it. You start to relax into the uncertainty instead of fighting it.

But trusting divine timing does not mean abdicating responsibility. You're still responsible for your choices. You're still responsible for your actions. You're still responsible for your healing. You don't get to blame circumstances when things don't work out. You don't get to say "If it matters, create the conditions and measure your inputs" without examining your role in the outcome.

This is where spiritual bypassing shows up. People use manifestation language to avoid accountability. "Context is protecting me from that job." Maybe. Or maybe you didn't prepare for the interview. "It's not the right time for a relationship." Maybe. Or maybe you're not doing the work to heal your attachment wounds. "Money will come when I'm ready." Maybe. Or maybe you need to take financial responsibility instead of waiting for a windfall.

Divine timing and personal responsibility are not opposites. They're partners. You take responsibility for what's in your control. Your beliefs. Your actions. Your healing. Your choices. And you surrender what's not in your control. The timing. The how. The specific path. You do your part and trust that the sequence will do its part.

Another aspect of trusting divine timing is patience. Most people want instant results. They take action for a week and expect their life to transform. But real change takes time. The shifts you're making internally need time to integrate. The actions you're taking need time to compound. The seeds you're planting need time to grow. Patience is continued throughput at a sustainable cadence in the absence of immediate reward.

This is hard in a culture that's addicted to instant gratification. But manifestation doesn't work on social media timelines. It works on life timelines. And life moves slower than your impatience wants it to. So you have to cultivate patience. You have to trust that the work you're doing matters, even when you can't see the evidence yet. You have to keep going, even when it feels like nothing is happening.

Trusting divine timing also requires you to stay present. Most people are so focused on the future, on when their manifestation will arrive, that they miss the present moment. They miss the lessons. They miss the growth. They miss the smaller manifestations that are showing up along the way. But the present moment is where your power is. It's where your choices are. It's where your life is actually happening.

When you're constantly focused on the future, you're not here. You're not engaged. You're not noticing the opportunities that are right in front of you. You're not appreciating what you already have. And that lack of presence creates resistance. It sends a signal that where you are right now isn't good enough. And that signal blocks the very thing you're trying to manifest.

So practice being here. Fully. Not as a way to stop wanting. But as a way to appreciate the journey. To notice the progress. To celebrate the small wins. To recognize that the life you're building is happening now, not in some distant future. And the more present you are, the more you can respond to what's unfolding instead of being stuck in your head about what's not here yet.

Finally, trusting divine timing means trusting yourself. Trusting that you'll know what to do when the moment comes. Trusting that you're capable of handling whatever shows up. Trusting that you're being guided, even when you can't see the path. This trust is not arrogance. It's faith. Faith in yourself. Faith in the process. Faith that you're exactly where you need to be, learning exactly what you need to learn, becoming exactly who you need to become.

Try this responsibility versus surrender check:

What's in my control this week?

What will I release control over?

How will I measure progress without fixating on timing?

Manifestation is not about controlling outcomes. It's about aligning yourself so fully with what you want that when the opportunity arrives, you're ready. And then trusting that the timing of that arrival is perfect, even when it doesn't match your timeline. You do the work. You take the action. You stay aligned. And then you let go. You trust. You surrender. Hold the plan, flex the path, and keep your throughput.

Do the work, make room, meet the moment. That is how timing finds you.

Key Takeaways

- Manifestation isn't about wishful thinking or magical solutions; it's about aligning your beliefs, decisions, and actions.
- Spiritual bypassing occurs when you use positive thinking to avoid taking responsibility for changing subconscious patterns.
- Your subconscious beliefs drive your results; until you align those beliefs with your conscious desires, your results won't change.
- Aligned action—taking steps consistent with your desired outcome—is essential; visualization without action is fantasy.
- Trusting divine timing means preparing yourself and creating the conditions for your desires, rather than passively waiting.
- Manifestation involves becoming the version of yourself who naturally attracts and sustains the results you seek.
- You block your own blessings when subconscious beliefs contradict your stated goals, creating resistance instead of flow.
- Receiving requires allowing good things without guilt or the constant urge to earn, prove, or immediately reciprocate.
- Release scarcity by consciously noticing and shifting your internal narrative from lack to sufficiency and possibility.
- Manifestation works best when you focus your attention on what you can control, while trusting the timing and process of your growth.

Chapter 18:
Thriving as the Most Powerful Version of You

"Your life becomes a masterpiece when you learn to master peace." — Nikki Rowe

You've spent seventeen chapters learning how to reclaim your power, set boundaries, communicate clearly, heal your body, choose better relationships, and align your beliefs with your actions. But knowledge without synthesis is just information. Understanding these principles intellectually is not the same as living them. And living them occasionally is not the same as embodying them so deeply that they become your default way of being.

This final chapter is about synthesis. About folding everything you've learned into a life that reflects your worth. About moving from knowing to being. From understanding to embodiment. From trying to thriving. Because the goal was never just to feel better for a moment. It was to become the version of yourself who doesn't need to keep fixing, healing, or proving. The version who simply is.

Most women approach personal growth as a series of problems to solve. They read books, attend workshops, hire coaches, all in pursuit of finally being enough. But growth is not about becoming someone new. It's about remembering who you've always been beneath the conditioning, the wounds, the fear. It's about bringing every part of yourself into coherence. It's about building daily practices that sustain you instead of deplete you. And it's about living in a way that honors the woman you're becoming while respecting the woman you've been.

Women who thrive don't wait until everything is perfect to start living fully. They don't postpone joy until they've healed every wound or achieved every goal. They build lives that feel good now, while continuing to grow, evolve, and expand. They understand that thriving is not a destination. It's a practice. A series of choices made daily that compound over time into a life worth living.

This chapter will teach you how to reconcile your contradictions into wholeness instead of rejecting the parts of yourself you've been taught to hide.

How to build daily rituals that sustain your worth instead of deplete it. How to create a personalized roadmap for success that aligns with who you actually are, not who you think you should be. And how to live your legacy starting today, instead of waiting for someday when conditions are perfect.

You thrive when you stop performing and start being. That version is already here. This chapter shows you how to embody her fully.

Integrating Shadow and Light Into Wholeness

You've been taught to present only your light. The parts of yourself that are palatable, acceptable, easy for others to digest. The successful parts. The kind parts. The parts that don't threaten anyone. And you've been taught to hide your shadow. The anger. The ambition. The selfishness. The messiness. The parts that make people uncomfortable. The parts you've been told make you too much or not enough.

But you are not whole when you're only showing half of yourself. Self-reconciliation requires bringing all of you into the light, not just the parts that get applauded. It requires accepting that you contain contradictions, that you're allowed to be complex, that being multifaceted is not a flaw. It's what makes you human.

Your shadow is not the enemy. It's the parts of yourself you've rejected, repressed, or disowned because they weren't acceptable in the environments where you were raised. Maybe you were told that anger was unladylike, so you pushed it down until you couldn't access it anymore. Maybe you were shamed for wanting attention, so you learned to make yourself invisible. Maybe you were punished for being selfish, so you became a chronic people-pleaser who lost herself in the process.

These rejected parts don't disappear. They go underground. They leak out in passive-aggressive comments, in self-sabotage, in patterns you can't explain. They show up as the parts of other people that trigger you most, because what you can't accept in yourself, you can't tolerate in others. Shadow work is about bringing these unclaimed qualities back into consciousness, examining them without judgment, and folding them back into your whole self.

Start by noticing what you judge most harshly in others. The woman who's too loud. The woman who's too ambitious. The woman who puts herself first.

Whatever quality irritates you most is likely a quality you've rejected in yourself. Not because it's bad, but because you were taught it was unacceptable. And now it's trying to get your attention.

Ask yourself: What would happen if I allowed myself to be that? What would happen if I let myself be loud, ambitious, selfish, angry, messy, demanding, whatever quality I've been suppressing? Usually, the fear is that you'll be rejected. That people will leave. That you'll be too much. But the truth is, the people who can't handle your wholeness aren't your people. And the ones who can will love you more for it.

Acknowledging these parts doesn't mean acting on every impulse. It means giving them space, listening to what they're trying to tell you, and understanding that your full emotional spectrum serves you. Your anger protects boundaries that have been violated. Your selfishness redirects you toward your own neglected needs. Your messiness signals that perfection has become a cage.

Shadow work also means owning the parts of yourself you're proud of but afraid to claim. The parts that are too bright, too powerful, too successful. Many women suppress their light as much as their shadow because being fully visible feels dangerous. You've been taught that shining too brightly threatens other people, that success makes you a target, that power makes you unfeminine.

But dimming your light to make others comfortable is another form of self-rejection. It's choosing other people's comfort over your own expansion. And it keeps you small in ways that serve no one. When you own your light fully, when you stop apologizing for your intelligence, your beauty, your success, your presence, you give other women permission to do the same.

Union is about holding both. The shadow and the light. The strength and the softness. The ambition and the rest. The independence and the need for connection. You don't have to choose. You don't have to be one thing all the time. You're allowed to be fierce in one moment and tender in the next. Confident and uncertain. Powerful and vulnerable. All of it is true. All of it belongs.

Wholeness isn't flawlessness. It's functional self-acceptance in motion. Not the absence of contradictions, but the acceptance of them. Not the erasure of complexity, but the embrace of it. When you stop trying to be one-dimensional, when you stop performing the version of yourself you think people want, you relax. You stop spending so much energy managing your image and start using that energy to live.

Union also requires forgiveness. Not of other people, though that may come. But of yourself. For all the times you betrayed yourself to keep the peace. For all the times you chose safety over truth. For all the times you made yourself small to fit into spaces that were never meant for you. You did the best you could with the tools you had. And now you have better tools. Now you get to choose differently.

Part of coherence is recognizing that the version of yourself you've been criticizing is the version that kept you alive. The people-pleaser protected you from conflict. The perfectionist kept you safe from criticism. The overachiever proved you were valuable. These strategies worked. They got you here. And now they're no longer serving you. So you thank them for what they did, and you release them with compassion.

Another aspect of synthesis is reclaiming the parts of yourself you gave away. The hobbies you abandoned because someone told you they were frivolous. The dreams you buried because they seemed impractical. The desires you suppressed because they felt selfish. All of those parts are still there, waiting for you to remember them. And when you do, when you bring them back into your life, you become more of who you are. Not who you think you should be. Who you are.

When you bring shadow and light into union, you stop being at war with yourself. You stop trying to be someone you're not. You stop performing for an audience that doesn't matter. And you start living from a place of unfiltered presence that makes everything else easier. Because when you're whole, you're not wasting energy hiding, suppressing, or pretending. You're just being. And being is where your power lives.

Daily Rituals of a Woman Who Knows Her Worth

Knowing your worth intellectually is different from living it daily. You can understand the concepts in this book, agree with every principle, and still fall back into old patterns if you don't have structures in place to support you. Daily rituals are those structures. They're the small, repeated actions that keep you rooted in who you're becoming instead of who you used to be.

A woman anchored in self-respect doesn't rely on motivation. Motivation is fleeting. It shows up when you feel inspired and disappears when life gets hard. Rituals are different. Rituals are non-negotiable. They're the things you do regardless of how you feel because you know they keep you grounded, connected, and clear. They're the daily practices that remind you of your value when the world tries to make you forget.

The first ritual is a morning practice that sets your tone for the day. This doesn't have to be elaborate. It doesn't require an hour of meditation, journaling, yoga, and green juice unless that genuinely serves you. It can be as simple as five minutes of intentional silence before you check your phone. Five minutes where you breathe, ground yourself, and decide how you want to show up today.

Many women start their day reacting. They wake up, immediately check their phone, scroll through emails or social media, and let the chaos of the world set their emotional state. By the time they've had coffee, they're already stressed, distracted, and disconnected from themselves. A morning ritual interrupts that pattern. It gives you space to choose your state instead of inheriting one from your inbox.

Try this: Before you reach for your phone, place your hand on your chest and take three deep breaths. Ask yourself: How do I want to feel today? What's one intention I'm setting? What's one thing I'm grateful for? This takes less than two minutes. But it roots you in yourself before the world makes demands.

Another ritual is protecting your energy throughout the day. This means being intentional about what you consume and who you spend time with. It means saying no to commitments that drain you. It means setting boundaries around your time, your attention, your emotional capacity. Someone living from internal authority doesn't give their energy away indiscriminately. She protects it like the finite resource it is.

Energy protection also means curating your inputs. What are you reading? What are you watching? Who are you listening to? If you're consuming content that makes you feel anxious, inadequate, or overwhelmed, that's affecting your state. You don't have to cut everything out, but you do have to be conscious of what you're letting in. Your mental diet matters as much as your physical one.

A third ritual is a midday check-in. Set a timer for midday and pause. Ask yourself: Am I still consistent with my values? Am I operating from my values or from old patterns? Am I in integrity with who I want to be? This check-in takes thirty seconds, but it prevents you from spending an entire day on autopilot. It gives you the chance to course-correct before the day is over.

Another essential ritual is movement. Not exercise as punishment for eating or to earn your body. Movement as a way to stay connected to your physical form. Movement that feels good. Walking. Dancing. Stretching. Yoga. Whatever helps you feel present in your body instead of trapped in your head. A woman grounded in self-worth doesn't ignore her body. She listens to it. She honors it. She treats it as a partner, not an obstacle.

An evening ritual closes the loop on your day. You reflect on what went well. You acknowledge what you accomplished. You release what didn't work. You prepare yourself for rest instead of carrying the day's stress into your sleep. An evening ritual signals to your nervous system that the day is complete. That you can let go. That you're safe. Write down three things that went well today. Not big achievements. Small moments. A good conversation. A decision you're proud of. A boundary you held. This practice trains your brain to notice what's working instead of obsessing over what's not.

Another ritual is a weekly review. Once a week, take twenty minutes to assess how you're doing. Are you living rooted in your values? Are you honoring your boundaries? Are you moving toward your goals or drifting? This review keeps you accountable to yourself. It's not about perfection. It's about noticing patterns and adjusting before small drifts become major detours.

A ritual that sustains worth is also about rest. Women anchored in self-respect rest without guilt. They understand that rest is not earned. It's required. They don't wait until they're burned out to stop. They protect idle space as part of their work cycle. One day where they do less. One evening where they don't produce. One hour where they just exist without an agenda. Rest is not laziness. Rest is maintenance.

Solitude recalibrates your self-trust. Use it as a reset, not a punishment. Spend time alone. Not scrolling. Not consuming content. Just being with yourself. Many women avoid being alone because they don't like their own company. They've spent so many years rejecting themselves that sitting with themselves feels uncomfortable. But you can't know your worth if you're afraid to be alone with yourself.

Rituals also include celebration. Someone living from internal authority celebrates her wins. Not just the big ones. The small ones. Every step forward. Every boundary held. Every choice made from integrity instead of fear. Celebration reinforces the behavior. It signals to your brain that you're moving in the right direction. And it makes the journey sustainable instead of a grind.

Finally, a ritual of release. Once a month, archive one commitment that no longer matches your current season. A belief. A relationship. A commitment. A habit. Synthesis requires space. And you can't make space for new growth if you're gripping tightly to everything old. Release is not failure. Release is discernment. It's choosing what stays and what goes based on who you're becoming.

These rituals are not for performance tracking but for nervous-system stability. They don't have to be time-consuming. They don't have to be perfect. They just have to be consistent. Because consistency is what builds identity. Every time you honor a ritual, you're proving to yourself that you're the kind of woman who values herself enough to prioritize her well-being. And over time, those small acts compound into a life that reflects your worth in every area.

Rituals are not about control. They're about care. They're how you love yourself daily, not just in theory but in practice. And when you build your life on rituals that honor who you are, thriving becomes your default. Not because life stops being hard. But because you've built a foundation strong enough to hold you through it.

Your Personalized Roadmap to Sustainable Success

Success cannot be franchised. It must be locally designed. The roadmap that worked for someone else won't necessarily work for you because you're not starting from the same place, you don't have the same strengths, and you're not building toward the same destination. Sustainable success requires a personalized approach. One that's designed around your values, your capacity, your season of life, and your definition of what success actually means to you.

Most women are following roadmaps designed by other people. They're chasing goals they think they should want. Climbing ladders that lead to places they don't actually want to go. And wondering why success, when they achieve it, feels hollow. Because it was never their version of success. It was someone else's. And no amount of external achievement will satisfy an internal misalignment.

The first step in creating your personalized roadmap is defining what success means to you. Not what your parents think it should be. Not what society says it is. Not what your peers are doing. What does it mean to you? What does a successful life look like in your mind? What does it feel like? What are you doing? Who are you with? How are you spending your time?

Get specific. Definition creates movement. "I want to be successful" is not a roadmap. "I want to build a business that generates enough income to support my family while giving me flexibility to be present for my kids" is a roadmap. "I want to feel fulfilled" is not a roadmap. "I want work that uses my skills, relationships that feel reciprocal, and time to rest without guilt" is a roadmap.

Once you've defined success for yourself, the next step is auditing where you are now. Not from a place of judgment, but from a place of assessment. What's working? What's not? Where are you already consistent with your values? Where are you out of integrity? This audit shows you the gap between where you are and where you want to be. And that gap is your roadmap.

But here's what most women get wrong. They look at the gap and try to close it all at once. They set ten goals, overhaul their entire life, burn out in three weeks, and then feel like failures. Sustainable success is not built through massive overhauls. It's built through small, consistent actions that compound over time. You don't need to change everything. You need to change one thing. And then another. And then another.

Prioritize. What's the one area of your life that, if improved, would create the most positive ripple effect? Start there. Pour your energy into that one area until you see traction. Then move to the next. Trying to transform everything simultaneously is how you stay stuck.

Your roadmap also needs to account for your capacity. Not your ideal capacity. Your actual capacity. How much energy do you have? How much time? How much support? How much mental bandwidth? Building a roadmap that requires more than you have is setting yourself up to fail. You have to design success around your real life, not a fantasy version of it.

This means being honest about your season. If you have young children, you're not going to have the same capacity as someone whose kids are grown. If you're healing from trauma, you're not going to have the same energy as someone who isn't. If you're working two jobs to make ends meet, you're not going to have the same time as someone with financial cushion. Your roadmap has to reflect your reality. And your reality will change. That's why the roadmap needs to be flexible.

Systems make growth automatic. Design ones that express your values instead of proving them. If your goal is to write a book, your system is writing for twenty minutes every morning. If your goal is financial security, your system is automating savings and scheduling energy recovery the way you schedule output. Systems are the daily behaviors that make the goal inevitable. Focus on building systems that fit into your life seamlessly. Systems you can maintain even on hard days.

Your roadmap also needs built-in recovery. You can't operate at maximum capacity all the time. You'll burn out. Sustainable success includes rest, recalibration, and reassessment. Build in quarterly reviews where you pause, reflect, and adjust. Is this still working? Is this still what I want? Am I still rooted in my values? Give yourself permission to change direction if needed. Flexibility is not failure. Rigidity is.

Another key to sustainability is support. You're not meant to do this alone. Who's in your corner? Who can you call when you're struggling? Who celebrates your wins? If you don't have that support, build it. Find a mentor. Join a community. Hire a coach. Invest in relationships that fuel you instead of drain you. Success is not a solo endeavor. And trying to make it one is why so many women collapse under the weight of their own ambition.

Your roadmap should also include measures of success that aren't just external. Yes, you want to hit financial targets, career milestones, relationship goals. But sustainable success also includes how you feel. Are you sleeping well? Are you enjoying your life? Do you have time for things that matter to you? Are you present with the people you love? These internal measures are just as important as external ones. Because what's the point of achieving everything if you're miserable in the process?

Finally, your roadmap needs to honor your values. Every decision you make should be filtered through your values. When your schedule reflects your values, achievement becomes regulation, not resistance. If one of your values is family, but your roadmap has you working eighty hours a week, there's a misalignment. If one of your values is creativity, but your roadmap has you in a job that's purely analytical, there's a misalignment. When your roadmap aligns with your values, success feels good. When it doesn't, success feels empty.

Review your values annually. They evolve as you do. What mattered to you five years ago might not matter now. And that's okay. Your roadmap should evolve with you. It's not set in stone. It's a living document that shifts as your life shifts. And the more it reflects who you are right now, the more sustainable your success will be.

Sustainable success is not about doing more. It's about doing what matters. It's not about being busy. It's about being intentional. It's not about keeping up with anyone else. It's about building a life that feels good to you. And when you create a roadmap that's personalized, realistic, values-aligned, and flexible, success stops being something you chase. It becomes something you live.

Try this integration review monthly: List three actions that made your life lighter, three that drained it, one you'll release.

Living Your Legacy Starting Today

Most people think about legacy as something that happens after they're gone. The impact they leave. The way they'll be remembered. But legacy is accumulated proof of how you spend your attention. Every action you take, every boundary you set, every value you honor, every person you influence, that's your legacy in motion.

You don't have to wait until you've achieved something monumental to start living your legacy. You don't have to wait until you're older, wiser, more successful, more healed. Your legacy is happening now. In how you show up. In how you treat people. In how you treat yourself. In the example you set for the people watching you, whether you realize they're watching or not.

Legacy starts with the life you're modeling. If you have children, they're learning how to live by watching you. Not by what you tell them, but by what you do. If you want them to have healthy boundaries, they need to see you setting them. If you want them to value themselves, they need to see you valuing yourself. If you want them to pursue their dreams, they need to see you pursuing yours. You teach more through your actions than you ever will through your words.

But legacy isn't just about children. It's about everyone in your orbit. Your friends. Your colleagues. Your family. The women who are watching you navigate your life, even when you don't know they're paying attention. Every time you choose integrity over approval, you expand what's possible for everyone watching. When you hold a boundary, you show them it's possible. When you walk away from what doesn't serve you, you model what self-respect looks like. Your life is a template. And the more you live consistent with your worth, the more you create space for others to do the same.

Legacy is also about the work you do. Not just your career, but the contribution you make. What are you building, creating, and solving? What are you offering to the world that wouldn't exist without you? This doesn't have to be grand. It doesn't have to be famous. It just has to matter to you. And it has to reflect your values.

Some women build legacy through business. Some through art. Some through service. Some through raising conscious, compassionate children. Some through mentoring the next generation. Some through healing work that ripples out into their communities. There's no hierarchy of impact. Your legacy is not measured by scale. It's measured by integrity. Are you doing what you're here to do? Are you using your gifts? Are you showing up fully?

Living your legacy also means being intentional about your relationships. The people you invest in are part of your legacy. The love you give. The care you provide. The space you hold. The ways you show up when it matters. Relationships are not separate from legacy. They are legacy. The way you love people, the way you support them, the way you challenge them to grow, that's what they'll carry forward.

Another aspect of legacy is the healing you do. When you heal, you don't just heal yourself. You heal your lineage. You break cycles that have been running in your family for generations. You stop passing down trauma. You stop repeating patterns. You become the one who says "This ends with me." And that decision, that commitment to doing your work, that's legacy. Because the generations that come after you won't have to carry what you chose to release.

Legacy is also about courage. Visible courage recalibrates collective permission. The risks you take. The times you choose truth over comfort. The moments you stand up for what's right even when it costs you something. When people see you living boldly, they start to question their own limitations.

They start to wonder what's possible for them. And that questioning is how change happens. Not through lectures, but through examples.

Living your legacy also means knowing when to rest. Burnout is not a legacy. Martyrdom is not a legacy. Sacrificing yourself to the point of depletion is not noble. It's unsustainable. And it teaches people that worthiness requires suffering. Your legacy includes modeling balance. Showing that you can be ambitious and rested. Successful and present. Driven and at peace. That you don't have to destroy yourself to matter. The calm you model in pressure becomes part of what you leave behind.

Another component of legacy is generosity. Not just financial generosity, though that matters if you have resources to share. But generosity of spirit. Generosity with your time, your wisdom, your encouragement. Being the person who shows up. Who listens. Who believes in people when they don't believe in themselves. Who opens doors. Who shares resources. Who lifts as she climbs. Scarcity made you conserve. Thriving teaches you to circulate. That generosity compounds. It ripples. And it's remembered.

Legacy also includes what you refuse. The dynamics you won't participate in. The conversations you won't engage. The values you won't compromise. What you stand against is as important as what you stand for. When you refuse to tolerate disrespect, you set a standard. When you refuse to engage in gossip, you create a culture of integrity. When you refuse to dim your light, you give others permission to shine. Your refusals shape the world around you.

Living your legacy means being honest. Not perfect. Honest. About your struggles. About your growth. About the ways you've messed up and what you've learned. When you're honest about your humanity, you make it easier for others to be honest about theirs. You remove the pressure to perform perfection. And you create space for real connection, real growth, real change.

Finally, living your legacy means trusting that your life matters. Even when you can't see the impact. Even when it feels small. Even when no one's watching. You matter. The choices you make matter. The way you live matters. And you don't have to wait for permission, recognition, or the perfect moment to start living in a way that reflects that.

Your legacy is not something that happens to you. It's something you create. Daily. Through your choices. Through your courage. Through your commitment to being the fullest version of yourself. And the beautiful thing about legacy is that it's never too late to start. Wherever you are right now, whatever you've done or haven't done, today is the day you can choose to live in a way that honors who you are and what you're here to do.

Try this legacy checkpoint quarterly: Write one sentence describing what your daily behavior currently teaches others.

You are most powerful when you live now, unguarded, unperforming, and fully engaged. That version of you is not in the future. She's here. She's been here all along. And she's ready. So stop waiting. Start living. Your legacy is calling. Power lives in present action. Begin now.

Key Takeaways

- Thriving means fully embodying your worth instead of merely understanding it intellectually.

- Real growth comes from becoming more yourself rather than constantly fixing or proving something.

- True integration happens when you accept both your shadow and your light as natural aspects of your whole self.

- Sustainable transformation is built on daily rituals that consistently reinforce your values and clarity.

- Your personal roadmap to success must align with your actual capacity and unique values, not someone else's definition.

- Self-worth isn't earned through achievement; it's claimed daily by making choices that reflect your inherent value.

- Legacy isn't something you leave behind after you're gone; it's how intentionally you live and impact others right now.

- Thriving is a continuous practice based on consistent choices, meaningful rituals, and strong boundaries that protect your energy.

- Your external circumstances always mirror your internal beliefs about your worth, so shift those beliefs to change your life.

- Power comes from choosing peace, clarity, and alignment every single day, exactly as you are.

Help Another Woman Find This Book

I have a simple question: Would you help someone you've never met if it didn't cost you anything and you didn't receive any credit for it?

If so, I have an ask to make on behalf of someone you do not know. And likely never will. She is just like you, or like you were before reading this book: tired of abandoning herself, seeking clarity about relationships, unsure where to find real answers... this is where you come in.

The only way for me to reach women who need this message is through readers like you. And most people do judge a book by its reviews. If you found this book valuable, would you please take a brief moment now and leave an honest review? It will cost you nothing and take less than 60 seconds.

I appreciate all reviews, whether positive or negative, and I will read them personally. Your review helps:

- One more woman see the truth she's been avoiding
- One more soul begin choosing herself
- One more life change for the better

Scan to leave a review

Thank you from the bottom of my heart.

Bibliography

Chapter 1 – The Woman You've Been Pretending to Be

- Brown, B. (2006). Shame resilience theory: A grounded theory study on women and shame. *Families in Society, 87*(1), 43–52.
- Brown, B. (2010). *The Gifts of Imperfection.* Hazelden.
- Brown, B. (2012). *Daring Greatly: How the Courage to Be Vulnerable Transforms the Way We Live, Love, Parent, and Lead.* Gotham Books.
- Gilbert, P. (2003). Evolution, social roles, and the differences in shame and guilt. *Social Research, 70*(4), 1205–1230.

Chapter 2 – The Invisible Cage You Built for Safety

- van der Kolk, B. A. (2014). *The Body Keeps the Score: Brain, Mind, and Body in the Healing of Trauma.* Viking.
- Herman, J. L. (1992). *Trauma and Recovery: The Aftermath of Violence.* Basic Books.
- Porges, S. W. (2011). *The Polyvagal Theory: Neurophysiological Foundations of Emotions, Attachment, Communication, and Self-Regulation.* W. W. Norton.
- Walker, P. (2013). *Complex PTSD: From Surviving to Thriving.* Azure Coyote Publishing.

Chapter 3 – Your Feminine Essence Was Never Lost

- Estés, C. P. (1992). *Women Who Run with the Wolves: Myths and Stories of the Wild Woman Archetype.* Ballantine Books.
- Gilligan, C. (1982). *In a Different Voice: Psychological Theory and Women's Development.* Harvard University Press.
- Fredrickson, B. L., & Roberts, T. A. (1997). Objectification theory: Toward understanding women's lived experiences. *Psychology of Women Quarterly, 21*(2), 173–206.
- Northrup, C. (2006). *Women's Bodies, Women's Wisdom.* Bantam.

Chapter 4 – The Root of Your Self-Sabotage

- LePera, N. (2021). *How to Do the Work: Recognize Your Patterns, Heal from Your Past, and Create Your Self.* Harper Wave.
- Maté, G. (2003). *When the Body Says No: The Cost of Hidden Stress.* Vintage Canada.
- Bandura, A. (1977). Self-efficacy: Toward a unifying theory of behavioral change. *Psychological Review, 84*(2), 191–215.
- Elliot, A. J., & Church, M. A. (2002). Client-articulated avoidance goals in the therapy context. *Journal of Counseling Psychology, 49*(2), 243–254.

Chapter 5 – Healing the Wounded Feminine Within

- Gibson, L. C. (2015). *Adult Children of Emotionally Immature Parents.* New Harbinger.
- Courtois, C. A. (2014). *It's Not You, It's What Happened to You.* Telemachus Press.
- Fosha, D. (2000). *The Transforming Power of Affect.* Basic Books.
- Gilbert, P. (2009). *The Compassionate Mind.* Constable & Robinson.

Chapter 6 – You Can Have Yourself AND Have Love

- Levine, A., & Heller, R. (2010). *Attached: The New Science of Adult Attachment and How It Can Help You Find — and Keep — Love.* TarcherPerigee.
- Gottman, J., & Silver, N. (1999). *The Seven Principles for Making Marriage Work.* Harmony Books.
- Johnson, S. M. (2008). *Hold Me Tight: Seven Conversations for a Lifetime of Love.* Little, Brown.
- Tatkin, S. (2016). *Wired for Love.* New Harbinger.

Chapter 7 – Boundaries Are Love Not Walls

- Tawwab, N. G. (2021). *Set Boundaries, Find Peace: A Guide to Reclaiming Yourself.* TarcherPerigee.
- Cloud, H., & Townsend, J. (1992). *Boundaries: When to Say Yes, How to Say No.* Zondervan.
- Rosenberg, M. B. (2003). *Nonviolent Communication: A Language of Life.* PuddleDancer Press.
- Brown, B. (2018). *Dare to Lead: Brave Work, Tough Conversations, Whole Hearts.* Random House.

Chapter 8 – Dangerous Confidence From the Inside Out

- Robbins, M. (2017). *The 5 Second Rule: Transform Your Life, Work, and Confidence with Everyday Courage.* Savio Republic.
- Neff, K. D. (2011). *Self-Compassion: The Proven Power of Being Kind to Yourself.* HarperCollins.
- Dweck, C. (2006). *Mindset: The New Psychology of Success.* Random House.
- Clear, J. (2018). *Atomic Habits: Tiny Changes, Remarkable Results.* Avery.

Chapter 9 – Embodying Your Magnetic Feminine Power

- Northrup, C. (2013). *Goddesses Never Age.* Hay House.
- Perel, E. (2006). *Mating in Captivity: Unlocking Erotic Intelligence.* Harper.
- Estés, C. P. (2005). *The Faithful Gardener.* HarperOne.
- Fredrickson, B. L. (2009). *Positivity: Top-Notch Research Reveals the Upward Spiral That Will Change Your Life.* Crown.

Chapter 10 – The Language of High Value Communication

- Rosenberg, M. B. (2003). *Nonviolent Communication: A Language of Life.* PuddleDancer Press.
- Scott, S. (2017). *Fierce Conversations: Achieving Success at Work and in Life.* Berkley.
- Gottman, J. (2011). *The Relationship Cure: A 5 Step Guide to Strengthening Your Marriage, Family, and Friendships.* Crown.
- Linehan, M. M. (1993). *Cognitive-Behavioral Treatment of Borderline Personality Disorder.* Guilford Press.

Chapter 11 – Your Body Is Your Temple Not Your Enemy

- Roth, G. (2010). *Women, Food and God.* Scribner.
- Bacon, L. (2010). *Health at Every Size.* BenBella Books.
- Maté, G., & Maté, D. (2022). *The Myth of Normal: Trauma, Illness, and Healing in a Toxic Culture.* Knopf Canada.
- Siegel, D. J. (2010). *The Mindful Therapist: A Clinician's Guide to Mindsight and Neural Integration.* W. W. Norton.

Chapter 12 – Recognizing Love From Trauma Bonds

- Carnes, P. (1997). *The Betrayal Bond: Breaking Free of Exploitive Relationships.* Health Communications.
- Bancroft, L. (2003). *Why Does He Do That? Inside the Minds of Angry and Controlling Men.* Berkley.
- Walker, P. (2013). *Complex PTSD: From Surviving to Thriving.* Azure Coyote Publishing.
- Herman, J. L. (1992). *Trauma and Recovery.* Basic Books.

Chapter 13 – Dating as a High Value Woman

- Carter, S., & Sokol, J. (1996). *Men Like Women Who Like Themselves.* Dell.
- Argov, S. (2002). *Why Men Love Bitches: From Doormat to Dreamgirl.* Adams Media.
- Perel, E. (2017). *The State of Affairs: Rethinking Infidelity.* Harper.
- Johnson, S. M. (2019). *Attachment Theory in Practice.* Guilford Press.

Chapter 14 – Creating Relationships Where You Feel Safe

- Tatkin, S. (2016). *Wired for Love.* New Harbinger.
- Johnson, S. M. (2008). *Hold Me Tight.* Little, Brown.
- Porges, S. W. (2011). *The Polyvagal Theory.* W. W. Norton.
- Fonagy, P., Gergely, G., Jurist, E., & Target, M. (2002). *Affect Regulation, Mentalization, and*

Chapter 5 – Healing the Wounded Feminine Within

- Gibson, L. C. (2015). *Adult Children of Emotionally Immature Parents.* New Harbinger.
- Courtois, C. A. (2014). *It's Not You, It's What Happened to You.* Telemachus Press.
- Fosha, D. (2000). *The Transforming Power of Affect.* Basic Books.
- Gilbert, P. (2009). *The Compassionate Mind.* Constable & Robinson.

Chapter 6 – You Can Have Yourself AND Have Love

- Levine, A., & Heller, R. (2010). *Attached: The New Science of Adult Attachment and How It Can Help You Find — and Keep — Love.* TarcherPerigee.
- Gottman, J., & Silver, N. (1999). *The Seven Principles for Making Marriage Work.* Harmony Books.
- Johnson, S. M. (2008). *Hold Me Tight: Seven Conversations for a Lifetime of Love.* Little, Brown.
- Tatkin, S. (2016). *Wired for Love.* New Harbinger.

Chapter 7 – Boundaries Are Love Not Walls

- Tawwab, N. G. (2021). *Set Boundaries, Find Peace: A Guide to Reclaiming Yourself.* TarcherPerigee.
- Cloud, H., & Townsend, J. (1992). *Boundaries: When to Say Yes, How to Say No.* Zondervan.
- Rosenberg, M. B. (2003). *Nonviolent Communication: A Language of Life.* PuddleDancer Press.
- Brown, B. (2018). *Dare to Lead: Brave Work, Tough Conversations, Whole Hearts.* Random House.

Chapter 8 – Dangerous Confidence From the Inside Out

- Robbins, M. (2017). *The 5 Second Rule: Transform Your Life, Work, and Confidence with Everyday Courage.* Savio Republic.
- Neff, K. D. (2011). *Self-Compassion: The Proven Power of Being Kind to Yourself.* HarperCollins.
- Dweck, C. (2006). *Mindset: The New Psychology of Success.* Random House.
- Clear, J. (2018). *Atomic Habits: Tiny Changes, Remarkable Results.* Avery.

Chapter 9 – Embodying Your Magnetic Feminine Power

- Northrup, C. (2013). *Goddesses Never Age.* Hay House.
- Perel, E. (2006). *Mating in Captivity: Unlocking Erotic Intelligence.* Harper.
- Estés, C. P. (2005). *The Faithful Gardener.* HarperOne.
- Fredrickson, B. L. (2009). *Positivity: Top-Notch Research Reveals the Upward Spiral That Will Change Your Life.* Crown.

Chapter 10 – The Language of High Value Communication

- Rosenberg, M. B. (2003). *Nonviolent Communication: A Language of Life.* PuddleDancer Press.
- Scott, S. (2017). *Fierce Conversations: Achieving Success at Work and in Life.* Berkley.
- Gottman, J. (2011). *The Relationship Cure: A 5 Step Guide to Strengthening Your Marriage, Family, and Friendships.* Crown.
- Linehan, M. M. (1993). *Cognitive-Behavioral Treatment of Borderline Personality Disorder.* Guilford Press.

Chapter 11 – Your Body Is Your Temple Not Your Enemy

- Roth, G. (2010). *Women, Food and God.* Scribner.
- Bacon, L. (2010). *Health at Every Size.* BenBella Books.
- Maté, G., & Maté, D. (2022). *The Myth of Normal: Trauma, Illness, and Healing in a Toxic Culture.* Knopf Canada.
- Siegel, D. J. (2010). *The Mindful Therapist: A Clinician's Guide to Mindsight and Neural Integration.* W. W. Norton.

Chapter 12 – Recognizing Love From Trauma Bonds

- Carnes, P. (1997). *The Betrayal Bond: Breaking Free of Exploitive Relationships.* Health Communications.
- Bancroft, L. (2003). *Why Does He Do That? Inside the Minds of Angry and Controlling Men.* Berkley.
- Walker, P. (2013). *Complex PTSD: From Surviving to Thriving.* Azure Coyote Publishing.
- Herman, J. L. (1992). *Trauma and Recovery.* Basic Books.

Chapter 13 – Dating as a High Value Woman

- Carter, S., & Sokol, J. (1996). *Men Like Women Who Like Themselves.* Dell.
- Argov, S. (2002). *Why Men Love Bitches: From Doormat to Dreamgirl.* Adams Media.
- Perel, E. (2017). *The State of Affairs: Rethinking Infidelity.* Harper.
- Johnson, S. M. (2019). *Attachment Theory in Practice.* Guilford Press.

Chapter 14 – Creating Relationships Where You Feel Safe

- Tatkin, S. (2016). *Wired for Love.* New Harbinger.
- Johnson, S. M. (2008). *Hold Me Tight.* Little, Brown.
- Porges, S. W. (2011). *The Polyvagal Theory.* W. W. Norton.
- Fonagy, P., Gergely, G., Jurist, E., & Target, M. (2002). *Affect Regulation, Mentalization, and*

the Development of the Self. Other Press.

Chapter 15 – The Sacred Feminine in Sisterhood

- hooks, b. (2002). *Communion: The Female Search for Love.* William Morrow.
- Gilligan, C., & Richards, D. A. J. (2009). *The Deepening Darkness: Patriarchy, Resistance, and Democracy's Future.* Cambridge University Press.
- Estés, C. P. (1992). *Women Who Run with the Wolves.* Ballantine Books.
- Gilligan, C. (2011). *Joining the Resistance.* Polity Press.

Chapter 16 – Abundance Is Your Natural State

- Hicks, E., & Hicks, J. (2006). *Ask and It Is Given: Learning to Manifest Your Desires.* Hay House.
- Wattles, W. D. (1910). *The Science of Getting Rich.* Elizabeth Towne.
- Seligman, M. E. P. (2011). *Flourish: A Visionary New Understanding of Happiness and Well-Being.* Free Press.
- Frankl, V. E. (1959). *Man's Search for Meaning.* Beacon Press.

Chapter 17 – Manifestation Without Spiritual Bypassing

- Dispenza, J. (2012). *Breaking the Habit of Being Yourself.* Hay House.
- Bernstein, G. (2016). *The Universe Has Your Back.* Hay House.
- Duhigg, C. (2012). *The Power of Habit.* Random House.
- Neville, G. (2005). *The Power of Awareness.* Wilder Publications.

Chapter 18 – Thriving as the Most Powerful Version of You

- Clear, J. (2018). *Atomic Habits.* Avery.
- Ruiz, D. M. (1997). *The Four Agreements.* Amber-Allen Publishing.
- Frankl, V. E. (1969). *The Will to Meaning.* Penguin.
- Neff, K. D., & Germer, C. K. (2018). *The Mindful Self-Compassion Workbook.* Guilford Press.
- Seligman, M. E. P. (2011). *Flourish.* Free Press.

www.ingramcontent.com/pod-product-compliance
Lightning Source LLC
Chambersburg PA
CBHW050557170426
43201CB00011B/1724